# "An Ecstasy of Folly":

# Prophecy and Authority in Early Christianity

# HARVARD THEOLOGICAL STUDIES
## 52

CAMBRIDGE, MASSACHUSETTS

# "AN ECSTASY OF FOLLY":

## PROPHECY AND AUTHORITY IN EARLY CHRISTIANITY

Laura Salah Nasrallah

DISTRIBUTED BY

HARVARD UNIVERSITY PRESS

FOR

HARVARD THEOLOGICAL STUDIES

HARVARD DIVINITY SCHOOL

"An Ecstasy of Folly":
Prophecy and Authority in Early Christianity

Harvard Theological Studies 52

Series Editors:
François Bovon
Francis Schüssler Fiorenza
Peter B. Machinist

Cover design: Eric Edstam
Cover art: Villa dei Misteri, Pompeii, Italy. Sala dei Misteri, panels III and IV, 2nd century B.C.E. Photography by Giovanni Lattanzi/Archart. Reproduced with permission

Nasrallah, Laura Salah, 1969–
An ecstasy of folly : prophecy and authority in early Christianity / Laura Salah Nasrallah.
p. cm. -- (Harvard theological studies ; no. 52)
Includes bibliographical references and index.
ISBN 0-674-01228-3
1. Prophecy--Christianity--History of doctrines--Early church, ca. 30-600. 2. Ecstasy--History of doctrines--Early church, ca. 30-600. 3. Authority--Religious aspects--Christianity--Early church, ca. 30-600. 4. Folly--Religious aspects--Christianity--History of doctrines--Early church, ca. 30-600. 5. Dispensationalism--History of doctrines--Early church, ca. 30-600. I. Title. II. Series.
BR195.P74N37 2003
231.7'45'09015--dc22

200306940

To my father

Salah Mitri Nasrallah

with love

# Contents

*Preface*                                                                    *ix*
*Abbreviations*                                                               *xi*

*Introduction*                                                                 1
   Prophecy and Rationality                                     5
   Prophecy and History                                        11
   A Model of Struggle                                         20
   Conclusions                                                  26

*Chapter One*
**TAXONOMIES OF ECSTASY, MADNESS, AND DREAMS**                                29
   Platonism and Madness                                       32
   "Stand Outside of Yourself": Philo's Taxonomy of Ecstasy    36
   The Early-Third-Century Debate                              44
     *The Anti-Phrygian Source*                      46
     *Tertullian*                                    51
   Conclusions                                                  58

*Chapter Two*
**"FOR WE KNOW ONLY IN PART AND WE PROPHESY ONLY IN PART":**
**SPIRITUAL GIFTS AND EPISTEMOLOGY IN 1 CORINTHIANS**                         61
   1 Corinthians and "Christian" Prophecy                      63
   Human Wisdom, Divine Folly, and the Politics of Identity: Who
     Are the *Pneumatikoi*?                          70
   One Body                                                     77
   Ranking *Pneumatika*                                        83
   1 Corinthians 13: Love Trumps Wisdom                        87
   Conclusions                                                  91

*Chapter Three*
**TERTULLIAN AND THE SOUL'S CONDITION**                              95
  Locating Tertullian                                                97
  Tertullian the Philosopher, Tertullian the Antiphilosopher        101
  *De anima*                                                        111
     The status animae *(De anima 4–22)*                            115
     *The Birth and Development of the Soul (De anima 23–41)*        122
     *The Soul at Death and in Sleep (De anima 42–58)*              125
  Conclusions                                                       126

*Chapter Four*
**ECSTASY AS MADNESS: TERTULLIAN AND THE COMPETITION**
**OVER SPIRITUAL GIFTS**                                            129
  The Soul and the Spirit                                           130
     *"For What Was Spiritual in Adam?"*                            131
     Amentia                                                        134
  Tertullian's Debate with the *Psychici*                           140
  Spiritual Gifts and the Periodization of History                  148
  Conclusions                                                       153

*Chapter Five*
**"AN ECSTASY OF FOLLY": THE SOUND AND UNSOUND MIND IN**
**EPIPHANIUS'S ANTI-PHRYGIAN SOURCE**                               155
  Inventing Montanism                                               156
  Reading With Epiphanius                                           162
  Reading Without Epiphanius: The Anti-Phrygian Source
     *(Pan.* 48.1.4–13.8)                                           167
     *What's the Difference? Identity and Otherness, Truth and Falsehood*  171
     *Reason and Mental Instability in the Anti-Phrygian*           178
  The Discourse of Periodizing History: The Catalog of Past
     Prophets                                                       187
  Conclusions                                                       194

*Conclusions*                                                       197
  Authority, Identity, and Epistemology                             198
  Ancient and Modern Discourses                                     201

**Selected Bibliography**                                           205
**Index**                                                           221

# Preface

There is no end of thanks I wish to give to those who have helped me to reach the completion of this project, which is a revision of my dissertation. My first thanks go to my advisor, Karen King, who sacrificed many hours of her own work to peruse mine. Her comments have been insightful and challenging, and the hours spent in enjoyable discussions of early Christian materials and various aspects of theory and method are sweet memories from graduate school. I also thank Helmut Koester for his many years of teaching me from his store of encyclopedic knowledge and for his model of hospitality and intellectual community. I am grateful to Elisabeth Schüssler Fiorenza for her incisive comments, for her warm care and wise advice, and for her models and methods which have challenged me and are a cornerstone for my work. All three have provided me many opportunities to grow as a scholar and a teacher.

During the time I worked on this project, I was supported in many ways, and I am grateful for the time for writing provided by the Charlotte W. Newcombe Doctoral Dissertation Fellowship as well as the Clarence G. Campbell Scholarship at the Harvard Divinity School. I am also grateful for the supportive atmosphere I found during my time teaching at Occidental College, especially in my colleagues D. Keith Naylor and Dale Wright in the Department of Religious Studies. The staff of Harvard Theological Studies has also been very helpful throughout this process: managing editor Dr. Margaret Studier, copy editor Eugene McGarry, and staff assistants Mindy Newman and Rachel Haut-Castañeda Billings deserve special thanks.

My thanks go to the students and professors of the Advanced New Testament Seminar at Harvard who have read my work and encouraged me at many stages. I am especially grateful to a variety of colleagues who have commented upon parts of the manuscript: Susan Abraham, Denise Buell, Lisa Cody, Charlotte Eyerman, Andrew Jacobs, Melanie Johnson-DeBaufre, Amy Lyford, AnneMarie Luijendijk, Shelly Matthews, Catherine Playoust,

Lawrence Wills, and Andres Zervigon. My colleagues and friends Melanie Johnson-DeBaufre, Valerie Cooper, and Lori Pearson were especially faithful, in Cambridge and at a distance.

Finally, I thank my father and stepmother, Salah and Nancy Nasrallah, who patiently encouraged and loved me throughout. Memories of my brother Marc Nasrallah's sense of humor and of my mother E. Eileen Nasrallah's support and love, as well as her interest in politics and religion, also sustained me. And I give my grateful thanks to my sweet husband, August Muench, who in addition to caring for me in very practical ways in the midst of his own research and work, adds joy to my every moment and gives me hope of great things to come.

Laura Nasrallah
Harvard Divinity School
October 2003

# Abbreviations

All other abbreviations throughout the text are taken from *The Society of Biblical Literature Manual of Style*.

| | |
|---|---|
| AAR | American Academy of Religion |
| ANF | Ante-Nicene Fathers |
| ANRW | Aufstieg und Niedergang der römische Welt |
| BETL | Bibliotheca Ephemeridum Theologicarum Lovaniensium |
| CCSL | Corpus Christianorum Series Latina |
| Dummer | Epiphanius, *Panarion haer.* Berlin: Akademie-Verlag, 1980. |
| ET | English translation |
| FoC | Fathers of the Church |
| GCS | Die griechischen christlichen Schriftsteller |
| *HTR* | *Harvard Theological Review* |
| HTS | Harvard Theological Studies |
| *JECS* | *Journal of Early Christian Studies* |
| JSNTSup | Supplement to the Journal for the Study of the New Testament |
| *JSOT* | *Journal for the Study of the Old Testament* |
| *JTS* | *Journal of Theological Studies* |
| Lampe | G. W. H. Lampe, *A Patristic Greek Lexicon.* Oxford: Clarendon, 1961–1968. |
| LCL | Loeb Classical Library |
| LSJ | H. G. Liddell and R. Scott, *Greek-English Lexicon with a Revised Supplement.* Oxford: Clarendon, 1996. |
| NAPS | North American Patristics Society |
| NRSV | New Revised Standard Version |
| *NTS* | *New Testament Studies* |
| RSV | Revised Standard Version |

| | |
|---|---|
| SBL | Society of Biblical Literature |
| SBLDS | Society of Biblical Literature Dissertation Series |
| SC | Sources chrétiennes |
| *Stud. Pat.* | *Studia Patristica* |
| *TDNT* | Kittel, Gerhard, ed. *Theological Dictionary of the New Testament*. Trans. Geoffrey W. Bromiley. 10 vols. Grand Rapids, Mich.: Eerdmans, 1964–1973. |
| TLG | Thesaurus linguae graecae |
| Waszink | Jan H. Waszink, *Quinti Septimi Florentis Tertulliani De anima*. Amsterdam: J. M. Meulenhoff, 1947. |
| WUNT | Wissenschaftliche Untersuchungen zum Neuen Testament |

# Introduction

In antiquity, dreams, prophecies, visions, and oracles were understood to be part of the same basic phenomenon[1] — the communication of the divine with the human. Marcus Tullius Cicero, in his *De divinatione*, claims to record a debate over divination between himself and his brother Quintus. Following Stoic philosophy, Quintus argues that the gods in their providence communicate constantly with humans through dreams, frenzy, and forms of divination such as astrology, augury, and oracles.[2] Marcus retorts:

> The question now arises as to which is the more probable: do the immortal gods, who are of surpassing excellence in all things, constantly flit about, not only the beds, but even the lowly pallets of mortals, wherever they may be, and when they find someone snoring, throw at him dark and twisted visions, which scare him from his sleep and which he carries in the morning to a dream-expert to unravel? Or does nature bring it to pass that the ever-active soul sees in sleep phantoms of what it saw when the body was awake? . . . If the gods send us these unintelligible and inexplicable dream-messages they are acting as Carthaginians and Spaniards would if they were to address our Senate in their own vernacular without the aid of an interpreter.[3]

This critique not only amuses; it also reveals that two deeper concerns lie at the heart of the matter of divination and prophecy: the question of

---

[1] Regarding the unity of this phenomenon, see John Hanson, "Dreams and Visions in the Graeco-Roman World and Early Christianity," *ANRW* 23.2:1395–1427.

[2] See especially Cicero, *De div.* 1.1.1–2.3 and 1.6.12. These forms of divination are usually defined as "artificial" — that is, a diviner employs a certain art or technique — over and against natural forms of divination, which include sleep and unsolicited ecstasies, for example.

[3] Cicero, *De div.* 2.63–64, in *Cicero: De senectute, De amicitia, De divinatione* (trans. William A. Falconer; LCL; Cambridge, Mass.: Harvard University Press, 1923) 515–19.

how the divine communicates with humans (and thus whether and how the divine cares for humans), as well as the question of the intelligibility of such communications, and thus how to understand them properly. Even more significantly, Cicero's mocking rejoinder to his brother points to the rhetoricity of debates over prophecy, visions, and ecstasy. Arguments about the phenomenon that encompasses divination, prophecy, dreams, visions, and ecstasy—a phenomenon to which I shall refer using the term "prophetic experience(s)"—are launched in contexts of struggle and debate. These struggles are especially concerned with epistemology, with what can and cannot be known, and with the authority gained and religious identity constructed from claims to perceive the communication and intervention of the divine in the present day.

Cicero is not alone in his interest in prophetic experience. The Hebrew Bible is full of such concerns, and early Christian communities also partook in this debate about how and what the divine communicates to humans, who had the right to speak as a prophet, and who had true prophetic authority. The first-century C.E. *Didache*, a set of community rules, attempts to give advice for recognizing false prophets: "No prophet who orders a meal in a spirit shall eat of it; otherwise he is a false prophet. . . . Whoever shall say in a spirit, 'Give me money, or something else,' you shall not listen to him."[4] Among early Christian prophets, there was to be no itinerant profiteering, no spontaneous prophetic requests for takeout dinners. Other early Christian communities accused each other of having prophets whose predictions did not come true;[5] who were "pseudo-prophets" or "false prophets";[6] who were in fact crazy—not divinely inspired, but demon-possessed;[7] who spoke incoherently or strangely;[8] or who were avaricious, wore eye makeup, and falsely claimed

---

[4]*Didache* 11.9, in *The Apostolic Fathers* (trans. Kirsopp Lake; 2 vols.; LCL; Cambridge, Mass.: Harvard University Press, 1912–1913) 1:327.

[5]Epiphanius, *Pan.* 48.2.4–9.

[6]See, for example, Mark 13:22 and parallels.

[7]See the anonymous source in Eusebius, *Hist. eccl.* 5.16.7.

[8]Eusebius, *Hist. eccl.* 5.16.7. Also, in an extramural debate, Celsus launches an accusation to which Origen will later respond: "they [the Palestinian prophets of Celsus's day] then go on to add incomprehensible, incoherent, and utterly obscure utterances, the meaning of which no intelligent person could discover, for they are meaningless and nonsensical, and give a chance for any fool or sorcerer to take the words in whatever sense he likes" (7.9; ET Origen, *Contra Celsum* [trans. Henry Chadwick; Cambridge: Cambridge University Press, 1953] 403).

to be virgins.[9] One source, preserved in Epiphanius's *Panarion*, accuses its opponents of engaging in an "ecstasy of folly,"[10] a phrase so precise, succinct, and harsh in its critique that I found it a compelling title for this book. These examples provide only a few glimpses of the far broader discussion of prophetic experience in the Greco-Roman world.

Discussions of dreams, visions, and prophecy were a prime location for philosophical speculation about the nature of the human soul, its origins and properties, its similarity to and difference from the divine, and human susceptibility to invasion by good or evil spirits (*daimones*). This book focuses on a selection of debates over the nature of prophetic experience in antiquity, arguing that these critical philosophical and theological speculations were also the locus of important discursive struggles over identity, authority, and epistemology. Discussions of dreams, visions, and prophecies often led to strong polemics, as interlocutors accused each other's communities of madness or irrationality, and of transgressing the normal, or of mistaking the demonic for the divine. These accusations are not transparent descriptions of problems within a community or between communities. Rather, they are rhetorically constructed charges that attempt to claim the side of truth, integrity, and proper knowledge. At the same time, the accusers question both the content of the knowledge and the means of knowing of those who claim to be prophets or ecstatic, challenging the new realms of knowledge that—or so the prophets claim—the divine has communicated. Prophets are accused of false claims to "authentic" prophecy and ecstasy, and thus of false claims to special knowledge from the divine.

The story of prophetic experiences in the New Testament and early Christian history—and the related topics of spirit and charismata, or "gifts"—almost always addresses both Paul's 1 Corinthians and early Christian communities interested in new prophecies, which scholars often characterize as "Montanism." The two are seen as bookends to the story of early Christian prophecy: its first articulations are found in Paul; the last charismatic gasps, inappropriately out of time with the evolution and progress of Christianity, are found in the late-second- and early-third-century C.E. struggle over Montanism. In this book, I take up these texts, but not to trace a story about the vibrant origins of Christian prophecy and the aberrance of Montanism's belated prophetic claims.

---

[9]Apollonius in Eusebius, *Hist. eccl.* 5.18.
[10]ἐν ἐκστάσει γέγονεν ἀφροσύνης. *Pan.* 48.5.8.

Modern investigations of both Paul and Montanism have performed a variety of tasks in the construction of a particular version of early Christian history, especially in discussions of church office and institutionalization, canon development, and a "decline of prophecy" within early Christian communities. I do not assume that Paul is the authoritative and original voice in the early Christian debates over prophecy, or that Montanism is the *locus classicus* for a study of struggle over early Christian prophecy, or that it represents a last blaze of prophetic and charismatic energy in the face of increasing ecclesiastical routinization and organization. Indeed, "Montanism" is not a term used by its affiliates, if indeed it is possible to isolate them; it is not even a frequent third-century slur for the "New Prophecy," which seems to have been the name embraced by those convinced of the Spirit's activity in the present. As is true of so-called heresies in general, what we do know of Montanism is based on scholarly reconstructions based on a variety of contentious and partial sources. This same Montanism, however, becomes the shaky foundation from which many historians debate the decline of early Christian prophecy. What if we were to set aside the term "Montanism" for a moment, and instead investigate a group of texts that deal with issues of prophecy and ecstasy, paying particular attention to their constructions of group identity and to the authority they seek to establish?[11] And what if we challenged the notion that 1 Corinthians, which many consider our earliest source, is the authoritative and originary story of early Christian prophecy? What if we set aside the idea that Paul is a Christian author? What image of ancient debates over prophecy would then emerge?

In this book, I dive into the ancient Greco-Roman world, with its proliferating discussions of prophecy, visions, dreams, and ecstasy. I primarily examine the rhetoric of three texts: Paul's first letter to the Corinthians, written in the 50s C.E., and two early third-century works—the Carthaginian Tertullian's *De anima*, and a source I call the Anti-Phrygian, which is embedded in Epiphanius's *Panarion*. I have chosen these three texts because they have been key sources for scholarly reconstructions of the origins and decline of

---

[11]The task of culling, isolating, and then grouping texts concerned with "Montanism" on the basis of their geographical provenance or time period was begun very well by Pierre de Labriolle (*Les sources de l'histoire du montanism. Textes grecs, latins, syriaques* [Freiburg: O. Gschwend and Paris: Ernest Leroux, 1913]; *La crise montaniste* [Paris: E. Leroux, 1913]), and continued by Ronald Heine (*Montanist Oracles and Testimonia* [NAPS Monograph Series 14; Macon, Ga.: Mercer University Press, 1989]; "Role of the Gospel of John in the Montanist Controversy," *Second Century* 6 [1987–1988] 1–19).

Christian prophecy. Moreover, all three wrestle with the topic of prophecy, especially debating prophecy's intersection with madness and reason and with the role of the spirit in history. I approach these texts with a particular interest in their use of rhetoric, and this book elucidates these texts' reliance on two different discourses current in the Greco-Roman world: a discourse of madness and rationality, and a discourse of the periodization of history.

The term "discourse," as utilized and developed by Michel Foucault, has been subject to multiple understandings and explications.[12] My use of the term is grounded in Foucault's remark that discourses are linguistic "practices that systematically form the objects of which they speak."[13] By participating in a given discourse, a text constructs through rhetoric a vision of the world as it should be, and seeks to exercise language in order to convince its audience of the power and reality of that vision. This book engages in an analysis of two such discourses in order "to examine the ways power/knowledge complexes operate at a micro-social level in order to produce regimes of truth."[14]

In this book, I explore the way in which the discourses of madness and rationality and of the periodization of history are intertwined in several ancient sources in order to demonstrate that much is at stake in the debate over prophecy. Both of these discourses are invoked in struggles over epistemology, authority, and religious identity. To put it another way, while engaging in a debate about prophecy, these texts contest who has access to the divine and to divine knowledge, and who has the authority to define the identity of a community. Such disputes, of course, did not end in antiquity, and it is my hope that this study may prove useful to those who seek to elucidate the discourses that shape more recent—and even current—debates and struggles.

## Prophecy and Rationality

Given the importance of the *logos*, "reason," to the philosophies of the ancient Greco-Roman world, we might expect our texts to work out precise

---

[12]For the terms "discourse" and "discursive formation," see Michel Foucault, *Archaeology of Knowledge and the Discourse on Language* (trans. A. M. Sheridan Smith; New York: Pantheon, 1972). For a useful discussion of the concepts involved, see Michèle Barrett, *The Politics of Truth: From Marx to Foucault* (Cambridge, England: Polity Press, 1991) 123–56.

[13]Foucault, *Archaeology of Knowledge*, 49.

[14]I quote the formulation of Elisabeth Schüssler Fiorenza, "Re-Visioning Christian Origins: *In Memory of Her* Revisited," in *Christian Origins: Worship, Belief, and Society* (ed. Kiernan J. O. Mahoney; JSNTSup 241; New York: Sheffield Academic Press, 2003) 226.

definitions of rationality and madness. When I began my research, I wanted
to explore the way in which several ancient authors use the terminology
of rationality and madness in their debates about prophecy and ecstasy. I
attempted to tease out how rationality is implicitly and explicitly defined
in these sources, by looking not only at terms denoting rationality and
madness (*logos* and *mania*, *ratio* and *amentia*) but at a wider field of
similar terminology. I found, however, that the authors investigated were
interested in discussing, but not defining, rationality and madness. Ancient texts employ terminology of a "sound mind" (ἐρρωμένη διάνοια),
or "reasoning" (λογισμός), or "knowledge" and "wisdom" (γνῶσις and
σοφία), or "folly" (μωρία), or "madness" (μανία and *amentia*). Indeed,
in antiquity, the topic of the *logos* or "reason" that structures the cosmos
was ubiquitous: it formed the bedrock of much philosophical and theological speculation. But in the texts that I studied, I discovered that the
terminology of reason and madness had no clear set of referents, and that
there was no undisputed definition of the essence of reason to which these
texts appealed or even which they tried to debate. In the midst of heated
arguments about another community's mad prophets and the sobriety and
reasonableness of one's own, we might expect to find some elaboration
of a theory of *logos* or a detailing of the mechanics of madness; but we
find none. I have found instead that accusations of madness and claims to
rationality are part of a larger discourse. Texts participate in a discourse
of madness and rationality as they attempt to delineate the realms of
knowledge and the means of knowing that are accessible to and permitted
for a given community.

Such rhetoric also serves to bolster a given text's authority, and to assert
the superiority of its particular view of religious identity, over and against
other communities. Of course, after Foucault, we recognize that claims to
knowledge are at the same time claims to power and authority. I grew up in
Atlanta in the 1970s, and teachers at my conservative religious elementary
school intoned, "If you're too open-minded, your brain might fall out." This
amusing image captures the way in which those adults sought to use their
authority to constrain the realms of knowledge to which young students
might be attracted in their religious and intellectual explorations. Excessive
pursuit of knowledge might result in what was posited as its opposite: the
loss of one's mind.

In this first decade of the twenty-first century, some may find this book's
topic of prophecies, visions, ecstasies, and dreams to be strange, a subject

normally reserved for psychics, the extremely religious, or those near death. Despite their importance in antiquity, dreams, ecstasy, and the like have often not been treated seriously by modern-day scholars; they have either been dismissed, or the methods used to study them are less than ideal.[15] This post-Enlightenment embarrassment toward a phenomenon difficult to explain and to control, a phenomenon which might border on the irrational, emerges out of scholarly commitments to modernity, a term which sometimes serves as a synonym for "rationality" or "progress." Sometimes, such scholarly commitments translate into an understanding of the orthodox or truly Christian as representing rationality, and the heretical or marginally Christian as exhibiting irrational or questionable behaviors.

Thus, pages have been written explaining why Paul's definition of glossolalia is "rational" and paradigmatic for Christianity,[16] or, in contrast, why ecstasy in Montanism was frenzied, a barbarian and heretical aberration erupting at the edges of the Roman empire. Writers in antiquity used similar approaches, creating a plethora of definitions of ecstasies and dreams in order to control the meaning of these terms. For example, we shall see the Anti-Phrygian source limiting ecstasy to an "ecstasy of sleep," rather than a frenzied standing outside of oneself (the literal meaning of the verb *ex-istēmi*, cognate to the noun *ekstasis*). But in ancient times as in modern, this narrowing of definitions was not an innocent phenomenon unconnected to broader issues of social and political control, as this book will demonstrate.[17]

---

[15]Works that do take seriously the scholarly importance of investigating dreams in antiquity include Michel Foucault, *The Care of the Self* (vol. 3 of *The History of Sexuality*; trans. Robert Hurley; New York: Vintage Books, 1988) esp. 4–36; Patricia Cox Miller, *Dreams in Late Antiquity: Studies in the Imagination of a Culture* (Princeton, N.J.: Princeton University Press, 1994); and François Bovon, "Ces chrétiens qui rêvent: L'autorité du rêve dans les premier siècles du christianisme," in *Geschichte, Tradition, Reflexion. Festschrift für Martin Hengel* (ed. Hubert Cancik et al.; Tübingen: Mohr/Siebeck, 1996) 631–53. Note especially Bovon's critique of Oepke's article on ὄναρ in the *Theological Dictionary of the New Testament*.

[16]See, for example, Christopher Forbes, *Prophecy and Inspired Speech in Early Christianity and its Hellenistic Environment* (Peabody, Mass.: Hendrickson, 1997). See also the discussion in the conclusion of ch. 2, pp. 91–93, below.

[17]Michel Foucault's *Madness and Civilization: A History of Insanity in the Age of Reason* (1961; trans. Richard Howard; New York: Vintage Books, 1988) traces the way in which phenomena classified as "mad" have been increasingly medicalized and quarantined over the past few centuries. Conflict between cultures over the relationship between ecstasy and medicine is explored in Anne Fadiman's *The Spirit Catches You and You Fall Down* (New York: Farrar, Strauss & Giroux, 1997), an ethnography of the incommensurably different

The meaning of terms such as reason, rationality, and madness is hardly transparent in present-day North America. While one might think that the answer is, so to speak, a matter of common sense, the subtle workings of contemporary North American culture belie that idea, in contexts ranging from the use of insanity defenses in courts of law to the stereotype of the tortured, mad artist; from the popularity of antidepressants to Christian communities' arguments over how the Spirit manifests itself in congregational worship. In recent decades, the question of what constitutes a normal frame of mind has been debated, and depression and "deviance" are increasingly treated with pharmaceuticals.[18] Beneath the volume of the debate, an idea of "rationality" itself is constructed according to unspoken norms, and is connected implicitly, quietly, to social control.

Today, the concepts of rationality and madness might be variously addressed by philosophers, or psychologists, or psychiatrists. The blurred lines that we find in antiquity between dreams and visions, prophecies and ecstasies, are now more clearly delineated into specialties and disciplines.[19] Often, prophecies are addressed by scholars of the study of religion; ecstasies are investigated by anthropologists; the content and mechanics of dreams are the purview of psychology or medicine. This present-day fragmentation of the study of dreams, visions, ecstasy, and prophecy into distinct disciplines presided over by experts makes it difficult to understand the unity and breadth of the category of prophetic experience in antiquity, when ecstasies, prophecies, visions, and dreams were considered aspects of the same phenomenon.

In the Greco-Roman world, speculation about prophetic experience formed a kind of cutting-edge discussion, which sliced across what we today think of as disciplinary fields. Ancient students of medicine, philosophy, theology, history, astrology, and dream interpretation all exhibited an interest in this topic. Accounts of dreams, visions, prophecy, and ecstasy were a privileged site

---

understandings of soul, health, and epilepsy maintained by a Hmong family and by doctors in central California.

[18]On the connection between madness, punishment, and the penal system, see Michel Foucault, *Discipline and Punish: The Birth of the Prison* (1975; trans. Alan Sheridan; 2d ed.; New York: Vintage Books, 1995) esp. 16–22. Consider also such books as Kay R. Jamison, *An Unquiet Mind* (New York: Knopf, 1995); Peter D. Kramer, *Listening to Prozac* (New York: Viking, 1993); and Fadiman, *The Spirit Catches You.*

[19]Ann Taves also makes this argument in the introduction to her study of religious experience in eighteenth-, nineteenth-, and early-twentieth-century American religion, *Fits, Trances, and Visions: Experiencing Religion and Explaining Experience from Wesley to James* (Princeton, N.J.: Princeton University Press, 1999) 7.

for philosophical, theological, and even medical discussion. The significance of prophetic experience was recognized by all social classes and all nations, and grounded the ancient mythic history of a nation or people, or ensured the continued health of the individual and the community.[20] For example, Cicero's *On Divination* and Plutarch's *On the Obsolescence of Oracles*, which may be characterized respectively as a philosophical treatise and as a kind of apologia for the oracle at Delphi, range widely in their discussions; some of the topics treated are the difference between natural and artificial divination, the nature of the gods' communication with humans, the importance of prophecies and divination for state religion, and the reasons for the decline of prophecy at Delphi. Soranus's *Peri psyche* and Tertullian's treatise *De anima* (which depends heavily on Soranus) use examples from medical observations to discuss the makeup of the human and the nature of sleep and dreams. Artemidorus's *Oneirokritikon* weaves together dream interpretation and sociopolitical analysis, insisting that the meaning of one's dreams lies, in part, in one's status and identity.[21] Dreams and visions move the plot along not only in Greco-Roman biographies or romances such as Philostratus's *Vita Apollonii*[22] or *Joseph and Aseneth*, but in numerous New Testament texts as well. In the Gospel of Matthew, for example, an angel appears to Joseph in a dream and instructs him to flee to Egypt;[23] in Luke-Acts, Zechariah prophesies at the birth of John, Anna the prophetess praises Jesus, the apostles receive the Spirit, and visions and dreams propel Peter and Paul around the Mediterranean basin.[24] Similar events pepper the apocryphal acts of the apostles.[25]

---

[20]See Cicero, *De div.* book 1. See also Artemidorus, *Oneirokritikon*.

[21]On Artemidorus and medicine, see S. R. F. Price's "The Future of Dreams: From Freud to Artemidorus," *Past and Present* 113 (1986) 3–37, esp. 4: "Artemidorus's work rested on an epistemology and a practice which are identical to those of one of the ancient schools of medicine (a connection which is normally overlooked in histories of science)."

[22]Hanson ("Dreams and Visions") mentions Philostratus.

[23]Matt 2:19–20.

[24]Luke-Acts is particularly interested in dreams and prophecy. See Bovon, "Ces chrétiens." For Zechariah's prophecy, see Luke 1:67; for Anna the προφῆτις, see Luke 2:36; for one example of Peter's "ecstasy," see Acts 10; for one example of Paul's visions, see Acts 16:6–12.

[25]Hanson, "Dreams and Visions," 1424; see, e.g., *Acts of John* 97–102, where Jesus appears to John and gives him a vision of the Cross of Light; Thecla's vision of the Lord, "sitting in the form of Paul" (*Acts of Paul and Thecla* 21); and Mygdonia's interpretation of a dream (*Acts of Thomas* 91).

Dreams, visions, ecstasy, and prophecy were thus a major site in the Greco-Roman world for speculation on important topics ranging from piety and the connection between the human and the divine to the maintenance of health, order, and control in sleep as in waking life. Scholarship on prophecy in early Christianity or in the Greco-Roman world, because of its disciplinary specializations and its occasional embarrassment about irrationality, often has not discussed the importance of these debates, or perceived the discursive nature of ancient struggles over prophecy. While the work of Hermann Gunkel and the history-of-religions school demonstrated that, in antiquity, those who observed or experienced activities of the spirit often understood them as "irrational" phenomena,[26] such scholars also interpreted their data within the framework of modern notions of rationality. What scholarship until now has not clearly discussed is how early Christian debates over prophecy construct and contest definitions of rationality and stability of reason—definitions that do not necessarily correspond to modern constructions—and how these debates about *ekstasis* and rationality are woven into questions of a community's religious identity and its understanding of its place within history. For years, scholars have studied a variety of issues in early Christian prophecy—leadership, prophets' itinerancy, prophetic versus ecclesiastical authority, and the genres and forms of prophetic utterances and literature, for example[27]—and have investigated the rise of Montanism, or the New Prophecy, as part of the history of early Christian prophecy.[28] Yet few have studied the ways in which arguments about prophecy are rhe-

[26]Hermann Gunkel, *The Influence of the Holy Spirit: The Popular View of the Apostolic Age and the Teaching of the Apostle Paul* (1888; trans. Roy A. Harrisville et al.; Philadelphia: Fortress, 1979). See also E. R. Dodds, *The Greeks and the Irrational* (1951; repr., Berkeley: University of California Press, 1956) esp. ch. 8.

[27]See, e.g., ibid.; Hans von Campenhausen, *Ecclesiastical Authority and Spiritual Power in the Church of the First Three Centuries* (trans. J. A. Barker; Stanford, Calif.: Stanford University Press, 1969); David Aune, *Prophecy in Early Christianity and the Ancient Mediterranean World* (Grand Rapids, Mich.: Eerdmans, 1983); Gunnar af Hällström, *Charismatic Succession: A Study of Origen's Consept* [sic] *of Prophecy* (Helsinki: Toimittanut Anne-Marit Enroth, 1985); and Cecil M. Robeck, Jr., *Prophecy in Carthage: Perpetua, Tertullian, and Cyprian* (Cleveland, Ohio: Pilgrim, 1992).

[28]See, for example, Labriolle, *La crise montaniste*; Heine, "Role of the Gospel of John in the Montanist Controversy"; Christine Trevett, *Montanism: Gender, Authority and the New Prophecy* (Cambridge: Cambridge University Press, 1996); William Tabbernee, *Montanist Inscriptions and Testimonia: Epigraphic Sources Illustrating the History of Montanism* (Macon, Ga.: Mercer University Press, 1997).

torically constructed.[29] Moreover, while many have investigated *mania* and glossolalia,[30] often focusing on prophecy in Corinth, a sustained study of the rhetoric of *ekstasis*, rationality, and soundness of mind is lacking.

## Prophecy and History

The second discourse which is common to the sources that I will discuss is the discourse of the periodization of history. The texts that I shall discuss use a particular understanding of history as a tool with which to argue.[31] In a situation of struggle over prophecy and spiritual gifts, Paul argues that complete knowledge through prophecy will exist only in the future; Tertullian, the Anti-Phrygian's contemporary, insists that prophecy is more vibrant in the present than ever before; the Anti-Phrygian insists that true prophecy existed only in the past. These texts' understandings of history are not neutral or natural, but seek to limit or extend human access to the divine and divine knowledge. 1 Corinthians, the Anti-Phrygian source, and Tertullian's writings all make claims about how God and God's spiritual

[29]See, however, Robert Hauck, *The More Divine Proof: Prophecy and Inspiration in Celsus and Origen* (AAR 69; Atlanta, Ga.: Scholars Press, 1989). Hauck clearly outlines Origen's debate with Celsus over prophecy, demonstrating the inadequacy of the traditional understanding of Celsus as a rationalist and Origen as a mystic. He does not, however, use these materials to discuss other aspects of their debate over prophecy. See also Karen King, "Prophetic Power and Women's Authority: The Case of the *Gospel of Mary (Magdalene)*," in *Women Preachers and Prophets through Two Millennia of Christianity* (ed. Beverly M. Kienzle and Pamela J. Walter; Berkeley: University of California Press, 1998) 21–41; King discusses Tertullian's *De anima* and sets forth a set of questions that have influenced my own.

[30]On *mania*, see, for example, Ruth Padel, "Women: Model for Possession by Greek Daemons," in *Images of Women in Antiquity* (ed. Averil Cameron and Amélie Kuhrt; Detroit, Mich.: Wayne State University Press, 1993) 3–19; and idem, *In and Out of the Mind: Greek Images of the Tragic Self* (Princeton, N.J.: Princeton University Press, 1992). Regarding Corinth, *mania*, and glossolalia, see, for example, Krister Stendahl, "Glossolalia: The New Testament Evidence," in *Paul Among Jews and Gentiles and Other Essays* (Philadelphia: Fortress, 1976) 109–24; or Forbes, *Prophecy and Inspired Speech*.

[31]A perfect example of a Christian source employing a discourse of history's periodization to establish the superiority of Christian religious identity and knowledge over and against Judaism is found in Justin Martyr, *Dial. Tryph.* 51–52. On how prophecy and history figure in terms of Jewish identity, see Eric M. Meyers, "The Crisis of the Mid-Fifth Century B.C.E. Second Zechariah and the 'End' of Prophecy," in *Pomegranates and Golden Bells: Studies in Biblical, Jewish, and Near Eastern Ritual, Law, and Literature in Honor of Jacob Milgrom* (ed. David P. Wright et al.; Winona Lake, Ind.: Eisenbraun, 1995) 713–23; Jacob Neusner, "In the

gifts function at different periods in history. They use this discourse in order to do three things: to delimit the realms of knowledge that they think are accessible and true, to claim authority for their own points of view, and to define the religious identities of the communities to whom they write. Yet these three texts are also primary resources for scholarly attempts to reconstruct early Christian history and for our own periodization of that history, which embodies our assumptions about how religions and communities develop over time. Scholars have read 1 Corinthians as a discussion of Christian prophecy at its origins, notwithstanding Paul's Jewishness. Tertullian and the Anti-Phrygian source have been characterized as part of the "Montanist controversy." That controversy is interpreted as a last struggle over prophetic gifts, as Christianity finally accepted as authoritative articulated structures of ecclesiastical order, rather than charismatic gifts and spiritual power.

These texts have thus been used to construct the dominant model of the history of New Testament and early Christian prophecy: that of Christianity's charismatic, prophetic origins, and subsequent declines of spirit into institution. This model of charismatic origins devolving into institution and office is a compelling metanarrative; indeed, it is the explanatory device for prophecy and spirit in early Christianity that is most frequently employed by ancient and modern writers alike. Like the discourse of rationality and madness, the model of decline too has to do with constructing epistemic boundaries, answering several implicit questions that have to do with knowledge. What can be known? That is, do humans have access to greater, divine realms of knowledge, beyond the usual epistemic faculties of the mind and of sense perception? Who can know? That is, who has the authority to claim such access to special epistemic realms, and how might his or her authority or truthfulness be challenged? And when can certain things be known? Are there limits in history, times when the divine interacts more vibrantly with humans, ushering them into new realms of knowledge?

---

View of Rabbinic Judaism, What, Exactly, Ended with Prophecy?" in *Mediators of the Divine: Horizons of Prophecy, Divination, Dreams and Theurgy in Mediterranean Antiquity* (ed. Robert M. Berchman; Atlanta, Ga.: Scholars Press, 1998) 45–60; Stephen Reid, "The End of Prophecy in the Light of Contemporary Social Theory: A Draft," in *SBL 1985 Seminar Papers* (ed. Kent Harold Richards; Atlanta, Ga.: Scholars Press, 1985) 515–23; and Thomas W. Overholt, "The End of Prophecy: No Players Without a Program," *JSOT* 42 (1998) 103–15.

Like the discourse of rationality and madness, a model of charismatic origins and subsequent routinization has to do with authority and identity: a model of decline is founded on the assumption that origins are monogenetic and that they represent a true, authentic, and pure essence of religion, community, belief, or practice. That the "moment of origin" is a historiographical construct, and not a historical datum, however, is forgotten. Hence arguments based upon this origin come to have authority to define the identity of current community according to Jesus himself, or "the first Christians," or "the Jesus movement," or "the early Church." This model is sometimes complexified as subsequent charismatic groups or movements are mapped as mimetic of but unequal to charismatic origins; they are characterized as faint copies in comparison to the original moment of spirit.

This model of charismatic origins and subsequent institutionalization, derived in part from the rhetoric of ancient texts themselves,[32] was perhaps made most famous by Max Weber's theories.[33] Weber discusses charisma as one of three pure types of legitimate authority.[34] Charismatic authority, he argues, is the antithesis of rational and traditional authority; it is of divine origin, and not accessible to the ordinary person.[35] It is revolutionary,

---

[32]See, e.g., Eusebius, *Hist. eccl.*; Tertullian, *Praes. haer.*

[33]I describe this model of decline according to Weber's formulation. I do not mean to imply, however, that the scholars whom I mention use Weber overtly or are even familiar with his assertions, but rather that their conclusions are in harmony with the theories that Weber made famous. Modern historiography employs this narrative of decline without taking into account its ancient and modern rhetorical contexts and the arguments served by this story. See also Dipesh Chakrabarty, *Provincializing Europe: Postcolonial Thought and Historical Difference* (Princeton, N.J.: Princeton University Press, 2000) esp. 6–16, 30–34, for a discussion of this concern in another field of materials. See also pp. 24–26, below.

[34]In his *Theory of Social and Economic Organization*, published posthumously in 1922, Weber discusses the three pure types of legitimate authority: rational or legal authority; traditional authority, which appeals to established beliefs; and charismatic authority, predicated on a leader's heroism and exemplary character. See Max Weber, *On Charisma and Institution Building: Selected Papers* (ed. S. N. Eisenstadt; Chicago: University of Chicago Press, 1968) 46–47. "Charisma," Weber states, is a term "applied to a certain quality of an individual personality by virtue of which he is set apart from ordinary men and treated as endowed with supernatural, superhuman, or at least specifically exceptional powers or qualities" (48).

[35]Weber, *On Charisma and Institution*, 48. The shaman or intellectual—two of the terms by which Weber characterizes this individual—has followers who exhibit "complete personal devotion" (49). "The role of charismatic is not subject to appointment or dismissal, is not characterized by hierarchy, by salary or benefits, and usually takes place in a 'communistic' environment, with no established administration" (49–50).

repudiating the past and unconcerned with daily economic burdens.[36] This original moment of charismatic authority "cannot remain stable, but becomes either traditionalized or rationalized, or a combination of both."[37] The model of charismatic decline posits that Christian origins were marked by vibrant prophecy, abundant charismata, and a lack of institutional structure, all of which gradually routinized into church institution and offices that organized and controlled these spiritual phenomena. In this institution, authority was not granted to prophets and charismatics—whose visions and knowledge were so difficult to guarantee—but to bishops, presbyters, and similar institutional leaders. Often, this story is told with a twinge of sadness over the loss of such vibrant and authentic origins, but also with a resigned confidence in the staying power of rationality and of institutions and organization.

Anthropologists of religion had already reinforced this model of charisma and decline by expanding its explanatory scope, theorizing that spirit religion or animism is the origin of all religion. As Weber argued that charisma exists at origins and then fades, so anthropologists argued that the spirit and its manifestations, including prophecy, ecstasy, and shamanism, are the origin and authenticating moment of religion, and can be studied most clearly in "primitive religions." Yet this model of decline was intertwined with a model of evolutionary progress: spirit and charisma fade, to be replaced ultimately by forms of rational, sophisticated monotheism. Edward Tylor, writing at the turn of the twentieth century, thus states that "a *minimum* definition of religion" is "the belief in Spiritual Beings."[38] His idea of the evolution of religion from polytheism to monotheism is inextricably linked to ideas about human progress and to the colonialism and racism of his day.[39] "Animism

---

[36]Ibid., 51–52. "Charisma is a typical anti-economic force. It repudiates any sort of involvement in the every-day routine world" and often leads to asceticism and mendicant orders (52).

[37]"Indeed, in its pure form charismatic authority may be said to exist only in the process of originating" (ibid., 54). Weber further explains: "Routinization of charisma also takes the form of the appropriation of powers of control and of economic advantages by the followers or disciples, and of regulation of the recruitment of these groups" (58).

[38]Edward B. Tylor, "Animism," in *Reader in Comparative Religion: An Anthropological Approach* (ed. William A. Lessa and Evon Z. Vogt; Evanston, Ill.: Row, Peterson and Company, 1958) 1. My emphasis.

[39]Disturbing as this is, Tylor may have intended to be radical in his time by suggesting that "the theory of the soul is one principal part of a system of religious philosophy, which unites, in an unbroken line of mental connection, the savage fetish-worshiper and the civilized Christian" (Edward Tylor, *Primitive Culture* [2 vols. in 1; 7th ed.; New York: Brentano's, 1924] 501–2). He was also struggling against the notion that religion is located in the realm

characterizes tribes very low in the scale of humanity," he states, which evolve in "unbroken continuity" into "high modern culture."[40] These "tribes very low on the scale of humanity" survived in Africa and other colonized lands, according to Tylor. Thus, a historiographical method applied to religion and anthropology becomes the grounds by which one might classify other races and colonized peoples as primitive, even in Tylor's day, if those "tribes" were still animistic.

Thus in our ancient sources as in our modern ones, the discourse of rationality and madness intertwines with the discourse of the periodization of history, if in a variety of different ways. In modern times, there is an assumption that history and rationality are intimately linked: history progresses in such a way that human communities leave behind spirit and the ecstatic experiences it produces as they develop towards an ever-increasing rationality. The idea that spirit has declined over time, or is represented in mainly "primitive" religions, lurks in discussions of spirit, ecstasy, and anthropology in the works of the 1960s and 1970s.[41] These works have been particularly influential to scholars of the New Testament and early Christianity seeking helpful models for the analysis of ancient texts.[42] Mary Douglas, in her *Natural Symbols: Explorations in Cosmology*, attempted to break free of the sort of model that Tylor employs. In order to challenge the concept that communities uniformly and linearly develop from "primitive" to "modern," while simultaneously shifting their concern from ritual to ethical matters, she introduced two axes, which she named "group" and "grid," thus creating a conceptual plane on which one can plot communities.[43] Douglas's model does well to shatter a

---

of the supernatural; by focusing on the human soul and on spirit religion, he radicalized the definition of religion. See the editors' introduction to Tylor in Lessa and Vogt, *Comparative Religion*, 11–13.

[40]Tylor, "Animism," 13.

[41]Mary Keller also makes this argument in the introduction to her excellent study, *The Hammer and the Flute: Women, Power, and Spirit Possession* (Baltimore, Md.: Johns Hopkins University Press, 2002) 1–17.

[42]In studies of the Corinthian community, Antoinette Clark Wire and Dale Martin both utilize Mary Douglas's framework of group and grid. See also, for example, Ross Shepard Kraemer, *Her Share of the Blessings: Women's Religions among Pagans, Jews, and Christians in the Greco-Roman World* (New York: Oxford University Press, 1992) 13–21; and Rebecca Krawiec, *Shenoute and the Women of the White Monastery: Egyptian Monasticism in Late Antiquity* (Oxford: Oxford University Press, 2002) 136.

[43]Mary Douglas, *Natural Symbols: Explorations in Cosmology* (1970; London: Routledge, 1996) 1–3. "Grid" refers to shared or private systems of classification, while "group" refers to the relative pressure exerted upon the ego by others. See ch. 4, "Group and Grid," esp. 60.

unidirectional model of charismatic origins and subsequent decline by pointing to the complexities of social organization, to the variable relationships
between a community's inclination to hierarchy and its embrace of ritual,
and a community's concerns about control of the individual body and the
body politic. But Douglas's model remains problematic because it places
charismatic and ritual practices at opposite ends of the scale; it does not
take into account that charismatic practices are also ritually and rhetorically
constructed.[44] That is, her method assumes that ritual and charisma are anti-
thetical, two opposing and mutually exclusive possibilities:

> The confirmed anti-ritualist mistrusts external expression. He values
> a man's inner convictions. . . . In the same way, leaders in a Pente-
> costal church compete to demonstrate their holiness by "talking with
> tongues," that is by pouring out a stream of incoherent speech. The
> more unintelligible, the more evident to the congregation that the
> gift of tongues is present. At the same time the anti-ritualist suspects
> speech that comes in standard units, polished with constant use; this
> is the hard coin of social intercourse, not to be trusted as expressing
> the speaker's true mind.[45]

But prophecy and ecstatic speech often occur in established ritual contexts;
later we shall see, for example, how Paul attempts to frame charismata in a
new ritual context. Prophetic messages may even use set forms of speech,
as we shall see in the oracles of Montanus and Maximilla.[46] Douglas's opposition of ritual to ecstatic speech is a scholarly manufacture, emerging
out of a model that has no tools for examining the rhetorical context and
construction of ecstatic speech. Ecstasy and "mysticism" are segregated
in a privileged realm, where they cannot be analyzed.

---

[44]Douglas also sometimes argues according to a more Weberian model: "This [idea that
effervescence declines into formalism and sectarianism] is a recurring and well-attested
developmental sequence. But the historical approach is misleading if it seems to imply that the
stage of religious effervescence will always fizzle out whether or not it becomes a preliminary
step to sectarian organization. For it can be sustained indefinitely. Its only requirement is that
the level of social organization be sufficiently low. Whereas religious history has shown that
increases in social organization call for ritual forms of expression, the reverse is not sufficiently
recognized" ("Social Preconditions of Enthusiasm and Heterodoxy," in *Forms of Symbolic
Action: Proceedings of the 1969 Annual Spring Meeting of the American Ethnological Society*
[ed. Robert F. Spencer; Seattle: University of Washington Press, 1969] 74).

[45]Douglas, *Natural Symbols*, 51.

[46]See, for example, Aune's form-critical analysis in *Prophecy in Early Christianity*.

The work of anthropologists of religion contemporary to Mary Douglas, such as I. M. Lewis and Victor Turner, exhibits similar problems. Lewis's *Ecstatic Religion*, while attempting to analyze ecstatic behavior according to its social and political contexts, still falls into a Weberian framework. Lewis states that "new faiths may announce their advent with a flourish of ecstatic revelations, but once they become securely established they have little time or tolerance for enthusiasm."[47] For Lewis, charismatic phenomena are a kind of steam valve for the oppressed and marginalized: possession will continue to occur, he posits, as long as there are "oppressed" sections of the community that need to express resistance,[48] but that still operate within extant boundaries of control and authority. Similarly, Turner's famous *Ritual Theory*, while it struggles against a model of progress that pits charisma, spirit, and spontaneity against organization, a highly developed symbol system, and routinization, replaces that model with a tripartite schema in which institution is challenged and energized by spirit, and then declines again into routinized institution, and then is challenged again. Turner thus extrapolates a self-replicating, cyclical process from the Weberian model.[49] For these anthropologists, expression of charisma—in Turner's terms, communitas—is romanticized, seen as spontaneous, authentic. The rhetoricity of charismatic phenomena are ignored.

[47]I. M. Lewis, *Ecstatic Religion: A Study of Shamanism and Spirit Possession* (1971; 2d ed.; London: Routledge, 1989) 29. Possession continues to happen because of "constantly recurring social and environmental pressures which militate against the formation of large, secure social groups" (ibid.). "If, however, religions which are in the process of degenerating into marginal cults tend to attract followers from the lower strata of society by possession, there is an equally well-defined tendency for successful inspirational religions to lose their ecstatic fervour and harden into ecclesiastical establishments which claim a secure monopoly of doctrinal knowledge" (156).

[48]Ibid., 118.

[49]Victor Turner, *The Ritual Process: Structure and Anti-Structure* (1969; New York: de Gruyter, 1995). Although Turner argues that *societas* (structure) and communitas (a sort of ritual liminality) are a dialectical process (203), he also states that this idea of communitas is nevertheless fundamentally transient. It is experienced by communities who have some sense, true or illusory, that they are marginal. Communitas can "under certain conditions" be "an 'ecstatic' experience, in the etymological sense of the individual's 'standing outside' his structural status" (188). But this status reversal is a fleeting thing, which may purify "the accumulated sins and sunderings of structure" (185) but which devolves back to it. Turner's latent assumptions and conserving instincts become even more evident in this statement: "Wisdom is always to find the appropriate relationship between structure and communitas under the *given* circumstances of time and place, to accept each modality when it is paramount without rejecting the other, and not to cling to

Even from the brief discussion above, we can see how Enlightenment theories of human progress and development (including the idea of the evolution of religion itself) have been harnessed to Romantic constructions and valorizations of the primitive and of the spirit. The model of charismatic origins and decline into institution wraps within itself elements of both Enlightenment and Romantic thought. Progress toward institution, with its routinized and rational structures, is preferable, but the loss of vibrant charismatic and ecstatic origins is regrettable, in a way, even as those long past charismatic beginnings authenticate and guarantee the truth of the tradition. The study of the history of Christianity has often used this model, almost reflexively, since it seems to fit so well with the history of religion and with the history of Christianity. Scholarship that does not engage in serious study of the rhetorical context of ancient texts, and of the discourses in which they participate, however, may misunderstand those texts, shoehorning them into an extant model of decline, with little concern for the texts' carefully constructed worldview and attempts at persuasion. Such scholarship may also uncritically internalize the ancient texts' rhetorical strategies, thus reproducing or taking for granted ancient historiographies of the decline of "primitive" spirit and the progress of rationality which resemble our own.

Although still debated today, the model of charismatic origins and subsequent routinization often continues explicitly and implicitly to guide the study of early Christianity and early Christian prophecy, as can be seen in works ranging from Adolf von Harnack's *Mission and Expansion of Christianity* to David Aune's *Prophecy in Early Christianity*.[50] Even Hans von Campenhausen, whose measured *Ecclesiastical Authority and Spiritual Power in the*

---

one when its present impetus is spent. . . . Spontaneous communitas is nature in dialogue with structure, married to it as a woman is married to a man. Together they made up one stream of life, the one affluent supplying power, the other alluvial fertility" (139–40). Turner reveals that his discussion of communitas is not only based upon observations of rituals of liminality among the Ndembu, but is deeply entrenched in his own binaried worldview. See also Carol Walker Bynum's critique of Turner ("Women's Stories, Women's Symbols: A Critique of Victor Turner's Theory of Liminality," in *Fragmentation and Redemption: Essays on Gender and the Human Body in Medieval Religion* [New York: Zone Books, 1991] 27–51).

[50]Adolf von Harnack, *Mission and Expansion of Christianity in the First Three Centuries* (1908; trans. James Moffatt; Gloucester, Mass.: Peter Smith, 1972) ch. 4. See also Cecil Robeck's discussion of Harnack in *Prophecy in Carthage*, 7; David Hill, *New Testament Prophecy* (London: Marshall, Morgan & Scott, 1979) esp. ch. 8; James L. Ash, Jr., "The Decline of Ecstatic Prophecy in the Early Church," *JTS* 37 (1976) 227–37; and James Dunn, *Jesus and the Spirit: A Study of the Religious and Charismatic Experience of Jesus and the First Christians as Reflected*

*Church of the First Three Centuries* attempts to resist dichotomizing official and charismatic types of authority,[51] elsewhere implicitly participates in this model when he argues that Montanism was a "reactionary" movement that recalled "the spirit of primitive Christianity."[52] The current study instead seeks to contribute to an understanding of early Christian history by showing that no historiographical model of spiritual origins and a slow slide into institution and office can do justice to the complexity of early Christian communities. In the pages that follow, we shall see that early Christians appealed to ideas of madness as well as rationality in their struggles over prophecy, and that they also appealed to the trope, common in antiquity as in the present, that humans march through different periods of history. Even as these ancient texts argue about the decline or the vibrancy of prophecy and ecstasy, they do not provide an undistorting windowpane through which we can view these phenomena. Debates over the validity of prophecy and ecstasy at a given period in history are rhetorically constructed in complex conditions of struggle, and do not necessarily indicate that prophecy and ecstasy have declined, or become marginal.[53] Reading early Christian texts according to the model of charismatic decline has led scholars to conclude that some ancient communities became marginal, aberrant, or even heretical by continuing to pursue prophecy and ecstasy after the time for such gifts had passed. A historiographical model that highlights struggle and the negotiations of authority, identity, and access to realms of knowledge allows us to draw a different picture, and to locate references to prophecy's role in history within a debate that reflects the complexity and variety of early Christianities.

---

*in the New Testament* (1975; Grand Rapids, Mich.: Eerdmans, 1997). See also Aune, *Prophecy in Early Christianity*, 189 and Hill, *New Testament Prophecy*, 190, which are discussed in detail on p. 161, below.

[51] Von Campenhausen, *Ecclesiastical Authority and Spiritual Power*, e.g., 2.

[52] Hans von Campenhausen (*The Formation of the Christian Bible* [1967; trans. J. A. Baker; Mifflintown, Pa.: Sigler, 1997] 221) states that Montanism's emphasis on prophecy necessarily clashed with the "canonical norm." See also Lee McDonald's excellent summary of von Campenhausen's views in *The Formation of the Christian Biblical Canon* (rev. ed.; Peabody, Mass.: Hendrickson, 1995) 174–75.

[53] For the position that prophecy did suffer decline and marginalization, see, for example, von Harnack, *The Mission and Expansion of Christianity*, ch. 5. More recently, see Aune, *Prophecy in Early Christianity*; Ash "The Decline of Ecstatic Prophecy in the Early Church"; Dunn, *Jesus and the Spirit*; and Hill, *New Testament Prophecy*, esp. ch. 8.

## A Model of Struggle

The topic of early Christian prophecy, and of prophecy in general, has elicited influential scholarly treatments, usually in the form of narrative history, that provide diachronic analyses and generalizing conclusions. These sweeping tales, structured around grand narratives such as the model of charismatic origins and the decline of charisma into institution, are seductive precisely because they offer totalizing and coherent stories about a diverse range of phenomena, persons, and time periods. In this book, I do not assume that a comprehensive narrative of early Christian prophecy can be reconstructed, nor do I attempt to write a history that might become a chapter in such a narrative. Modern histories structured according to axioms of historical decline or progress subtly echo antiquity's own predilection for sweeping accounts of the progression of empires,[54] without sufficiently analyzing the rhetorical frameworks that govern such histories. As we shall see, some ancient sources employ a discourse of the periodization of history similar to the model of charismatic origins and decline into institution. This similarity can blind us to the rhetoricity of ancient texts. Their view of history, of the passing of charismatic gifts and the evolution of Christianity into institutions, is so natural to us that we can miss the way in which this very view of history is launched in a context of debate and struggle. Any historiography, including my own, is an attempt at persuasion, written from a certain standpoint and for a certain purpose; historical reconstruction is always an imaginative and ideological enterprise.[55] Instead of assuming that there is a grand narrative to early Christian history, waiting to be discovered, this book takes up a model of struggle, which analyzes the competing discourses of a given time period,

---

[54]Consider the *Histories* of Polybius and the *Jewish Antiquities* of Josephus.

[55]See the work of Elisabeth Schüssler Fiorenza in *But She Said: Feminist Practices of Biblical Interpretation* (Boston: Beacon Press, 1992); and Elizabeth A. Castelli and Hal Taussig, "Drawing Large and Startling Figures: Reimagining Christian Origins," *Reimagining Christian Origins: A Colloquium Honoring Burton L. Mack* (ed. idem; Valley Forge, Pa.: Trinity Press International) 2–20. Castelli and Taussig state that "reimagining Christian origins as a tableau or mural is epistemologically distinct from the more common metaphor of telling the story or narrative of early Christianity. If we understand the study of Christian origins as a tableau in production, we escape the reductionism of causality that stories of Christian beginnings often elicit" (19). In this study I present the texts which I have chosen as part of a "tableau in production," and recognize that my own historiographical attempts are part of the same.

and questions texts' attempts to construct a totalizing history. By choosing a model that privileges sites of conflict and moments of struggle, I join others in resisting some historiographical constructions of early Christian history, in which studies of early Christian charismata and prophecy are imagined as one strand of a totalized history of decline from charismatic origins or, differently articulated, spirited origins moving toward rational progress and *telos*.[56]

I borrow the term "model of struggle" from Elisabeth Schüssler Fiorenza's theoretical approach to the interpretation of the New Testament,[57] which emphasizes earliest Christianity's negotiations of power and uses of rhetoric. Thus, this book also employs rhetorical-critical method in the analysis of ancient texts—a method which focuses upon ancient forms of rhetoric, and also, on how rhetoric functions to persuade and convince. I use the analyses of those interested in classical rhetoric, such as Margaret Mitchell and George Kennedy,[58] but I am guided in particular by Schüssler Fiorenza's counsel regarding the practice of rhetorical criticism: "The task is not to rehabilitate rhetoric but to articulate it as a critical practice. As critical practice rhetoric is able to investigate the dimensions of domination and freedom in a cos-

[56]Ibid. Scholars such as Castelli and Taussig have emphasized that early Christian historiography must not be reduced to one story. Using the image of cubist painting, they propose that we "[retrain] the aesthetic and the scholarly optic" to enjoy the cubist aesthetic, in which nothing is flattened out as background, in which multiple perspectives compete on the canvas, and in which realism is eschewed (1–10, esp. 5). Such a framework, they argue, critiques the model of decline used so often in early Christian historiography, and the concept of pristine origins that undergirds it. Schüssler Fiorenza ("Re-Visioning Christian Origins," 238) states it even more boldly: "to read early Christian history in terms of the reconstructive model of rapid decline from the heights of radical equality to the valleys of patriarchal institution is to overlook the continuing struggles that have been ongoing throughout Christian history between those who understand Christian identity as radically inclusive and egalitarian and those who advocate kyriarchal domination and submission."

[57]Although this term appears in several of Elisabeth Schüssler Fiorenza's works, including *Jesus and the Politics of Interpretation* ([New York: Continuum, 2000] see esp. 149–73) and *Rhetoric and Ethic: The Politics of Biblical Studies* (Minneapolis: Augsburg, 1999), it is best explicated in "Re-Visioning Christian Origins," 237.

[58]See Margaret Mitchell, *Paul and the Rhetoric of Reconciliation: An Exegetical Investigation of the Language and Composition of 1 Corinthians* (Tübingen: Mohr/Siebeck, 1991); and George Kennedy, *A New Testament Interpretation through Rhetorical Criticism* (Chapel Hill, N.C.: University of North Carolina Press, 1984).

mopolitan world."[59] I therefore discuss ancient sources in terms of forms of classical rhetoric, but, like ancient rhetoricians, I am most interested in how rhetoric works to persuade and convince in a context of struggle. The text's rhetorical construction of both author and audience—in Schüssler Fiorenza's terms, the "inscribed author" and "inscribed audience"[60]—is a focal point of this study. I apply this model of struggle to moments of argument and debate over prophecy in antiquity. This study examines both Paul and early-third-century texts in light of Schüssler Fiorenza's idea that "as a public discourse, biblical studies could . . . understand biblical discourses as inscriptions of struggle and reconstruct them as public debates of the *ekklesia*."[61] A model of struggle allows for a critical reading of ancient (and more recent) texts that represent themselves as continuous with apostolic succession, the progress of truth, or the development of orthodoxy.[62] Such texts often point to the "heretic" or the "other" as moments of deviance or of rupture in the smooth, attenuated course of Christian history. Although these texts claim to be normative and continuous with some pure origin and correct practice of Christianity, their rhetoric, I shall demonstrate, reveals that these very claims to normativity participate in larger discourses embracing prophecy and ecstasy. Thus these texts seek to control the boundaries of knowledge and of community, and to concentrate authority in a community or in a subset of that community. In the pages that follow, I discuss moments of debate, discontinuity, and disruption, and I investigate how ancient texts employ arguments about rationality and arguments about history to construct their own authoritative place in time and in community over and against a "disruptive" other. Regarding both the

[59]Schüssler Fiorenza, *Rhetoric and Ethic*, 80. Schüssler Fiorenza states, "Rhetoric constitutes *doxastic* rather than epistemic knowledge." Here she follows the work of Rayme McKerrow, who emphasizes that rhetoric studies how symbols come to possess power, rather than what they are in and of themselves. See especially Schüssler Fiorenza's method as developed in *In Memory of Her: A Feminist Theological Reconstruction of Christian Origins* (New York: Crossroad, 1983) and *But She Said*. Form criticism has often been used to distinguish the prophetic forms and traditions imbedded in other texts (see, e.g., the work of Gunkel and Aune). Since I am not as interested in studying the rhetorical form of the earliest oracles as I am in determining how they function within the debates, rhetorical criticism serves this discussion best by allowing access to the insights of form criticism while providing other tools for study. See also Schüssler Fiorenza, *Rhetoric and Ethic*, 105–10.

[60]See, e.g., Schüssler Fiorenza, *Rhetoric and Ethic*, 128.

[61]Ibid., 10.

[62]On the problem of the hermeneutical circularity of assuming struggle and then finding it, see Michel Foucault, "Discursive Formations," in *Archaeology of Knowledge*, 31–39.

ancient and modern texts that are treated in this study, I repeatedly ask the questions: Who is served by a given historiography? What work do these grand narratives do?

To state it in another way, this study examines a topic, that of prophetic experience, as it is elaborated in a variety of rhetorical settings. By beginning with this topic, I attempt to disrupt both a linear history that would plot the course of early Christian prophecy, as well as the traditional categorization of sources according to their religious and philosophical affiliations. Foucault proposed something like this in his *Archaeology of Knowledge*, suggesting an analysis of history as "a population of dispersed events";[63] his theory deliberately uncouples humanism from historiography and thereby resists models that construct history as an ineluctable and rational progress toward some *telos*.[64] This study thus questions both ancient and modern rhetoric about the progress of history and about the norms of rationality. In treating the topic of prophetic experience, I isolate and analyze the discourses of rationality and madness and of the periodization of history, discourses that controlled discussions of this theme in antiquity. Furthermore, I have assembled and treated with equal respect and interest texts that are usually segregated from each other by normative identity boundaries such as Montanist (read: heretical) and orthodox, Stoic and Platonic, Jewish and Christian.[65] Thus, this study also investigates the way in which these identities are rhetorically constructed in ancient and modern texts.

My historiographical approach has been influenced not only by the feminist work of Elisabeth Schüssler Fiorenza and the historiographical method of Michel Foucault,[66] but also by the insights of postcolonial critics who

---

[63]Ibid., 22.

[64]Ibid., 11, 13. See also Schüssler Fiorenza, "Re-Visioning Christian Origins," 226–27.

[65]Recent scholarship has been challenging the construction of such normative boundaries in other ways. See Karen L. King, *What is Gnosticism?* (Cambridge, Mass.: Harvard University Press, 2003); Daniel Boyarin, *Dying for God: Martyrdom and the Making of Christianity and Judaism* (Stanford, Calif.: Stanford University Press, 1999); and idem, "The Gospel of the *Memra*: Jewish Binitarianism and the Prologue to John," *HTR* 94 (2001) 243–84.

[66]Earlier I mentioned Foucault's *Madness and Civilization*, which offers an outstanding articulation of the interconnection of authority/power and the delimitation of fields of knowledge. Foucault's methods in that study have informed my investigation of much earlier sources. In *Madness and Civilization*, Foucault explains how madness has been defined and made other, set aside and quarantined, especially in the hospitalization of the mentally ill in France in the seventeenth and eighteenth centuries. He exposes the way in which the government at the time manufactured connections between poverty, mental illness, and criminality that defined and justified the confinement of the "deviant."

challenge the very category of history. Ashis Nandy, for example, insists
that the modernist idea of historical consciousness is itself a phenomenon
produced at a particular moment in Western thought, and that the impulse
to "presume a perfect equivalence between history and the construction of
the past" prevents historians from criticizing their own methodology and
worldview.[67] Nandy explains:

> Millions of people still live outside "history." They do have theories
> of the past; they do believe that the past is important and shapes
> the present and the future, but they also recognize, confront, and
> live with a past different from that constructed by historians and
> historical consciousness. They even have a different way of arriv-
> ing at that past.[68]

Similarly, Dipesh Chakrabarty, a Marxist labor historian and postcolonial
critic, insists that the idea of history as the march of chronological time
toward some rational *telos* is not the only way of conceptualizing time and
the world. Indeed, such an idea of history leads to the sort of analysis that
we have already seen in Edward Tylor, where some peoples living today
are puzzlingly categorized as "primitive," perpetually in a state of the
"not yet," as if they just haven't caught up with the march of history, or
have stalled at some early stage in human progress. Chakrabarty critiques
historicist analysis because it implicitly relies on Enlightenment ideas of
progress and is imbricated with a colonial insistence that a subject people
are "not yet" ready for self-determination: not yet sufficiently literate, or
not yet fully educated—that is, not yet sufficiently inculcated with the
dominant culture. He counters the category of history with his ideas of
"timeknot" and "heterotemporality," terms intended to capture the experience of many today who live simultaneously both in the modern European
concept of history and in some other sense of time, whether mythic or
sacred, or merely distinctly nonlinear and unchronological.[69]

Not only in our ancient sources does the discourse of rationality and madness intertwine with the discourse of the periodization of history. Although

---

[67]Ashis Nandy, "History's Forgotten Doubles," *History and Theory* 34 (1995) 48.
[68]Ibid., 44.
[69]See Chakrabarty, *Provincializing Europe*, 30–34, 239–55. For a thoughtful critique of
a modern construction of history and its relation to the category of religion, see Talal Asad,
*Genealogies of Religion: Discipline and Reasons of Power in Christianity and Islam* (Baltimore,
Md.: Johns Hopkins University Press, 1993) esp. 1–24.

it may seem that the kind of totalizing history of anthropologists like Tylor is over, we can still find references to certain kinds of religious practice as primitive or even standing outside history. For example, even in the wake of Edward Said's 1978 *Orientalism*, we find such references in a persistent Orientalist rhetoric that implies that Islam is primitive and barbarian. Nearly twenty-five years later, Bernard Lewis, in *What Went Wrong? Western Impact and Middle Eastern Response* tries to answer the question of how "By all the standards that matter in the modern world—economic development and job creation, literacy and educational and scientific achievement, political freedom and respect for human rights—what was once a mighty civilization [Islam] has indeed fallen low."[70] An interviewer posed to Lewis the question: "In your book you talk about the reluctance of the Muslim world to learn from Europe and the West—how for many years Muslims weren't interested in reading European literature or learning about its history. Is that still the case?" He replied: "Generally speaking they [Muslims] have accepted the need to learn from more advanced societies. . . . But clearly they have a lot of catching up to do in order to be at the level of modern knowledge. For better or for worse, at the present time what we sometimes call Western civilization is modernity. It's no longer purely Western."[71] Moreover, for Lewis, part of Islam's inability to catch up to modernity lies precisely in its religiosity—its inability to split off state from religion—a problem he admits used to exist in Christianity, too.[72] *This* has led to what he implies is the backwardness of "Muslims" or "people in the Middle East." Surely this view of religion itself as a regressive force that is harmful and dangerous to politics is something that should concern scholars of religion. And Lewis's assumptions about how history advances and works—a history that progresses toward modernity, which is implicitly identified with the "West," despite his attempt to uncouple the two—has certainly led to dangerous and demeaning conclusions.

---

[70]Bernard Lewis, *What Went Wrong? Western Impact and Middle Eastern Response* (Oxford: Oxford University Press, 2002) 152.

[71]http://www.princeton.edu/~paw/. September 11, 2002: Features. Accessed January 2003.

[72]"Secularism in the Christian world was an attempt to resolve the long and destructive struggle of church and state. . . . This is a problem long seen as purely Christian, not relevant to Muslims or for that matter to Jews, for whom a similar problem has arisen in Israel. Looking at the contemporary Middle East, both Muslim and Jewish, one must ask whether this is still true—or whether Muslims and Jews may perhaps have caught a Christian disease and might therefore consider a Christian remedy" (Lewis, *What Went Wrong?*, 115–16).

## Conclusions

How we understand history and define its periods matters; how we argue about rationality and madness, the institutional and the primitive, also matters. This book seeks to avoid and to subvert the historiographical assumptions of scholars who understand history to be a clear march toward progress, modernity, or rationality, but who do not question the meaning of these terms. By using a model of struggle to read early Christian debates over prophecy, we shall see that their discussions of prophecy and ecstasy are not clear windows onto historical reality, but are rhetorically constructed to persuade an audience. Certain discourses come to the fore. As they debate prophecy and ecstasy, these texts use language of "sound mind" and of "madness." They also employ different understandings of history and of its periodization—of what spiritual gifts and realms of knowledge are possible and appropriate at a given time. While the debate in a given text may thus seem to be about a sound understanding, mental aberrancy, or God's action in history, I argue that these are elements in the text's more urgent struggle to assert its own authority, to validate its understanding of Christian identity, and, most of all, to limit the fields of knowledge that serve to construct both authority and identity. Thus, while making claims about prophecy and ecstasy, these authors are also formulating identity, constructing epistemic boundaries, and shoring up their own authority.

It is my thesis that these three categories—group boundaries or community identity, the control of knowledge, and the establishment of authority—are nodes within the larger debate over prophecy in antiquity. In our texts, the terminology of madness and rationality, and the rhetoric of history as well, function not descriptively but prescriptively to construct an author's or a community's identity over and against others. Arguments over prophecy and ecstasy are always also arguments over group boundaries. Moreover, debate over prophecy manufactures boundaries to knowledge. It sets limits—based on such elements as gender, status, ontology, and the interpretation of history—on what can be known and what must remain unknown, and by doing so stakes out certain fields of knowledge as legitimate. In the context of setting limits and constructing identity, the author asserts his own authority, and the authority of his, or his community's viewpoint, in order to manufacture the truth both of his community's identity and of the epistemic boundaries that he seeks to create.

In order to obtain a broader view of debates over prophetic experiences, in my first chapter I sketch a context for ancient Greco-Roman debates over prophecy and ecstasy and assemble the key texts for this study. Drawing from a range of writings, including Artemidorus's *Oneirokritikon*, Plato's *Phaedrus*, Philo's *Who is the Heir of Divine Things*, Tertullian's *De anima*, Epiphanius's early-third-century C.E. source, and Paul's 1 Corinthians, I show that many communities in antiquity sought to order and organize their understandings of ecstasy, prophecy, and dreams. Moreover, I demonstrate that these attempts at taxonomy are not neutral schemes of classification, but rather function in two ways: to situate the taxonomizing text as an authoritative source within this broader conversation, and to argue that one form of ecstasy, madness, or dreams is superior. The sources used in this chapter demonstrate the broad range of interest in the topic in antiquity—these texts traverse the boundaries of Platonic and Stoic, Jewish and Christian, "heretical" and "orthodox."

In the second chapter, I return to 1 Corinthians, to investigate further Paul's ranking and ordering of spiritual gifts. While Paul does not use the terminology of madness and rationality invoked by the other authors treated in this study, he does subtly employ the related terms of folly and wisdom in order to "correct" the Corinthians' understanding of spiritual gifts, especially prophecy and tongues, in their own community. His letter arrives in the midst of a community that understood itself to be richly endowed with spiritual gifts and spiritual knowledge, yet it accuses that community of not being spiritual people, but merely fleshly. Paul also employs a discourse of the periodization of history, insisting that knowledge, wisdom, prophecy, and tongues—charismata the Corinthians held dear!—are passing away. He asserts that full knowledge will only be possible in the future. I posit that Paul and some members of the Corinthian community are struggling over epistemic boundaries, and the question of who can have how much of what sort of knowledge. Paul tries to draw epistemic limits for—as he argues—the benefit, unity, and especially the identity of the community. At the same time, he attempts to shore up his own authority among the Corinthians, who place much—too much, argues Paul—value on wisdom and spiritual gifts.

Chapters 3, 4, and 5 treat early-third-century texts that are usually characterized as part of the Montanist controversy. Instead of reading them as evidence of an orthodox view, represented by Epiphanius's source, and a heretical view, expressed by Tertullian, I ask: how do these texts participate in the common discourses of madness and of historical periodization, even as they struggle over prophecy? In chapters 3 and 4, I offer a close reading of Tertullian's *De anima*, making sense of his argument about a corporeal soul that experiences *amentia* ("madness") or ecstasy. I discuss in detail his ideas about knowledge and about the construction of the human soul, ideas that allow Tertullian to embrace a broad range of sources of knowledge, including sense perception as well as the "madness" that prophecy and true spiritual gifts bring. I later turn to his intramural debates with the so-called *psychici* over anthropology, prophecy, and the periodization of the time and the presence of the Paraclete.

In chapter 5, I turn to Epiphanius's Anti-Phrygian source in *Panarion* 48, another text engaged in the early-third-century Christian debate over prophecy and ecstasy. I analyze its arguments from scripture, as well as its bitter polemic, which mocks certain oracles of Montanus and Maximilla and derides its opponents for their lack of sound mind. Thus, in chapters 3–5 I elucidate the discourse of madness and rationality and the discourse of the periodization of history that permeate the texts of Tertullian and the Anti-Phrygian, and I discuss the ways in which these roughly contemporary authors struggle to establish epistemic boundaries and the truth and reality of their communities' Christian identity.

In the pages that follow, we shall dive into the world of antiquity, where dream interpreters offer their services in the marketplace; where madness is conceived by some as the ascent of the soul into higher realms of knowledge; where a woman sees a vision of a bodied soul—clear and ethereal—during Sunday service; where fierce fights erupt over whether God's love for humanity is manifested by the gift of ecstasy; and where true Christian identity, in some circles, is measured by the spiritual gifts and divine grace manifest in one's community.

CHAPTER 1

# Taxonomies of Ecstasy, Madness, and Dreams

Some dreams, explains Artemidorus, the second-century C.E. author of the *Oneirokritikon*, usually translated the *Interpretation of Dreams*,[1] should be characterized by the term *enhypnion*; others he names *oneiros*. It is the latter that are true dreams, epistemically valuable, insightful, predictive, worth interpreting; the former are mere flickerings from bad digestion or the day's concerns. Artemidorus's *Oneirokritikon* preserves the richest extant example of a complex taxonomy of dreams and dream interpretation in the Greco-Roman world at his time. Luther Martin even argues that the best translation of the title is *A Taxonomic Science of Dreams*.[2] Artemidorus's taxonomy branches methodically: even *oneiroi* are divided into two categories, theorematic and allegorical.[3] The first category refers to straightforward dreams, where things are as they seem; the allegorical *oneiros*, in which meaning is cloaked in symbols, is the primary focus of the rest of his writing. Artemidorus's taxonomy branches quickly, like a fast-growing tree: the meaning of a given oneiric image depends upon the dreamer's status, gender, familial relations, and even homeland or ethnicity. For example, dreaming that one has been born has no fewer than twelve possible interpretations, depending upon the dreamer. For the artisan, it is an inauspicious sign: the hands will be somehow bound, as an infant

---

[1] The *Oneirokritikon* is difficult to date, and not much is known about its author. See Robert J. White's introduction to his translation, with commentary, of Artemidorus, *Interpretation of Dreams* (Park Ridge, N.J.: Noyes, 1975) 1–2, 6–10.

[2] Luther H. Martin, "Artemidorus: Dream Theory in Late Antiquity," *Second Century* 8 (1991) 107.

[3] Artemidorus, *Oneir.* 1.2.

is swaddled; for the male slave, it is an auspicious sign: it means that he will be cared for and coddled; for the male householder, it is inauspicious: he will be infantilized, belittled in his own domain. Some taxonomies of dreams branch further, involving not only the self, but others: dreams which "involve the body or part of the body, or external objects . . . have the tendency to affect others too" (1.2).[4] Artemidorus explains further: in this oneiric universe, the head represents the father, the foot the slave; the right hand the father, son, friend, or brother; the left hand the wife, mother, mistress, daughter, or sister; the penis the parents, wife, or children. The dream body does not escape the waking life, with its everyday patriarchy and kyriarchy, or "rule of the master";[5] rather, it is coded and stamped with the social, economic, and political structures of the waking world.

The *Oneirokritikon* discloses a fascination with dreams, visions, and their prophetic qualities that has no close parallel in twenty-first-century North America. In Greco-Roman antiquity, dreams, ecstasy, prophecies, visions, and even madness—all considered part of the same phenomenon—were approached in at least two ways that differ from our own time. First, while today we tend to define prophecy as a prediction of the future, in antiquity the definition was much broader. Prophecies—and the visions, ecstasies, and dreams that transported those prophecies—did not only have to do with the prediction of the future, but could serve as critiques of the present, as political commentaries, or as devices to warn or to heal.

Like genetics and cloning today, in Greco-Roman antiquity, dreams and ecstasy were the hot topic of scientific, political, philosophical, and theological discussion—as well as, admittedly, being the object of occasional ridicule: Artemidorus admits that others, unlike himself, would not deign to wander the agoras, speaking with dream interpreters of questionable repute. Thus, a second difference between dreams and prophecies in antiquity and our own time is this: if, in antiquity, dreams were at times dismissed or ridiculed, sometimes violently, it is not because they were considered unimportant, but precisely because their significance was so pervasive and powerful. Dreams, ecstasy, visions, and prophecy formed the ground for speculation among those whose work we (with our culture of expert academic disciplines) would define

---

[4]ET White, 17. Regarding the dream of being born, see Artemidorus, *Oneir.* 1.13. For an excellent survey and analysis of Artemidorus's interpretations, see Cox Miller, *Dreams in Late Antiquity*, ch. 2. Although many of Artemidorus's interpretations presume a male dreamer, some also indicate interpretations for the female dreamer.

[5]The term "kyriarchy" is taken from Elisabeth Schüssler Fiorenza's work. See, for example, *But She Said*, 7–9.

as medical, psychological, philosophical, political, literary or novelistic, or propagandistic. All such speculations about prophetic experience, of course, took place in conversation with the religions of antiquity, pursuing complex questions: What is the human soul, and how is it susceptible to dreams and ecstasy? What capacities for knowledge does a human have? How does the divine communicate to the human? What exactly happens to a person in death, or sleep, or madness?

Although Artemidorus, for one, is hesitant to say whether dreams come from the gods or not,[6] many in antiquity discuss a dream or an ecstasy—or, as we shall see in Plato, madness—as a particularly significant moment of contact between the human and the divine. This moment was epistemically transformative. In and through it, one was endowed with some knowledge not normally accessible to humans. Even Artemidorus's simplest taxonomy acknowledges that some dreams are significant for knowledge and some are not: he distinguishes between truth and falsehood and between dreams that *seem* significant or real, but are merely a result of indigestion or the day's events. But, as we shall see, other texts in antiquity make far more complex claims about the new realms of knowledge that one can access through ecstasies or dreams.

This chapter juxtaposes a variety of texts in order to provide a kind of wide-angle lens on the discussion of prophecy, ecstasy, madness, and dreams in Greco-Roman antiquity, and in order to show that this discussion is not unique to Christians or Jews or "pagans," Platonists or Stoics, so-called orthodox or so-called heretics. I introduce the idea of these widespread taxonomies by turning to two influential philosophical/theological sources: Plato and Philo. An analysis of their attempts to order and taxonomize madness and ecstasy provides a context for similar attempts on the part of two of the focal texts of this book—Tertullian's *De anima*, and the Anti-Phrygian source found within Epiphanius's *Panarion*. I conclude by suggesting that Paul's 1 Corinthians offers its own sort of taxonomy as it discusses and then ranks spiritual gifts.

In a variety of the works I shall discuss, lists and definitions of ecstasy, madness, and dreams function to sketch a sort of map for the reader—a map of the different routes that prophetic experiences can take through the topography of the soul. Even more, these lists and definitions function rhetorically to situate the author in the midst of a familiar debate and a broader philosophical conversation. The author also thus rhetorically constructs him- or herself as the next authoritative commentator on a common theme. "There are three kinds of dreams," or, "there are four kinds of ecstasies": the literature of antiquity echoes with the authoritative tones of those who list, order, and taxonomize dreams and the like. Moreover, even as these lists provide various definitions, they lead the reader to conclude that all ecstasies (or madnesses, or dreams, or spiritual gifts, as the case may be) are not equal.

In this chapter, I argue that while the texts studied here claim to provide a map of some prophetic phenomenon, each text in fact upholds and defines one form of ecstasy or dreams or madness. These taxonomies are not interested in recounting the complex branches and possibilities of others' dreams, as the *Oneirokritikon* is (although it too constructs a hierarchy of dreams). The author, in constructing this map, attempts to authorize one particular definition of ecstasy and to exclude others, which in turn will become the standard for future discussion and evaluation. As Rosamond Wolff Purcell and Stephen Jay Gould argue, "Taxonomy, or the science of classification, is the most underrated of all disciplines. Dismissed by the uninformed as philately gussied up with jargon, classification is truly the mirror of our thoughts, its changes through time the best guide to the history of human perceptions."[7]

The taxonomies proffered do not neutrally list three or four kinds of dreams or ecstasy, but rather highlight one form as correct or appropriate. At the same time, while the stated definitions may seem to have to do with a straightforward attempt to define ecstasy or dreams, together they reveal a pattern of what is at stake: what realms of knowledge people can access through dreams and ecstasy. These are not merely lists, but indeed are politically charged, hierarchical taxonomies—systems of ordering which exclude or dismiss other forms of ecstasy, preferring one as epistemically more significant.

## Platonism and Madness

Behind many of our later taxonomies of ecstasy or madness stands the powerful philosophical influence of Plato, or at least of the Middle Platonism that developed from his writings. Plato's *Phaedrus* offers four forms not of ecstasy, as the first-century C.E. author Philo will, but of *mania*, or "madness," which is contrasted to *sōphrosunē*, "prudence" or "sobermindedness." Plato offers this taxonomy in the context of one of Socrates'

---

[7]Rosamond Wolff Purcell and Stephen Jay Gould, *Illuminations: A Bestiary* (New York: W. W. Norton, 1986) 14.

dialogues. "This speech is not true," Socrates muses—the speech which immediately preceded, insisting that Phaedrus give himself to the man who is not in love with him, who is not sickened by lack of *sōphrosunē*.[8] Socrates overthrows rational calculation:[9]

> And thus I must say that that speech is not true, which says that it is necessary to indulge one who is not in love, rather than one who is presently in love, because the one is mad, and the other sober (διότι δὴ ὁ μὲν μαίνεται, ὁ δὲ σωφρονεῖ). For if it were simply that madness is an evil, what is said would be good, but now it appears to us that the greatest of good things come through madness, when it is given as a gift of the goddess. (*Phaedr.* 244A)[10]

To explain why *mania* can be a good thing, and, in the narrative framework of the *Phaedrus*, to retract advice that it is better to take as one's mate the distanced and detached nonlover over the "insane" lover, Socrates discusses different kinds of *mania*. This discussion has two effects: it asserts that there are a variety of good forms of madness, and it investigates the madness of love and bolsters Socrates' (or Plato's) assertion that one should choose the

---

[8]Martha Nussbaum, *The Fragility of Goodness: Luck and Ethics in Greek Tragedy and Philosophy* (New York: Cambridge University Press, 1986) 205; see also 202. Note, however, how well Nussbaum's reading correlates with a contemporary point of view from the United States, with its valorization of passionate love, and its general incomprehension of extirpation of the passions or of pursuit of abstraction (love for the general rather than the particular) as valuable disciplines (see 216–17). See also Dodds, *The Greeks and the Irrational*, ch. 3.

[9]It is interesting that Socrates speaks in a different voice, in the persona of Stesichorus, son of Euphemus, from Himera. These names are codes: "The one who establishes or leads the dances or choirs," son of "He who speaks well," from the town of "Desire." Socrates has been giving different speeches in different voices. The first lines of the current speech ("that speech is not true") echo a Homeric quotation he uses in an earlier speech (243B), further underscoring the playfulness and complexity of the arguments. This dialogue plays with rhetorical exercises for beginning students, who are expected not only to provide an argument in a speech, but also to be able to invent a range of convincing speeches that might refute each other. Regarding such elementary exercises, see George A. Kennedy, "Introduction," in *Progymnasmata: Greek Textbooks of Prose Composition and Rhetoric* (Atlanta, Ga.: SBL, 2003) x–xi.

[10]The Greek edition of the *Phaedrus* used here is that of John Burnet, in *Platonis Opera* (5 vols.; Oxford: Clarendon, 1900–1907). In this chapter, all translations of ancient texts are mine unless otherwise noted.

lover who is insane on account of love over the sober-minded nonlover.[11] This
suggestion may not seem shocking in a twenty-first-century U.S. context,
where jealous lovers plead insanity as a defense, and where romantic love
is characterized as a kind of mad passion. But in Greco-Roman antiquity,
the idea that being out of one's mind could be a positive thing is surprising,
given the cultural emphasis on self-control, on the training of the mind, and
on rationality and sober-mindedness, as we can even see in the speech that
preceded Socrates'—that one should take up with the man whose *sōphrosunē*
is not compromised.

In its taxonomy of *maniai*, the *Phaedrus* lists first a madness which is
manic or mantic—that is, which leads to prophecies that are god-given and
beneficial, such as those found at the oracles at Delphi and Dodona or in the
words of the Sibyl. Second is a madness that can provide release in times of
crisis;[12] third, a poetic madness; and finally, the madness of the soul trying to
ascend to the divine, which is akin to the madness of the lover. The *Phaedrus*
turns from the issue of the lover, who is nearer to madness than to sober
thinking, to an extended discussion about the soul, delving into the issue of
anthropology. The soul is immortal, always moving. In its perfect form, it is
winged and in its flight in the heavens sees above the mundane and perceives
reality and truth: that is, it has access to a different realm of knowledge than

---

[11]Nussbaum (*Fragility of Goodness*, 201) has eloquently read Plato's *Phaedrus* against the
famous *Symposium*, where the speech of Alcibiades, "the person 'possessed' by the 'madness'
of personal love," is perhaps trumped by Socrates' recollection of Diotima's calm teaching
regarding the soul's ascent through contemplation of increasing abstractions. Diotima argues
that one must shunt off one's mad love for one individual, and see that what one really longs
for is the Goodness or the Beauty manifested in part in that individual. Note, however, that
some scholars have wondered if Alcibiades' speech trumps Diotima's, in a way, or if at least the
eloquence and interest of the speech lightly veil Plato's resistance to agreeing with Diotima's
idea of love. On the soul's capacity for divination, see also *Tim*. 71E–72B (and Philo's re-
use of it in *Spec*. 1.219); see also Plato, *Rep*. 571C–572B, cited in Nussbaum, *Fragility of
Goodness*, 205. On the difficulty of defining reason in ancient philosophy, see also Michael
Frede, "Introduction," in idem and Gisela Striker, eds., *Rationality in Greek Thought* (Oxford: Clarendon, 1996) 1–28. But Nussbaum (*Fragility of Goodness*, 204) highlights Plato's
own ambivalence towards the conclusions he sometimes held about rationality and the soul,
and love and madness: "Consistently, in pre-*Phaedrus* dialogues, Plato has used '*mania*' and
related words to designate the state of soul in which the non-intellectual elements—appetites
and emotions—are in control and lead or guide the intellectual part. . . . It is linked particularly with the dominance of erotic appetite. . . . Clearly the pre-*Phaedrus* dialogues do attack
*mania* as a 'simple evil.'"

[12]See *Phaedr*. 244D–E for a longer explanation of this complicated form of *mania*.

the souls caught in bodies. The souls aloft see justice, sobriety, and especially knowledge (*epistēmē*): "not the kind of knowledge that is involved with change and differs according to which of the various existing things (to use the term 'existence' in its everyday sense) it makes its object, but the kind of knowledge whose object is things as they really are."[13] Trapped in bodies (*Phaedr.* 246C), souls still long for this flight and upper region. Only at the end of this long section about the nature of the soul does Plato return to what originally seemed to be the point of the story: whether one should take the (maddened) lover or the (sober) nonlover to oneself:

> Now we reach the point to which the whole discussion of the fourth kind of madness was tending. This fourth kind of madness is the kind which occurs when someone seeks beauty here on earth and is reminded of true beauty. His wings begin to grow and he wants to take to the air on his new plumage, but he cannot; like a bird he looks upwards, and because he ignores what is down here, he is accused of behaving like a madman. So the point is that this turns out to be the most thoroughly good of all kinds of possession, not only for the man who is possessed, but also for anyone who is touched by it, and the word "lover" refers to a lover of beauty who has been possessed by this kind of madness.[14]

As we shall see, centuries later, Philo's *Who is the Heir of Divine Things* constructs a similar fourfold pattern, but while the *Phaedrus* deftly switches from yearning for a beautiful human to yearning for the Form of Beauty, Philo's text articulates the best sort of ecstasy as the yearning for the divine.

The *Phaedrus*, in its attempt to justify the madness of the lover, provides a list of four kinds of madness which it positively evaluates. Nevertheless, it too suggests that one form of madness is better than all the others; indeed, the three forms of madness which precede it serve to persuade the reader that madness has been and can be evaluated positively. Think of the oracles inspired by Apollo, think of the madness wrought by Dionysus, think of the poetic genius brought on by the Muses, the text cajoles (*Phaedr.* 265B). Surely, in this cultural context, the reader will agree that some forms of madness

---

[13]*Phaedr.* 247D–E; translated by Robin Waterfield, in Plato, *Phaedrus* (Oxford: Oxford University Press, 2002) 30.

[14]*Phaedr.* 249D–E; ET Waterfield, *Phaedrus*, 33.

have salutary results. And one form of madness is better than all the others: the lover's madness, which spirals upwards toward something divine.

## "Stand Outside of Yourself": Philo's Taxonomy of Ecstasy

Philo's philosophical approach is part of the Middle Platonism widespread in his hometown of Alexandria—a vital intellectual center of Greco-Roman antiquity—and abroad in the first century C.E.[15] Allegorical interpretation and Middle Platonic thinking characterize his *Who is the Heir of Divine Things*, a long, speculative, allegorical approach to Genesis 15 that contains a taxonomy of ecstasy. *Who is the Heir of Divine Things* does not immediately reveal a polemical context, but rather is a fragment of evidence of early-first-century C.E. speculation, in this case urban and Jewish, about ecstasy and knowledge.[16] Despite the absence of obvious polemics, Philo does not offer a neutral taxonomy, but insists that one form of ecstasy is the best. His taxonomy, and Plato's in the *Phaedrus*, provide examples of the kinds of philosophical debates and taxonomies of madness and ecstasy which provide a context for the early-third-century Christian debates.

Philo borrows from Plato and adopts a Platonic anthropology, or understanding of the human, as his own; moreover, his fourfold taxonomy of ecstasy roughly echoes Plato's in its form, if not in its content. Philo sets forth this taxonomy within the broader context of an allegorical interpretation of Genesis 15, and within the even broader context, well known and much discussed in scholarship, of his positive valuation of ecstatic experience.[17] Philo's *Who*

---

[15]David Runia, *Philo of Alexandria and the* Timaeus *of Plato* (Leiden: Brill, 1986) ch. 1. On early Christians' use of Philo, and their embarrassment about appropriating a Jewish thinker, see idem, "Philo and Origen: A Preliminary Survey," in Robert J. Daly, ed., *Origeniana Quinta: Historica, Text and Method, Biblica, Philosophica, Theologica, Origenism and Later Developments: Papers of the Fifth International Origen Congress, Boston College, 14–18 August 1989* (BETL 105; Leuven: Peeters, 1992) 333–38. On Origen's use of Philo, see also, in the same volume, Annewies van den Hoek, "Origen and the Intellectual Heritage of Alexandria: Continuity or Disjunction?," 40–50; and idem, "The 'Catechetical' School of Early Christian Alexandria and Its Philonic Heritage," *HTR* 90 (1997) 59–87. Philo died in approximately 50 C.E., around the time of Paul's first extant letters.

[16]Philo also authored *De Somniis*, from which only two treatises survive; these preserve two categories of dreams out of the three he originally discussed. For an outline of his three-fold taxonomy, see *Somn.* 2.1-2.

[17]Peder Borgen ("Philo of Alexandria," in *Jewish Writings of the Second Temple Period: Apocrypha, Pseudepigrapha, Qumran Sectarian Writings, Philo, Josephus* [ed. Michael E.

*is the Heir of Divine Things* begins with the question of who will be Abram's heir. Gen 15:2 depicts Abram questioning God: "What wilt you give me, for I continue childless, and the heir of my house is Eliezer of Damascus?" God immediately responds, "This man shall not be your heir."

Philo moves past the literal meaning of this story about Abram's desire for a flesh-and-blood heir. Instead he understands the text allegorically: the story describes the characteristics of anyone who wishes to inherit divine things. The true heir is not Eliezer, nor even a child of flesh and blood, a body caught in sense perception, but rather is something intellectual. Abram's heir is "the purest mind, which disregards not only the body, but also the other part of the soul, which is unreasonable and jumbled together in the blood" (*Her.* 64).[18] Philo goes on to offer a surprising conclusion: among other things, the "heirs of intellectual things are incorporeal natures"[19] and the true heir "stands

---

Stone; Philadelphia: Fortress, 1984] 233–82) outlines those works of Philo which belong to Philo's extended interpretation of Genesis. *Who is the Heir of Divine Things* is part of a larger set of works which "continue the verse by verse commentary on Genesis now taking in Gen 11–18, but bring in other parts of the Bible when systematic and topical interests vary the structure" (244). Regarding Philo and mysticism, see, for example, Hauck, *The More Divine Proof*, 142; and Andrew Louth, *The Origins of the Christian Mystical Tradition From Plato to Denys* (Oxford: Clarendon, 1981) 72. Philo's mysticism and Origen's are often compared. Note how Henri Crouzel's characterization of Origen's mysticism becomes an ad hominem attack on "Montanism": for Origen, Crouzel states (*Origen* [1985; trans. A. S. Worrall; San Francisco, Calif.: Harper & Row, 1989] 100), "the grace of knowledge is a free gift of the divine love. It must be received freely by man and ascesis is the witness to this will on man's part. Origen criticized the conception held by the Montanists of trance as unconsciousness and that shows that God does not take possession of a soul without its consent." However, in Origen's corpus there is, to my knowledge, only one explicit negative reference to the *Cataphryges* in *In epistolam ad Titum*. See Heine, *Montanist Oracles and Testimonia*, 8–9. For more on this, see my "'An Ecstasy of Folly': Rhetorical Strategies in Early Christian Debates over Prophecy" (Th.D. diss., Harvard Divinity School, 2002) 85–88, which discusses scholarly treatments of Philo and Origen, and which treats in detail Origen's view on prophecy and the soul.

[18]This passage occurs within a context that speculates about gender (*Her.* 61–62): The irrational is connected with animals, and the female line; Sarah, however, as the allegorical stand-in for virtue, is a female with no mother (see Philo's allegorical interpretation of Gen 20:12) and thus produces "male descent." This dramatic connection of irrationality and the feminine may find its root in the description of the soul in Plato's *Timaeus*, but also represents a tinkering with Plato's conception.

[19]ἀσώματοι γὰρ φύσεις νοητῶν πραγμάτων εἰσὶ κληρονόμοι. *Her.* 66. The edition used is that of Leopold Cohn and Paul Wendland, *Philonis Alexandrini Opera Quae Supersunt* (7 vols. in 8; Berlin: Georg Reimer, 1896) 3:16.

outside of himself" (*Her.* 68)—that is, the true heir "is in ecstasy," as the verb ἐξίστημι and the noun ἔκστασις are etymologically related.

Using Gen 12:1 ("Now the LORD said to Abram, 'Go from your country and your kindred and your father's house to the land that I will show you' ") as a touchstone, Philo enjoins this soul (ψυχή) or understanding (διάνοια) to be like Abram: if it yearns to inherit divine things, it should abandon land, kin, and father's house. These are understood allegorically to represent the body, sense perception, and, most surprisingly, reason (λόγος). This abandonment takes the form of ecstasy—a wild, Dionysian ecstasy. Philo easily uses a spread of vocabulary associated with madness:

> Therefore, soul, if some yearning to inherit the good and divine things should enter you, leave not only "the land"[20]—that is, the body—and "kindred"—that is, sense perception—and "your father's house"—that is, *logos*, but also flee from yourself and stand outside of yourself (ἔκστηθι σεαυτῆς); as those who are possessed and corybants, be inspired with frenzy[21] and be possessed by some prophetic inspiration. For the understanding (διάνοια) which is inspired and is no longer in itself, but has been violently agitated and driven mad by heavenly love, and is led by the truly Existent, and is drawn along upwards toward it (while truth advances and removes obstacles before the feet) so that the understanding may advance down the road as upon a highway—this is the heir.[22]

Philo adopts the language of Dionysian cult in order to describe this inspired and noetic experience. Possession occurs only with the shearing off of sense perception and the mad ascent of the mind. The mind is unmoored from the limits of human reason and spins upwards into something that looks like madness.

---

[20]The three quoted terms refer to Gen 12:1, where Abram is instructed to "Go from your country and your kindred and your father's house to the land that I will show you."

[21]Literally, "be bacchants."

[22]πόθος οὖν εἴ τις εἰσέρχεταί σε, ψυχή, τῶν θείων ἀγαθῶν κληρονομῆσαι, μὴ μόνον γῆν, τὸ σῶμα, καὶ συγγένειαν, <τὴν> αἴσθησιν, καὶ οἶκον πατρὸς (Gen 12:1), τὸν λόγον, καταλίπῃς, ἀλλὰ καὶ σαυτὴν ἀπόδραθι καὶ ἔκστηθι σεαυτῆς, ὥσπερ οἱ κατεχόμενοι καὶ κορυβαντιῶντες βακχευθεῖσα καὶ θεοφορηθεῖσα κατά τινα προφητικὸν ἐπιθειασμόν· ἐνθουσιώσης γὰρ καὶ οὐκέτ' οὔσης ἐν ἑαυτῇ διανοίας, ἀλλ' ἔρωτι οὐρανίῳ σεσοβημένης κἀκμεμηνυίας καὶ ὑπὸ τοῦ ὄντως ὄντος ἠγμένης καὶ ἄνω πρὸς αὐτὸ εἱλκυσμένης, προϊούσης ἀληθείας καὶ τὰν ποσὶν ἀναστελλούσης, ἵνα κατὰ λεωφόρου βαίνοι τῆς ὁδοῦ, κλῆρος οὗτος. *Her.* 69–70; Cohn and Wendland, 3:16–17. For the same interpretation (but of a different text), see Philo, *Mig.* 7–12.

Philo even uses the rhetorical technique of prosopopeia to "interview" this inspired "understanding" or *dianoia*, asking it to tell the story of its departure from land, kin, and its father's house. The *dianoia* responds:

> I changed my abode from the body when I paid no regard to the flesh; and from sense perception, when I put before my mind that all sensible things did not truly exist. I charged sense perception with having standards of judgment which were adulterated and corrupted and filled with falsehoods of opinion, and I also charged sense perception with sentences of judgment that were prepared to entice and grasp and to snatch away truth from the midst of outward appearance. I also turned away from reason when I observed its great lack of reason (μετανέστην καὶ τοῦ λόγου, ἡνίκα πολλὴν ἀλογίαν κατέγνων) and, further, I turned away from its self-elevation and self-aggrandizement. For it [the *logos*] dared (with not a little recklessness) to show me bodies [i.e., substantive things] through shadows, real things through speeches—bodies and words which were impossibilities. And, even as it was tripped up, it chattered and broke off into vagueness, powerless to render by a clear, outward appearance the peculiar natures of the established signifiers (ὀνόματων). Having suffered like a foolish and infantile child, I learned to withdraw, as it was better, from all these things, but to dedicate the powers of each to God, who fixed the body to be corporeal and who prepared sense perception to perceive and who extends speech to the *logos*.[23]

The *dianoia* asserts that it has left behind certain incorrect epistemological approaches; namely, ways of knowing through sense perception or through reason. The true heir inherits only after abandoning certain approaches, and only after entering a kind of madness or ecstasy. The body fails. Sense perception's deluding powers offer objects that seem to be real, but in truth are only part of false opinion. Even that element usually held to be highest in ancient philosophical thought, the *logos*—"reason," "word," or "speech"—is rejected because of its shadowy imprecision, its semiotic crisis: words claim to represent reality while offering only blunders, vagueness, and chattering.[24]

---

[23]*Her*. 71; Cohn and Wendland, 3:17.

[24]Philo suggests that all three elements—the body, sense perception, and reason—be turned over as dedications or votives to God (reminiscent of Romans 12:1) to be enshrined in two sanctuaries, one intellectual and the other sensible.

Philo later returns to the issue of the loss of mental power as he presents a taxonomy of ecstasies. This fourfold model neutrally sets forth three kinds of ecstasy, and then, like the taxonomy in the *Phaedrus*, focuses on the last, best ecstasy. The first sort of ecstasy is "a fury like madness, producing derangement and due to old age or melancholy or some other similar cause"; as Philo understands it, this is the sort of ecstasy and blindness that might overtake the impious (*Her.* 249–50). The second sort of ecstasy is extreme amazement (ἡ . . . σφοδρὰ κατάπληξις), such as that which Jacob felt when he heard that Joseph was still alive and ruling in Egypt (Gen 45:26, *Her.* 251), or that which the congregation at Sinai experienced when it saw God in fire and smoke (Exod 19:18, *Her.* 251). The third kind is "a rest of the understanding, if indeed the mind can ever produce quiet" (ἡ . . . ἠρεμία διανοίας, εἰ δὴ πέφυκέ ποτε ἡσυχάζειν, *Her.* 249). Tertullian will later echo this ambivalence about the idea of the mind at rest. Philo, Tertullian, and Epiphanius's source contain glimpses of a great debate over this idea of ecstasy as the mind at rest, and simultaneously over the interpretation of Gen 2:21, in which (according to the language of the Septuagint) God cast an ecstasy upon Adam while Adam slept. Philo explains that this is an "ecstasy of quiet and of rest for the mind. For the mind's sleep is the awakening of the senses, and the understanding's awakening is senses' inaction."[25] This inverse relation between sense perception and the activity of the mind clarifies further Philo's belief that sense perception must be shunted off in order for clarity of mind to be achieved, even if the result paradoxically appears to be madness, strange behavior, or disconnection with one's environment.

The fourth kind of ecstasy, illustrated by a story about Abraham that begins in Gen 15:2, is the best and involves the "setting" of the human mind and the rising of the divine as "ecstasy and inspired possession and madness fall" (*Her.* 264). Echoing Plato's fourth category of *mania* in the *Phaedrus*, Philo concludes that the best form of ecstasy is a frenzy or madness. This eviction of the human mind and rising of the divine mind is "what the inspired and God-possessed experience" (*Her.* 258). Philo moves further in Genesis 15 to analyze verse 12: "As the sun was going down, a deep sleep fell upon Abram, and a deep and terrifying darkness descended upon him." The verse's reference to the sun leads Philo into an extensive allegorical interpretation, where the sun represents the human mind:

---

[25]ἔκστασιν τὴν ἡσυχίαν καὶ ἠρεμίαν . . . · ὕπνος γὰρ νοῦ ἐγρήγορσίς ἐστιν αἰσθήσεως, καὶ γὰρ ἐγρήγορσις διανοίας αἰσθήσεως ἀπραξία. *Her.* 257; Cohn and Wendland, 3:59.

For the reasoning faculty (λογισμός) in us is equivalent to the sun in the cosmos, since both bear light. For what the reasoning faculty is in us, the sun is in the world, since both of them are light-bringers, one light sending out to all with respect to sense perception, the other illumining us through grasping the mental faculties. So therefore while the mind still shines and traverses us as at noonday, such a light pouring forth in every soul, we are in ourselves, we are not possessed (ἐν ἑαυτοῖς ὄντες οὐ κατεχόμεθα). But when sunset comes, as is likely, ecstasy and inspired possession and madness fall (ἔκστασις καὶ ἡ ἔνθεος ἐπιπίπτει κατοκωχή τε καὶ μανία). For when the divine light shines, the human sets; when the former sets, the human light emerges and rises. This happens often to the prophetic class. Among us the mind is evicted at the arrival of the divine spirit, and it enters again at the spirit's removal. It is not willed that mortal should cohabitate with the immortal. Therefore the setting of the reasoning power and the darkness which surrounds it produce ecstasy and madness which is from divine possession (διὰ τοῦτο ἡ δύσις τοῦ λογισμοῦ καὶ τὸ περὶ αὐτὸν σκότος ἔκστασιν καὶ θεοφόρητον μανίαν ἐγέννησε).[26]

Here Philo uses both νοῦς and λογισμός, and makes absolutely clear that the human and the divine mind are incommensurable. The divine mind, during ecstasy and prophecy, evicts the human intellect, the "soul's soul."[27]

For Philo, paradoxically, an epistemic high point looks like drunkenness or madness. Such assertions about the best form of ecstasy echo elsewhere in his

---

[26]*Her.* 263–65; Cohn and Wendland, 3:15.

[27]Lest we think that Philo is here bound to the scripture, and so uses the image of the mind as setting sun because the sun is setting in the Genesis account, we can find a similar image elsewhere. We also find allegorical exegesis of the "sun" in *De somniis*, where it can mean many things, but one understanding is particularly close to the sense here in *Who is the Heir of Divine Things*: "When this shines upon the understanding (διάνοια) it causes those lesser luminaries of words to set, and in a far higher degree casts into shade all the places of sense-perception" (*Somn.* 13). Philo elaborates the inverse relation between the human mind and reasoning and the divine mind: "For as long as mind and sense-perception imagine that they get a firm grasp . . . the divine Word is far away. But when each of them acknowledges its weakness, and going through a kind of setting passes out of sight, right reason (ὀρθὸς λόγος; stands in parallel use to θεῖος λόγος) is forward to meet and greet at once the practising soul, whose willing champion he is when it despairs of itself and waits for him who invisibly comes from without to its succour" (*Somn.* 11; ET in *Philo: Works* [trans. F. H. Colson and G. H. Whitaker; 12 vols.; LCL; Cambridge, Mass.: Harvard University Press, 1929–1962] 5:360–61). Elsewhere, the senses alone are pushed aside: *On the Contemplative Life* refers to soaring "above the sun of our senses" (*Contempl.* 2.11–12; ET *Philo: Works*, 9:119).

corpus. Sometimes, Philo uses the terms κορυβαντίος and βακχεύομαι and their cognates just as we would expect: as terms to critique drunken behavior.[28] But in *On Drunkenness* (*Ebr.* 146.2), as in the passage just discussed, Philo weaves together the usually negative language of drunkenness and *mania* with the extremely positive terms of ecstasy. Philo here explains 1 Samuel 1, where Eli observes Hannah praying silently and concludes that she is drunk. Eli's confusion of intoxication and ecstasy becomes a perfect platform from which Philo can launch his commentary on drunken behavior and strange ecstasy. Hannah's name, Philo explains, means "grace," and "without divine grace it is impossible either to leave the ranks of mortality, or to stay for ever among the immortal. Now when grace fills the soul, that soul thereby rejoices and smiles and dances, for it is possessed and inspired, so that to many of the unenlightened it may seen to be drunken, crazy and beside itself."[29] The constellation of terms is interesting: as in *Her.* 69–70, "being bacchic"[30] and being in ecstasy are set side by side. Later in the passage, Philo explains that those who bear God within them (θεοφόρητοι) experience a hot flush over the body, along with the rising of the soul. Explaining this odd phenomenon and its behavioral effects, here as elsewhere Philo riffs on the paradox that those who are most austere and most sober, like Hannah, seem to be drunk in their ecstasy.[31]

---

[28]While cognates of κορυβαντιάω, used six times in the Philonic corpus, are wholly neutral or positive, βακχεύω and cognates are used to depict bad forms of drunkenness three out of seven times, once in the case of Noah's drunkenness after he planted a vineyard and drank its wine (*Plant.* 148.3). In this case as in others, terms of madness (μανία, παραφροσύνη) are used in conjunction with βακχεύω. *Ebr.* 124.1 uses the term negatively, comparing slavery and intoxication.

[29]βεβάκχευται γάρ, ὡς πολλοῖς τῶν ἀνοργιάστων μεθύει καὶ παρακινεῖν καὶ ἐξεστάναι ἂν δόξαι. ET *Philo: Works,* 3:394–95. On Philo and loss of mental control in prophecy, see also John R. Levison, *The Spirit in First Century Judaism* (Leiden: Brill, 1997) 30–55. The connection between the concept of grace (χάρις) and that of gifts (χαρίσματα) is a new subject of my research.

[30]"[T]o celebrate the mysteries of Bacchus; speak or act like one frenzy-stricken" (*LSJ*, s.v. βακχεύω).

[31]One could argue that Philo's use of such terms (and frequent early Christian avoidance of them, or use of them only in polemic) may be explained by the historical context of Jews in Alexandria. That is, Philo, writing to establish Jewish identity for Jewish readers and to explicate and praise it before Gentile readers, appeals to the congruence between phenomena in Hellenistic philosophy/cult and Jewish religion. Perhaps Philo even reverses the tradition of ancient oppressions by Ptolemy IV Philopater, who tried to assimilate Alexandrian Jews into the cult of Dionysos, according to 3 Maccabees: instead, Philo assimilates Dionysian

This sort of language appears again in an autobiographical reference in *On the Migration of Abraham* (*Migr.* 34–35); Philo states that at times he cannot write, but "at other times, I have come empty and have suddenly become full, the ideas descending like snow and invisibly sown, so that under the impact of divine possession I had been filled with corybantic frenzy and become ignorant of everything, place, people present, myself, what was said and what was written." This frenzy and even "ignorance" (πάντα ἀγνοιεῖν) are accompanied by unusual focus: "sharp-sighted vision, exceedingly distinct clarity of objects, such as might occur through the eyes as the result of the clearest display."[32]

Philo makes it clear that this "corybantic frenzy," characterized by madness and irrational behavior, is deeply connected to an individual epistemic revolution, a revolution that, at least according to *Who is the Heir of Divine Things*, involves the absence of the human mind. Philo's story of creation, *On the Origin of the World*, explains how the human mind is modeled after the "Mind of the Universe" (*Opif.* 69) and then proceeds to describe the investigatory power of this mind, a potential which is natural to it:

> Following the love of wisdom, which guides it, transcending every sensible being, then aiming at the province of the mind, it also beholds in that [place] the models and Ideas—things of surpassing beauty—of the sensible objects which it saw here; it is seized with sober drunkenness, like possessed Corybants, filled with a different yearning for an even better desire. (*Opif.* 70–71)

Here we see the ascent of the soul, an echo of the last, best form of ecstasy discussed in the *Phaedrus*. Again and again, Philo's corybantic frenzy is juxtaposed with sobriety, albeit drunken sobriety, and the clarity of vision during the moment of ecstasy is emphasized.

It is odd that Philo, rooted in Middle Platonic philosophy and its emphasis upon the mind, refers easily and so often to the human mind's dimming and

---

language into Jewish interpretation. Philo uses the phrase "sober drunkenness" to describe the pure worship of the Therapeutai and Therapeutides (*Contempl.* 11–12; see also 88–89) who "desire the vision of the Existent and soar above the sun of our senses" (ET *Philo: Works*, 9:119). The term "sober drunkenness" is found in various places, including *Leg.* 1.84 (μεθύει τὴν νήφουσαν μέθην) and *Opif.* 71. This idea certainly becomes significant in the contemplative tradition found in later Christian writers, such as Gregory of Nyssa.

[32] Translated by David Winston, *Philo of Alexandria: The Contemplative Life, The Giants, and Selections* (Classics of Western Spirituality; New York: Paulist Press, 1981) 76.

even expulsion during the best sort of ecstasy. But perhaps this move into what looks like madness could be called hyperrationality. In Philo's framework, the mind is akin to God and to the divine Logos, and is ontologically different from the rest of the human.[33] The human mind is expelled only as the person approaches the divine, stretching up into the realm of the Logos, which mediates between human and divine. In *On the Creation of the World*, Philo depicts a cosmos where the ontological gap between God and the human is such a deep chasm that the Logos must stand within it as sympathetic mediator. The human mind, although it is akin to the divine Logos, cannot bridge this gap on its own, because the human is him- or herself a borderland—immortal with respect to the mind, and weighed down by body and lower soul.[34] In ecstasy, the mind is carried over the gap, moved into the realm of the Logos even as it loses its own *logos* and *logismoi*.

Philo constructs a taxonomy of ecstasy not so much to discuss the intricacies of forms of ecstasy as to highlight one particular form as best. Moreover, this form of ecstasy is best precisely because of its epistemic potential to effect a revolution in knowledge within the person experiencing the ecstasy. Who is the heir of divine things? The person who rejects all normal forms of gathering knowledge—the body, sense perception, and *logos*, which is simultaneously reason and the expression of knowledge through language. The heir of divine things is the person whose possibilities of knowing are paradoxically transformed by the absence of his or her own mind, and by the rising of the divine mind. The fourfold taxonomy of ecstasy serves to make several points about knowledge: that normal realms of knowledge are shallow; that it is wise to abandon them; that a completely different—because divine—realm of knowledge yields a truly rich inheritance.

## The Early-Third-Century Debate

Like Philo and Plato, Tertullian and the Anti-Phrygian source also proffer taxonomies, orderings of ecstasy and dreams. But unlike Plato and Philo, these early-third-century texts formulate their taxonomies in a more ex-

---

[33]Philo, *Opif.* 145–46: "Now what is this kinship [between the humans and their divine father]? Every [hu]man, in respect of his mind, is allied to the divine Reason, having come into being as a copy or fragment or ray of that blessed nature, but in the structure of his body he is allied to all the world" (ET *Philo: Works*, 1:115). See also Bovon, "Ces chrétiens," 631–53.

[34]Philo, *Opif.* 135.

plicitly polemical context. Tertullian's *De anima* and the Anti-Phrygian source in Epiphanius (*Pan.* 48.1.4–13.8) are not in direct conversation with each other—Tertullian wrote from Carthage in North Africa, and the provenance of the Anti-Phrygian source is unknown.[35] But both of these works which discuss prophecy and ecstasy use the language of a sound mind and of madness in order to bolster their positions. Philo, as we saw, easily uses terms which either allude or directly refer to Dionysian frenzy and madness to talk about the best form of ecstasy. Although Tertullian does not go quite this far, he too uses the language of madness (*amentia*) as a positive term, in order to challenge the authenticity of his opponents' ecstasies and spiritual status. The Anti-Phrygian source, in contrast, deploys the terminology of madness polemically in precisely the opposite way, in order to challenge the authenticity or truth of its opponents' ecstasies and Christian identity. In chapters 3–5, Tertullian's and the Anti-Phrygian's arguments will be discussed in greater detail. The sections which follow introduce the fascinating third-century debate by focusing on one aspect of argumentation: interpretations of LXX Gen 2:21 and taxonomies of ecstasy (in the Anti-Phrygian's case) and dreams (in Tertullian's case).

As we have already seen, Philo uses Gen 2:21 to exemplify one kind of ecstasy—an ecstasy of rest or quiet—but dismisses this kind of ecstasy as he moves to discuss its more interesting form. The Anti-Phrygian will try to reclaim Gen 2:21's quiet, passive ecstasy as the only true kind of ecstasy, while Tertullian will interpret Gen 2:21 in a completely different way, as an *amentia* or madness which leads to active prophecy. Thus in the early-third-century context, interpretation of Gen 2:21, a moment in the story of Adam's sleep and Eve's creation from his rib, formed a focal point for Tertullian's and the Anti-Phrygian's debate about ecstasy and prophecy.[36] The verse and its context read:

> [21]So the Lord God caused a deep sleep to fall upon the man, and while he slept [in the Septuagint, this reads, "God cast an ecstasy upon Adam, and he slept"; καὶ ἐπέβαλεν ὁ Θεὸς ἔκστασιν ἐπὶ τὸν

[35]For a full introduction to Tertullian, the Anti-Phrygian, and the so-called Montanist controversy, see pp. 155–62, below.

[36]We also find hints elsewhere that Gen 2:21–23 is an important passage for interpretive debate, whether over prophecy and ecstasy or other issues; consider the data provided in *Biblia patristica: index des citations et allusions bibliques dans la littérature patristique.* Paris: Éditions du Centre national de la recherche scientifique, 1975– ). Vol. 1, *Des origins*

Αδαμ, καὶ ὕπνωσεν][37] took one of his ribs and closed up its place with flesh; [22]and the rib which the Lord God had taken from the man he made into a woman and brought her to the man. [23]Then the man said, "This at last is bone of my bones and flesh of my flesh; she shall be called Woman, because she was taken out of Man." [24]Therefore a man leaves his father and his mother and clings to his wife, and they become one flesh. (Gen 2:21-24)[38]

The questions of what happened to Adam as a result of that ecstasy — Did he sleep and rest? Did he awake and prophesy? What are the implications for one's own soul's abilities? — become central to the Anti-Phrygian's and to Tertullian's taxonomies of ecstasy and dreams.

## The Anti-Phrygian Source

In the late-fourth-century C.E. *Panarion*, or *Medicine Box* against the heresies, Epiphanius cobbles together his own writing with various sources he finds in order to develop a list of eighty heresies, which he terms "concubines," over and against the true bride of Christ, which is the pure church.[39] Among the arguments against these eighty heresies is one usually titled "Against the Montanists" (*Panarion* 48-49). But, as we shall discuss more fully in chapter 5, the text does not use the term "Montanist," a later designation. The section is actually directed against the "Phrygians." The source identifies its opponents with a geographical marker that denigrates both Phrygia, a wild and barbarian land, and its inhabitants, who are often

---

à *Clément d'Alexandrie et Tertullien* notes 51 uses of one or more verses of Gen 2:21-23. By far it is Tertullian who is most interested in this passage (24 uses). *Hypostasis of the Archons* and Clement of Alexandria cite it next most frequently (14 uses). Vol. 2, *Le troisième siècle [Origène excepté]* shows reduced interest in the passage, with only 26 citations listed. Origen uses the passage 22 times, according to Vol. 3, *Origène*. Vol. 4, *Eusèbe de Césarée, Cyrille de Jérusalem, Épiphane de Salamine* indicates that among these three authors, it is Epiphanius who is most interested in the passage: 26 out of 34 uses are his, and seven of these, the largest single clustering, are from *Panarion* 48. This raw data provides more support for my argument that Tertullian and Epiphanius's source are engaged in the same discourse, although they are not in direct contact with each other.

[37]The Septuagint edition used is *Septuaginta* (ed. Alfred Rahlfs; Stuttgart: Deutsche Bibelgesellschaft, 1979).

[38]Unless otherwise noted, English translations of the Bible are from the RSV. The Greek edition of the New Testament used is Nestle-Aland's *Novum Testamentum Graece* (26th ed.; Stuttgart: Deutsch Bibelstiftung, 1979).

[39]For more on the *Panarion*, especially its use of gendered rhetoric, see pp. 162-67, below.

characterized as wild, barbarian, and unusually attracted to frenzied ecstasy. Epiphanius's section against the Phrygians is an early-third-century document embedded in *Pan.* 48.1.4–13.8.[40] This text is concerned to argue that the Phrygians are not part of the true church, doing so primarily by challenging the veracity and sound-mindedness of several oracles from the Phrygian prophets Maximilla and Montanus. As part of its argument, the Anti-Phrygian source proffers a tripartite taxonomy of ecstasy, a taxonomy which engages in an interpretive debate over LXX Gen 2:21.

The way in which the Anti-Phrygian source introduces its interpretation of Gen 2:21–24 indicates that these verses are part of a larger and contentious debate, one in which truth is hard to discern because it looks awfully similar to falsehood. (Unfortunately, the Anti-Phrygian's text is also hard to discern because of a lacuna in the text, indicated by the asterisk below). The Phrygians, it says,

> braid a lie to the truth and void of intelligence the mind of those who care for rigid discipline. They heap up for themselves speeches, through which they falsify their own error, saying that certain things are similar, indeed, that they set alongside* from the fact that the holy scripture has said: "The Lord cast an ecstasy upon Adam and he slept." But this is not at all similar to that.[41]

For the Anti-Phrygian source, part of the problem of interpreting Gen 2:21 lies in the fact that it is difficult for the source to differentiate its own position from that of the Phrygians: both use the same scriptures, and the Phrygians' "braided" argument, looked at one way, could seem quite true. The Anti-Phrygian source thus seeks to emphasize difference—difference between its opinion and that of the Phrygians, difference between the Phrygians' behavior in ecstasy and Adam's ecstasy in Genesis 2.

The Anti-Phrygian's interpretation of Gen 2:21 draws on the narrative situation of the passage in Genesis in order to support its definition of ecstasy over

---

[40]Regarding the extent of the source, see pp. 167–70, below.
[41]Εἰ δὲ θελήσουσι παραπλέκειν τῇ ἀληθείᾳ τὸ ψεῦδος καὶ ἀνοητεῖν τὸν νοῦν τῶν τῆς ἀκριβείας ἐπιμελομένων, ἑαυτοῖς τε ἐπισωρεύουσι λόγους, δι' ὧν παραποιητεύονται τὴν ἑαυτῶν πλάνην, ὅμοιά τινα εἶναι λέγοντες, ἵνα δὴ παραστήσωσιν * ἀπὸ τοῦ τὴν ἁγίαν γραφὴν εἰρηκέναι >>ἐπέβαλεν ὁ θεὸς ἔκστασιν ἐπὶ τὸν Ἀδὰμ καὶ ὕπνωσε<<, ἀλλὰ οὐκέτι ὅμοιον τοῦτο εἴη ἐκείνῳ. For Greek edition and information on problems in the text, see Epiphanius, *Panarion haer. 34–64* (ed. Karl Holl; 2d rev. ed. by Jürgen Dummer; GCS; Berlin: Akademie-Verlag, 1980) 225–26, hereafter referred to as Dummer.

and against that of the Phrygians. According to the source, Adam's ecstasy was a one-time affair, a kind of divine anesthetic administered out of God's love for Adam, so that he would not feel pain (*Pan.* 48.6.3).[42] Similarly, in the present, because of God's "compassion and love toward humanity," God has given sleep and rest "for the diversion of a person from care and for the diversion from needful things in life" (*Pan.* 48.6.2). Here the Anti-Phrygian may provide a glimpse of the opinion against which s/he argues: it seems that the Phrygians may have asserted that out of the abundant excess of God's love for humans, God brought similar things (ecstasies, one supposes) upon them as God did upon Adam (*Pan.* 48.4.5). God's *philanthropia* opened a channel between the divine and the human, a channel manifest in ecstasies and prophecies like that of Adam. The Anti-Phrygian effects a separation between its interpretation of Gen 2:21 and that of the Phrygians by arguing that the Phrygians have misunderstood the meaning of *ekstasis*: "For [God] placed upon Adam an ecstasy of sleep, not an ecstasy of wits" (τῆς ἔκστασιν τοῦ ὕπνου, οὐκ ἔκστασιν φρένων). The Anti-Phrygian resists any analogy between the Phrygians and Adam, and elaborates this argument by calling up a taxonomy of *ekstaseis*.

"Ecstasy has many different definitions," argues the Anti-Phrygian, and perfunctorily runs through two of them: "It is called ecstasy on account of an excess of amazement, and madness is called ecstasy on account of the fact that it 'stands outside' of what is prescribed." The source then gets to the heart of the matter—a "correction" of the Phrygians' misinterpretation of Adam's ecstasy:

> But that [referring to Gen 2:21] was called an ecstasy of sleep accord-
> ing to another definition, according to a natural operation, above all on

---

[42]For a late-fourth-century interpretation, see, for example, John Chrysostom, *Homiliae Genesis*, Homily 15 (on Gen 2:20–22). Chrysostom discusses the unusual drowsiness God placed upon Adam, and continues: "So, from man's rib God creates this rational being, and in his inventive wisdom he makes it complete and perfect, like man in every detail—rational, capable of rendering him what would be of assistance in times of need and the pressing necessities of life" (15.11; ET *Homilies on Genesis 1–17* [trans. Robert Hill; FoC 74; Washington, D.C.: Catholic University of America Press, 1986] 200). Chrysostom thinks that Adam "was endowed also with the prophetic grace": "I mean, the reason why this blessed author taught us in the preceding passages that Adam was overcome by drowsiness and sleep so as to have no sense at all of what happened was that when you come to know that on seeing the woman he describes her creation precisely, you may have no doubt that he is saying this under the influence of the prophetic grace and the inspiration of instruction by the Holy Spirit" (15.12; ET Hill, 201).

account of the fact that this ecstasy was brought very deeply upon holy Adam, even while he was being made by God's hand. (*Pan.* 48.4.6)

With the words "another definition, according to a natural operation," the Anti-Phrygian shadowboxes against what must have been the influential interpretive moves of the Phrygians, who understood Adam's ecstasy as the original and authoritative moment, the etiology and justification of their own ecstasies.

But the Anti-Phrygian insists that this form of ecstasy is merely one of rest, characterized by the absence of sense perception: "All the senses leave a person when s/he is sleeping, in order to offer rest."[43] Using Genesis 2's story of creation to draw larger conclusions about anthropology, the Anti-Phrygian argues: "The body (τὸ ὄργανον), which has an earthly nature and surrounds the soul," is "granted a time when it is freed from palpable sense perception into a settled condition of rest" (*Pan.* 48.5.6).

The Anti-Phrygian wants to emphasize that during this time of rest for the body, "the soul does not experience an ecstasy of its governing power or its thought."[44] In an argument very different from Tertullian's, as we shall see, the Anti-Phrygian asserts that dreaming does not bring about an ecstasy of the mind. When the soul "sees itself as if it were awake, and walks and works and crosses the sea and speaks to crowds," it

> never acts like a fool, in ecstasy having become an ecstatic person, who when awake in body and soul takes in hand frightening things, and often abuses himself and his neighbors in a frightening manner. S/he does not know what things s/he cries out, since such a person is in an ecstasy of folly.[45]

---

[43]ἐν τῷ γὰρ ὑπνοῦν τὸν ἄνθρωπον μεθίστανται πᾶσαι αἱ αἰσθήσεις, εἰς ἀνάπαυσιν τραπεῖσαι. *Pan.* 48.5.1; Dummer, 226. The text goes on to recount how each of the five senses lies dormant during this time. The discussion of touch is particularly riveting: "If some creatures pass over our body, we do not feel their touch on our body, except if the creatures run over us heavily, since every organ is in an ecstasy from activity, through rest, from sleep" (*Pan.* 48.5.5).

[44]αὐτὴ δὲ ἡ ψυχὴ οὐκ ἐξέστη τοῦ ἡγεμονικοῦ οὐδὲ φρονήματος. *Pan.* 48.5.6; Dummer, 227.

[45]οὐ μὴν κατὰ τὸν ἀφραίνοντα καὶ ἐν ἐκστάσει γινόμενον ἐκστατικὸν ἄνθρωπον, τὸν τῷ σώματι καὶ τῇ ψυχῇ ἐγρηγορότα τὰ δεινὰ μεταχειριζόμενον καὶ πολλάκις ἑαυτῷ

This passage, with its double-barreled reference to ecstasy (ἔκστασις and ἐκστατικός) juxtaposed with the ideas of foolishness, fear, abuse, and ignorance, reveals that the Anti-Phrygian source does not control the terms of the debate. The very behavior that the Anti-Phrygian marks as foolish and frightening is often understood to be a by-product or marker of ecstasy.[46] It is against an ecstasy that results in such behavior that the Anti-Phrygian source constructs its taxonomy: ecstasy can be defined as amazement, and it can be defined as madness, but Gen 2:21 must be read as evidence of a third sort of ecstasy: an "ecstasy of rest."

The Septuagint's translation of ἔκστασις in Gen 2:21 and subsequent interpretations of Gen 2:21–24 as evidence of an ecstatic and prophetic Adam dominate the discourse, and the Anti-Phrygian source seeks in that context to delimit the meaning of the term *ekstasis*. The author writes: "I have explained the reason why partaking in sleep is called 'an ecstasy from the Lord' in that passage" (*Pan*. 48.6.2). As at the beginning of the discussion of Gen 2:21 (*Pan*. 48.4.4–5), the Anti-Phrygian is concerned to emphasize that God's *philanthropia* consists in removing humans from worries and the troubles of daily life. Thus ecstasy—in Adam's case, as well as at the time of the Anti-Phrygian—is evidence of God's love not because it gives further access to the divine, and not because it represents a moment of God's intense and even violent contact with a human (as others may have argued, and as we recall from Philo) but merely because it gives rest, and, in Adam's case, anesthetizes him from the pain of the rib's removal (*Pan*. 48.6.3).

The Anti-Phrygian insists upon the unbroken and linear continuity of Adam's knowledge. Adam experienced merely an "ecstasy of rest," not one of mental capacities. The source's insistence that Adam "was not in an ecstasy of wits or of thoughts"[47] reminds the reader of the definition of ecstasy which

---

δεινῶς χρώμενον καὶ τοῖς πέλας· ἀγνοεῖ γὰρ ἃ φθέγγεται καὶ πράττει, ἐπειδήπερ ἐν ἐκστάσει γέγονεν ἀφροσύνης ὁ τοιοῦτος. *Pan*. 48.5.8; Dummer, 227.

[46]Eusebius's anonymous source takes a different approach, citing a certain Alcibiades who rejected the idea that a prophet must speak in an ecstasy. Eusebius (*Hist. eccl.* 5.17.1–2; ET Lake, 1:485) quotes his anonymous source: "He continues as follows, 'I have given this abstract of what I found in a work of theirs when they were attacking the work of Alcibiades the Christian in which he shows that a prophet need not speak in ecstasy.' And he goes on in the same work to give a catalogue of those who have been prophets of the New Testament, and among them he numbers a certain Ammia and Quadratus and says thus: 'But the false prophet speaks in ecstasy, after which follow ease and freedom from fear; he begins with voluntary ignorance, but turns to involuntary madness of soul, as has been said before.'"

[47]ἀλλὰ οὐκ ἦν ἐν ἐκστάσει φρενῶν καὶ διανοημάτων. *Pan*. 48.6.4; Dummer, 227.

the Anti-Phrygian resists. The Anti-Phrygian's opponents understand Adam's statement in Gen 2:23 ("This is flesh of my flesh . . ." ) to be prophecy, but the source attempts a different interpretation. The source grudgingly concedes that a prophecy occurred, but merely concludes that Adam "knew" or was aware of (ἐπέγνω) the past (saying "bone of my bone" reveals that he knew what had happened as he slept) and he "knew" the present (that the woman was taken from his body) and, to quote, "he prophesied about the future, that 'for this a person will leave his father and his mother. . . .' "[48] This knowledge and articulation of the past, present, and future gives the Anti-Phrygian further cause to emphasize: "These things are not from an ecstatic man, nor from one who does not follow (conceptually) but of one who has a sound understanding."[49] Unlike Tertullian, who, as we shall see, understands Adam to refer prophetically to Christ and the church, the Anti-Phrygian's interpretation has drained the text of its prophetic punch. Adam merely refers to past, present, and the future event of a man leaving his family and joining his wife—the slow march of linear history.[50] While this periodization of history is natural to us—easy to skim over, and take at face value—we see here that this discourse is launched in a polemical situation, in order to support the Anti-Phrygian's attempt to reclaim the term "ecstasy" away from what it sees as the irrational follies of Montanus, Maximilla, and their disciples.

## Tertullian

Tertullian probably wrote his *De anima* between 210 and 213 C.E., at roughly the same time that the Anti-Phrygian was writing.[51] In *De anima*, Tertullian engages in the debate over sleep, dreams, ecstasy, and the soul, utilizing key terms of ecstasy (*ecstasis*), madness (*amentia*), and dreams (*somnia*). Tertullian's complex ideas about the soul, epistemology, and *amentia* necessitate a thorough exploration in chapters 3 and 4. Here, I focus on some of his theories about sleep and dreaming, his development of a tripartite taxonomy of dreams, and his interpretation of Gen 2:21.

---

[48]*Pan.* 48.6.6; Dummer, 228. These verb tenses reflect an interaction not with the Hebrew text, but with the Septuagint. Indeed, it is because of the Septuagint's use of the term "ecstasy" that these verses are a subject of so much debate.

[49]ταῦτα δὲ οὐκ ἐκστατικοῦ ἀνδρὸς οὐδὲ ἀπαρακολουθήτου, ἀλλὰ ἐρρωμένην ἔχοντος τὴν διάνοιαν. Ibid.

[50]This flat interpretation may also subtly support the Anti-Phrygian's pro-second-marriage stance in *Pan.* 48.8.6–9.10.

[51]For more on the context of *De anima*, see pp. 96, 111–14, below.

In *De anima*, Tertullian argues that the soul's dreams are epistemically valuable. Indeed, he accepts a broad range of phenomena as useful to knowledge, in part because, influenced by Stoicism, he believes sense perception to be valuable epistemically. Moreover, he wants to assert, with the Stoics, that sleep is reasonable (*An.* 43.7), a temporary suspension of the activity of the senses, which procures rest for the body but not for the soul. Rest is "alien to immortality," and the soul, which is immortal and is itself a body,[52] is always active. Tertullian's idea of the soul cannot allow, as the Epicureans and others argue, that sleep represents some intermission or absence of the soul or spirit. From the phenomenon of dreams, he argues that the soul is not inactive in sleep.

Like the sleep centers of today, with their experiments and theories about brain activity during sleep, many in antiquity theorized the mechanics of sleep. In terms common to many sources—in fact, in almost the same words as the Anti-Phrygian source—Tertullian discusses the activity of the soul while dreaming. The Anti-Phrygian source reads:

> For in sleep, all the senses are changed in a person in order that the senses might receive rest. . . . For the body has an earthly character which also surrounds the soul; since God made it useful to us, a time was given to the body that it might cease from palpable sense perception into a state of rest. The soul itself is not in ecstasy, standing apart from its ruling portion (*hegemonikon*) or from thought. For many times it imagines and sees itself as in waking, and it walks and works and crosses the ocean and gives a public speech, seeing itself, through dreams, in more and greater situations. It is *not* become like an ecstatic person, in an ecstasy of foolishness. (*Pan.* 48.5.1, 6–7)

Tertullian echoes (or prefigures):

> [The soul] shows itself in constant motion: it traverses land and sea, it trades, it is excited, it works, it plays, it sorrows, it rejoices, it pursues things lawful and unlawful; it shows that it is capable of much even

---

[52]The Latin edition of *De anima* used throughout this book is that of Jan H. Waszink (*Quinti Septimi Florentis Tertulliani De anima* [Amsterdam: J. M. Meulenhoff, 1947]). Hereafter references to it and to the excellent commentary contained in this edition will be denoted only by his name and a page number. All translations are mine unless otherwise noted. I have found Edwin A. Quain's translation (*Tertullian: Apologetical Works and Minucius Felix Octavius* [FoC 10; 1950; Washington, D.C.: Catholic University of America Press, 1962]) immensely helpful in preparing my own, although I diverge quite a bit from his interpretations.

without the body, that it also is furnished with its own members, although it nonetheless needs the body again in order to accomplish something. Therefore, when the body awakens, resuming its functions, it asserts before your eyes the resurrection of the dead.[53]

The Anti-Phrygian and Tertullian describe the activities and abilities of the dreaming soul in similar ways. It even seems that they do so for similar reasons. The Anti-Phrygian insists that the dreaming soul loses its access to sense perception, but does not abandon governance of itself; it is not like a madman or an ecstatic. Tertullian insists that the dreaming soul "does not wholly rest or become inactive or yield its immortal nature as a servant of sleep"[54]—words that would seem to support the Anti-Phrygian's argument. Yet Tertullian uses the idea of the sleeping soul to different effect, arguing that the soul and the body are never separated. The soul does not exit the body during its dreams.

Tertullian also wants to insist, against other Christians' claims, that dreams are not merely "accidents of sleep" and minor disturbances of the soul.[55] For him, valuable knowledge can be gained through dreams, prophecy, and *amentia*, and this prophetic experience is nothing to be afraid of. Tertullian asserts that the perpetual activity of the soul is natural, and actually a sign that everything is working well: it is part of the soul's "divinity and immortality"—not, that is, merely evidence of something like Artemidorus's *enhypnion*, a dream which simply regurgitates the day's events or reflects difficult digestion. Because rest is natural to the body, but alien to the soul, and because Tertullian believes that the soul too is a body, he asserts that the soul uses its own limbs to continue its activity during the body's rest. Tertullian gives us an image of this: the gladiator without weapons, who fights without effect.[56]

---

[53]"Probat se mobilem semper; terra mari peregrinatur negotiatur agitatur laborat ludit dolet gaudet, licita atque inlicita persequitur, ostendit quod sine corpore etiam plurimum possit, quod et suis instructa sit membris, sed nihilominus necessitatem habeat rursus corporis agitandi. Ita cum evigilaverit corpus, redditum officiis eius resurrectionem mortuorum tibi affirmat." *An.* 43.12; Waszink, 60–61.

[54]"Nec quiescit nec ignavescit omnino nec naturam immoralitatis servam soporis addicit." *An.* 43.12; Waszink, 60.

[55]"de accidentibus somni et non modicis iactationibus animae." *An.* 45.1; Waszink, 62.

[56]"actu enim fiunt, effectu vero non fiunt." *An.* 45.2; Waszink, 62.

Before he develops his taxonomy of dreams, Tertullian uses Gen 2:21 to bolster his point that sleep and ecstasy are related, and that both are divinely sent. I offer Edwin Quain's translation, which is generally excellent, in order to debate his interpretation of this passage and to clarify Tertullian's use of *ecstasis* ("ecstasy") and *amentia*:

> This power we call "ecstasy," a deprivation of the activity of the senses which is an image of insanity. Thus, in the beginning, sleep was preceded by ecstasy, as we read: "And God sent an ecstasy upon Adam and he slept." Sleep brought rest to the body, but ecstasy came over the soul and prevented it from resting, and from that time this combination constitutes the natural and normal form of the dream.[57]

Tertullian sets up three equivalent terms in the first sentence: *ecstasis*, *excessus sensus*, and *amentiae instar*. Quain translates *excessum sensus* as "a departure of sense." While this translation is possible, I argue that a better translation is merely "ecstasy": that is, as in *Adversus Marcionem* Tertullian offers *amentia* as a Latin translation of *ecstasis*, as we shall see later,[58] here he throws in a third equivalent term to explain. *Excessus* is defined as "a leaving of the mental powers, loss of self-possession, = ἔκστασις." Moreover, after the Augustan period *sensus* refers not only to perception, feeling, and sense, but also to "sense, understanding, mind, and reason"; it is a synonym of *mens* and *ratio*.[59] Precisely because the term "ecstasy" is so difficult to define, and is often used polemically, lexica are of little help in situations like these. But here we see that in Tertullian's personal lexicon *excessus* is equivalent to *ecstasis*, as previously (and here again) we have seen that *ecstasis* is equivalent to *amentia*. Moreover, although Waszink recommends that the phrase be translated "a withdrawing of sense-perception and an image of insanity,"[60] *instar* with the genitive can also be a term of equivalency: "like, in the form of,

---

[57]ET Quain, 280. "Hanc vim ecstasin dicimus, excessum sensus et amentiae instar. Sic et in primordio somnus cum ecstasi dedicatus, et misit deus ecstasin in Adam et dormiit. Somnus enim corpori provenit in quietem, ecstasis animae accessit adversus quietem, et inde iam forma somnum ecstasi miscens et natura de forma." *An.* 45.3; Waszink, 62.

[58]*Marc.* 5.8.12; see ch. 4, below.

[59]Charlton T. Lewis and Charles Short, *A Latin Dictionary* (Oxford: Clarendon, 1975), s.v. *excessus* and s.v. *sensus*.

[60]Waszink, 480.

equal to."[61] Thus, while Epiphanius's source describes the shutdown of sense perception, while creatures crawl over the body without the sleeper's knowledge,[62] here we see that Tertullian is not in fact interested in talking about the departure of sense perception, as Quain and Waszink would have it.

Instead, because the Greek term *ekstasis* is so important to his thought, he offers two additional terms, with slightly different nuances, to explain it: "ecstasy, which is a loss of self-possession, which is equivalent to the Latin term *amentia*." Thus Quain's and Waszink's translations, while possible, are misleading and do not take into consideration Tertullian's high valuation of sense perception.

As we shall discuss more fully in later chapters, Tertullian here easily elides the words *ecstasis*—the Greek term for ecstasy—and *amentia*—the Latin term that is usually used to denote madness. Tertullian understands Adam's ecstasy in Gen 2:21 to be an example of the sort of ecstatic dreaming to which any human now has access, not through some natural privileged spiritual state, but through the normal processes of dreaming and ecstasy. Indeed, elsewhere in his corpus, he challenges other Christians to prove their Christianness precisely by producing "some psalm, some vision, some speech, insofar as it is spiritual, in ecstasy—that is, in *amentia*."[63] Unlike the Anti-Phrygian (and perhaps the Anti-Phrygian reacts to interpretations of Gen 2:21 that resemble Tertullian's), Tertullian argues that sleep can lead to ecstasy, an ecstasy that is synonymous with *amentia*, madness. Unlike the Anti-Phrygian, Tertullian insists that Adam's sleep led to the soul's ecstasy, to its tilting toward a kind of madness. This sort of dreaming is natural and normal.

So is every dream a window onto the greater realms of knowledge that ecstasy can offer? No. Tertullian offers a taxonomy that evaluates dreams according to their delusional or beneficial properties. The first kind of dream is sent by demons—the message can be favorable, but the intent is to delude the dreamer. The second class of dreams is from God, and is part of the outpouring of the Holy Spirit which is promised in Joel 2:28–32 (compare Acts 2:17–21): "they may be compared to the grace of God as being honest, holy, prophetic, inspired, edifying, and inducing to virtue."[64] The majority of

---

[61]Lewis and Short, s.v. *instar.*

[62]See n. 43, above.

[63]*Marc.* 5.8.12. This will be discussed in more detail on pp. 141–43, below.

[64]"Ea deputabuntur quae ipsi gratiae comparabuntur, si qua honesta sancta prophetica revelatoria aedificatoria vocatoria." *An.* 47.2; Waszink, 65.

people—the just and the unjust, as Tertullian emphasizes through his story of Nebuchadnezzar's dreams—receive their dreams from God.

The third class of dreams is hardest to understand, and Tertullian describes this class in more detail and with some confusion. They are the dreams "which the soul seems to induce by itself from directing its attention toward the things surrounding it."[65] But then Tertullian recalls that the soul cannot effect dreaming on its own, a point he had discussed in chapter 45. Thus he queries, "Moreover, since [the soul] is not able to dream voluntarily, . . . how can it itself be the cause of any vision? Therefore this class must be laid aside as a natural form [of dreams] which preserves the soul while the soul endures whatever happens to it in ecstasy."[66] This final category of dreams cannot be attributed to a demon or to God; they are "surpassing opinion and interpretation and power of exposition;[67] they are treated as distinct, as properly belonging to ecstasy and its mode."[68] Unlike the Anti-Phrygian, who wants to divorce dreams from the idea of ecstatic madness, Tertullian reaches for the word *ecstasis*—a word he associates with *amentia* and Adam's sleep, as we have seen—to define his third, most ambiguous category of dreams. This category resembles Artemidorus's *oneiros*: an epistemically significant dream that emerges out of something other than the events of the day or one's digestion. Thus Tertullian has constructed a taxonomy that retains two categories of epistemically valuable dreams: those from God and those which seem to be from the soul itself, that is, those which are in some special category, which belong to ecstasy.

Elsewhere in *De anima*, as he attempts to explain the experience of the soul in ecstasy, Tertullian uses Gen 2:21 to make two simultaneous arguments. First, he wants to argue from this verse and those following that Adam, in his ecstatic sleep, prophesied. Tertullian resists those Christians who would assert, like the Anti-Phrygian, that this mention of Adam's ecstasy refers to nothing more than an ecstasy of sleep, or the natural event of rest which overcomes

---

[65]"Tertia species erunt somnia quae sibimet ipsa anima videtur inducere ex intentione circumstantiarum." *An.* 47.3; Waszink, 65.

[66]"Porro quam non est ex arbitrio somniare, . . . quodmodo ipsa erit sibi causa alicuius visionis? Num ergo haec species naturali formae relinquenda est servans animae etiam in ecstasi res suas perpeti?" *An.* 47.3; Waszink, 65–66.

[67]See Waszink's commentary on the passage (p. 506).

[68]"Ea autem, quae neque a deo neque a daemonio neque ab anima videbuntur accidere, et praeter opinionem et praeter interpretationem et praeter ennarationem facultatis, ipsi proprie ecstasi et rationi eius separabuntur." *An.* 47.4; Waszink, 66.

the tired soul. Nor does Tertullian, like the Anti-Phrygian, concede grudgingly that a prophecy occurred, but then drain that prophecy of all power, saying that Adam merely recognized what was going on:

> Certainly, even if Adam immediately prophesied that great mystery with regard to Christ and the church—"Now this is bone of my bones and flesh of my flesh; for this reason a man will leave his father and mother and cling to his wife, and the two will become one flesh"—[this is because] he experienced an accident of the spirit, for an ecstasy fell upon him, a power of the holy spirit, effecting prophecy.[69]

Tertullian instead understands Adam's ecstasy to have brought about a real and powerful prophecy. Second, Tertullian argues that Adam's ecstasy and prophecy were secondary events, not ontologically given to human souls, but an *accidens* of the spirit. Tertullian wants to hedge against a possible misinterpretation—just because he says that Adam experienced a prophetic ecstasy, he does not mean that Adam is some prototype of an ontologically superior, prophetic and spiritual person—and at the same time to accuse other Christian communities of misunderstanding the status of a "spiritual person." Adam was indeed in a real and prophetic ecstasy, even one that is natural, Tertullian claims over and against certain Christian groups, but his spiritual state was a secondary phenomenon, not something ontologically fixed. Tertullian claims that some Christian communities wrongly think that certain humans are spiritual as part of their very being. Rather, he would insist, all humans have access to something like Adam's ecstatic sleep. All humans can enter ecstasy through dreams.

Tertullian, like his contemporaries, privileges origins (here Genesis and the first human) as a way to talk about the human condition in the present, and he understands the creation story to provide an etiology for various present-day ideas. Discussing Adam's "prophecy" in Gen 2:21–24 (*An.* 21.2), Tertullian follows the interpretive strategy of texts such as Eph 5:31–32, which cites Gen 2:24 and then offers its own interpretation of the events of Adam's sleep and awakening, namely, that a prophecy occurs: " 'For this reason a man shall leave his father and mother and be joined to his wife, and

---

[69]"Nam etsi Adam statim prophetavit magnum illud sacramentum in Christum et ecclesiam: hoc nunc os ex ossibus meis et caro ex carne mea; propter hoc relinquet homo patrem et matrem et agglutinabit se mulieri suae, et erunt duo in unam carnem, accidentiam spiritus passus est: cecidit enim ecstasis super illum, sancti spiritus vis operatrix prophetiae." *An.* 11.4; Waszink, 15.

the two shall become one flesh.' This is a great mystery, and I am saying that it refers to Christ and the church." Tertullian thus maintains that Adam in his ecstasy prophesied about Christ and the church, but that this prophecy is due to an *accidens* of the Holy Spirit—which he also calls an *ecstasis*—that is set in apposition to *sancti spiritus vis*—a power of the Holy Spirit, which is an *operatrix prophetiae*. Tertullian, in using the phrase *accidentiam spiritus passus est*, draws upon the common philosophical distinction between what is essential and what is accidental: an *accidens* is by definition secondary or not naturally a part of the essence of a thing. While others, according to Tertullian, would claim that some souls are implanted with spirit as a condition of their being, and thus have access to different realms of knowledge, Tertullian instead argues that all human souls are created equally, since all are the product of the breath of God. Both Tertullian and the Anti-Phrygian, oddly enough, want to argue that ecstasy is an accidental, secondary phenomenon. But the Anti-Phrygian wants a calm, restful, sleeping, entirely sane Adam, while Tertullian embraces the idea that Adam prophesied through a natural process, accessible to all, of madness and ecstasy.

## Conclusions

In 1 Corinthians, Paul also engages in a kind of taxonomizing, although not of the same sort that we have seen in Plato, Philo, the Anti-Phrygian source, and Tertullian. Their threefold and fourfold lists are formally very similar: they offer several definitions, but then settle on one as best. Paul offers a different kind of ordering. His general list of spiritual gifts in 1 Cor 12:8–10 is made more specific by the ranking proffered in 12:28: "And God has appointed in the church first apostles, second prophets, third teachers, then workers of miracles, then healers, helpers, administrators, speakers in various kinds of tongues." This ordering, marked so clearly by ordinal numbers, takes the Corinthians' gifts, their charismata, and divides and ranks them in a way that undoubtedly surprised the Corinthians. Paul separates the gifts of tongues and prophecy, and ranks tongues dead last; wisdom and knowledge, gifts which the Corinthians held dear, have disappeared altogether. As we shall see more fully in the next chapter, Paul ranks and orders spiritual gifts in the context of the rhetoric of unity and of one body.

Plato, Philo, Tertullian, and the Anti-Phrygian source present their taxonomies, whether of ecstasy, dreams, or madness, in different ways. Yet each of these taxonomies functions rhetorically to do two things: to situate the author within a familiar and authoritative tradition of commentary, and to advocate the text's own stance on ecstasy, dreams, or madness. The taxonomies thus dismiss others' ideas of the best sort of ecstasy and others' claims to knowledge received through such a phenomenon. These taxonomies are not neutral lists, but are ranked orderings of this phenomenon. Plato's *Phaedrus* mentions four forms of madness—manic/mantic, a madness that provides release in times of crisis, poetic madness, and the madness of the soul trying to ascend to the divine—but discusses only the last in detail, and with lavish attention and wonder: the ecstasy or madness of the soul which is trying to fly to the gods and the lover who is beside himself is the last and best *mania*. Philo's *Who is the Heir of Divine Things* again follows the fourfold pattern, listing ecstasy because of age or melancholy (a sort of dementia), ecstasy due to extreme amazement, and ecstasy due to passivity of mind (using LXX Gen 2:21 as an example); but he focuses on the fourth and "best" sort of ecstasy. This is "what the inspired and God-possessed experience" (*Her.* 258); it is the eviction of the human mind and the rising of the divine mind. Like Plato, Philo associates the best form of ecstasy with a kind of divine frenzy or madness.

So also Tertullian. In his discussion of dreams, he focuses on the third kind of dream, which is also an ecstasy. Tertullian states that dreams can be from the demons or from God, but focuses on the most ambiguous category of dreams, those which are "surpassing opinion and interpretation and power of exposition; they are treated as distinct, as properly belonging to ecstasy and its mode" (*An.* 47.4). The Anti-Phrygian source counters with three kinds of ecstasy, again engaging in a discussion of only one. Ecstasy can come from amazement, it can be a madness, it can emerge from fear, but the source is most interested in an ecstasy of rest, and argues that LXX Gen 2:21 uses the term "ecstasy" to signal God's granting rest to Adam. The soul is still thinking and self-governing, the source claims, and it is "not like a person who has become ecstatic through foolishness or in ecstasy," who "undertakes terrifying things, and often uses himself and those nearby in a frightening manner" (*Pan.* 48.5.8). The Anti-Phrygian and Tertullian agree that Genesis 2's story of Adam is a crucial text in the debate over ecstasy, but the Anti-Phrygian argues strenuously that Adam's ecstasy was one of sleep, not of "wits" or the mind (φρενῶν).

Tertullian also uses Gen 2:21 to argue about ecstasy, but employs it for different purposes than the Anti-Phrygian. In *De anima*, Tertullian targets his interpretation of Gen 2:21 over and against opponents who, he claims, use the text to argue that Adam is ontologically a spiritual person (and the prototypical spiritual person) because he fell into ecstasy and prophesied. Tertullian instead insists that the *amentia* that fell upon Adam was secondary; the soul is unitary, and the spirit which overcomes a person in ecstasy is an accidental phenomenon. Tertullian's argument is aimed not against those who would rehabilitate or domesticate a definition of ecstasy, as the Anti-Phrygian seeks to do, but against those who would argue that some people are ontologically more capable of experiencing ecstasies and thus of attaining the divine realm of knowledge which ecstasies make accessible.

While Plato, Philo, and Tertullian are interested in an ecstasy that produces unique epistemic possibilities, the Anti-Phrygian is interested in limiting ecstasy to an "ecstasy of sleep," a taxonomic category of little interest to Philo or Tertullian. The Anti-Phrygian source is interested in establishing an authoritative argument about the true nature of ecstasy. It does so not so much by defining ecstasy as by making the *claim* that it is doing so, and then by excluding certain definitions from the purview of what is proper.

Tertullian and the Anti-Phrygian adopt the rhetorical strategy, current in Greco-Roman antiquity, of taxonomizing ecstasy and dreams. They apply this trope to struggles over the boundaries of knowledge among early-third-century Christian communities. What do you know? How do you know it? What guarantees that knowledge is divine, not demonic, that an ecstasy is God's natural gift during sleep, or a madness that marks true Christian identity, rather than evidence of an "ecstasy of folly," of the absence of one's wits or mind? Or, as we turn to Paul's first letter to the Corinthians in the next chapter, what are spiritual gifts, and which are better than others? What sort of taxonomy does Paul shore up in 1 Corinthians? In this chapter and the next, we see that debates over ecstasy and prophecy were at heart also struggles over epistemology, struggles over the boundaries and access to special realms of knowledge, forged in the crucible of claims to true religious or true Christian identity.

# "For We Know Only in Part and We Prophesy Only in Part": Spiritual Gifts and Epistemology in 1 Corinthians

What kind of ecstasy is the best ecstasy? What kind of madness is epistemically transforming? What kind of dream renders knowledge? We have seen that taxonomies of dreams, madness, and ecstasies are not neutral, but participate in a common topos in order to make an argument about what an author thinks is the best form of the phenomenon. Through constructing a taxonomy, the author seeks to define ecstasy, dreams, and madness, and the realms of knowledge these confer. In 1 Corinthians, too, we find a text that is concerned with ordering and ranking, but here the terms of the debate are charismata, "gifts," and *pneumatika*, "spiritual things," usually translated "spiritual gifts." This chapter explores how Paul's letter attempts to persuade the Corinthians to accept certain conclusions about spiritual gifts and about knowledge.

The interwoven strands of epistemology, authority, and identity are the web to which this book returns again and again. By following these threads through 1 Corinthians, I hope to demonstrate that Paul, through his rhetoric about charismata and *pneumatika*, attempts to establish his authority, to limit the fields of knowledge to which the Corinthians had access, and to challenge one of the primary ways in which the Corinthian community was constructing its identity. This use of epistemology, authority, and identity as a lens does not provide perfect vision for untangling the threads of interpretive conundra evoked by 1 Corinthians. Rather, I hope to contribute to the ongoing debate over 1 Corinthians and to demonstrate that, like many texts involved in the debate over prophecy, 1 Corinthians utilizes both a discourse of madness and rationality and one of the periodization of history in order to make its larger point and to attempt to limit the realms of knowledge and the forms of religious identity to which the Corinthians had access.

1 Corinthians is most fruitfully read through the lens of a model of struggle, a struggle which includes debates over prophecy and spirit. The letter makes assertions about epistemology—what knowledge about the divine can be attained, and the proper (according to Paul) limits of that knowledge and the spiritual gifts which are associated with it. As we saw in the last chapter, arguments about prophecy and ecstasy are woven into a larger fabric of assertions about how humans know what they know about the divine, and what or how much they can know. Paul (waveringly, but consistently) tries through his rhetoric to construct boundaries between the human and divine as part of his larger argument regarding wisdom and spiritual gifts in Corinth. Throughout the letter, Paul works to re-form and reform notions of knowledge and wisdom in the Corinthian community. Although the most explicit discussion of knowledge (*gnōsis*) and wisdom (*sophia*) occurs in chapters 1–4, this concern runs like a consistent colored thread throughout the epistle. The discussion of charismata in later chapters is intimately woven into the attempts at epistemic boundary-building in these first chapters.

The Corinthians, it seems, were engaged in the same struggle over knowledge and identity, some questioning Paul's authority as they articulated their own views. Paul's critique of wisdom and knowledge functions to relativize what these Corinthians (think they) know of the divine, to exclude their notions of wisdom and knowledge without suggesting that they should be expelled from the community. Paul accomplishes this in part by employing a discourse of madness and rationality, configured as a discourse of folly and wisdom, and by employing a discourse of the periodization of history, where certain spiritual gifts are devalued, relegated to the realm of incomplete, partial, inadequate knowledge.

This chapter focuses on 1 Corinthians in order to see how the issues of spiritual gifts (especially prophecy and glossolalia) and wisdom and knowledge overlap in this important text—a text by a Jewish author to a primarily Gentile audience, which is often read as the earliest evidence of Christian prophecy.[1] Many of the materials discussed in this book, because they are

---

[1] On the traditional view of Paul (as a Jew who converted to Christianity) versus the newer assessment of Paul (as a Jew who propagated the message of a Judaism open to Gentiles, and Jesus as Christ), see John Gager, *Reinventing Paul* (Oxford: Oxford University Press, 2000) chs. 1–2. See also Daniel Boyarin, *A Radical Jew: Paul and the Politics of Identity* (Berkeley: University of California, 1994).

noncanonical or considered late, are thus not believed to impinge upon the "origins" of Christianity. Hence, they do not raise the kind of fierce scholarly debate that we see in commentaries and monographs on 1 Corinthians. There has been no shortage of sophisticated work on Paul or 1 Corinthians (especially among Protestant scholars), and the variety of methods employed has led to different insights about the letter. Observing even briefly the passion in these interpretations of Paul will allow us to understand better the diluted and thin streams of anxiety that still run through scholarly analyses of the later materials discussed in the following chapters of this book.

Scholars—especially those using anthropological and critical theory— have correctly understood that Paul is concerned with the boundaries of the body, individual and communal; others have studied Paul's interest in knowledge and epistemology. Theologian scholars of the past two centuries have asserted that Paul attempts to "correct" certain Corinthian understandings of wisdom, knowledge, and access to the divine, but frequently have not read this attempt in terms of rhetorical critical analysis or the anthropological theories that elucidate the issues of 1 Corinthians. I hope that the conclusions I reach in this chapter bring these streams of scholarship into conversation. Before I can turn to analyze 1 Corinthians itself, however, I must lay out some of the central issues in the study of 1 Corinthians.

## 1 Corinthians and "Christian" Prophecy

1 Corinthians is a unified letter[2] which employs deliberative rhetoric to convince its audience.[3] Deliberative rhetoric is the "political address of

---

[2]The majority of scholars regard 1 Corinthians as a unity. See Hans Conzelmann, *1 Corinthians: A Commentary on the First Epistle to the Corinthians* (Hermeneia; Philadelphia: Fortress, 1975) 3–4; and Margaret Mitchell, *Paul and the Rhetoric of Reconciliation*, the most complete and impressive monograph on classical rhetoric and 1 Corinthians to date. Martinus De Boer ("The Composition of 1 Corinthians," *NTS* 40 [1994] 229–45) argues unnecessarily that 1 Corinthians was written in two phases: chapters 1–4 respond to oral reports of division from "Chloe's people" while chapters 5–16 respond to new information from Stephanas, Fortunatus, and Achaicus. For arguments about partition hypotheses, see Conzelmann, *1 Corinthians*, 3–4, and especially Mitchell, *Paul and the Rhetoric of Reconciliation*, 2–5; her entire book comprises a careful defense of the letter as a unity.

[3]See Mitchell, *Paul and the Rhetoric of Reconciliation*, 20–64. See also Elisabeth Schüssler Fiorenza, "Rhetorical Situation and Historical Reconstruction in 1 Corinthians," *NTS* 33 (1987) 386–403, especially her review of several scholars' positions on the rhetorical form of 1 Corinthians on 390–93; see also her revision of this article in *Rhetoric and*

recommendation and dissuasion" (γένος συμβουλευτικόν, *genus delibera-tivum*)[4] which, according to Margaret Mitchell's culling of ancient hand-books of rhetoric, has four major characteristics: it focuses on the future time as its subject of deliberation, urging audiences to pursue a course of action for the future; it uses as a main argument appeals to that which is advantageous or beneficial (τὸ συμφέρον);[5] it offers proofs by example (παραδείγματα); and concord and factionalism are topics that it frequently addresses.[6] As part of his struggle with the Corinthians over epistemology and their self-identification as "spiritual people," Paul uses deliberative rhetoric in order to call that community to a particular religious identity and in order to establish the limits of what can be known.

A variety of theories have been presented regarding who these Corinthi-ans—with their interest in being "spiritual people"—were, and what their situation was. These theories usually reveal something about the era and com-mitments of the scholar who interprets the text. Over time, F. C. Baur's and others' thesis of outside opponents or Judaizers has largely been left behind.[7]

---

*Ethic,* 105–28. Note C. Joachim Classen's acerbic article, directed against Hans Dieter Betz's understanding of Hellenistic rhetoric: "St. Paul's Epistles and Ancient Greek and Roman Rhetoric," in *Rhetoric and the New Testament: Essays from the 1992 Heidelberg Conference* (ed. Stanley Porter and Thomas Olbricht; JSNTSup 90; Sheffield, England: JSOT, 1993) 265–91. See especially 269, where Classen points out that the rules for epistolography were at times different from those for rhetoric more generally.

[4]Joop Smit, "Argument and Genre of 1 Corinthians 12–14," in Porter and Olbricht, eds., *Rhetoric and the New Testament,* 222.

[5]On this, see also ibid., 223.

[6]See Mitchell, *Paul and the Rhetoric of Reconciliation,* ch. 2: "Corinthians as Delibera-tive Rhetoric."

[7]See, for example, Conzelmann, *1 Corinthians,* 14–15; and Dieter Georgi, *The Oppo-nents of Paul in Second Corinthians: A Study of Religious Propaganda in Late Antiquity* (Philadelphia: Fortress, 1986) 1–9. Those who hold to a thesis of outside opponents include Gerd Theissen (*The Social Setting of Pauline Christianity* [ed. and trans. John H. Schütz; Edinburgh: T&T Clark, 1982] 40–44), who thinks that the opponents are other itinerant charismatics challenging Paul's role as apostle; Michael Goulder ("Σοφία in 1 Corinthi-ans," *NTS* 37 [1991] 516–34), who thinks the opponents are Petrine Christians; and Walter Schmithals (*Gnosticism in Corinth: An Investigation of the Letters to the Corinthians* [trans. John E. Steely; Nashville, Tenn.: Abingdon, 1971] 113–16), who argues against Zahn that there are not three separate groups of opponents, but rather that there is one group, which identifies itself with Palestinian Judaism, but about which Paul is ill informed. Elizabeth Castelli ("Interpretations of Power in 1 Corinthians," *Semeia* 54 [1991] 198) critiques this search for opponents as part of scholars' construction of Paul as normative, and their "other-ing" of other viewpoints.

Unlike 2 Corinthians, where Paul fights opponents whom he mockingly calls "superapostles," in 1 Corinthians he struggles with the Corinthian community itself, or at least with some members of it. The cause of this struggle has been the subject of much debate. Conzelmann has suggested that the Corinthians exhibit "enthusiastic individualism,"[8] while Walter Schmithals's *Gnosticism in Corinth* moved even further and posited that the Corinthian community tended toward "a pneumatic-libertine Gnosticism" which was at the same time Jewish.[9] "Such pneumatic manifestations as emerge in the community in Corinth," Schmithals explains, "are throughout not specifically Christian. They were widespread in the Hellenistic-syncretistic religions of the primitive into the early church."[10] Hans Conzelmann qualifies this by calling the Corinthians "proto-Gnostic," but then pushes further with the term "Corinthian libertinism."[11] Antoinette Clark Wire tests her theory that the letter is really directed to the Corinthian women prophets.[12] Dale Martin,

[8]Conzelmann, *1 Corinthians*, 212; see also his introduction, where he discusses the "moral and religious disorders" at Corinth which are, in his opinion, bound up with "religious enthusiasm" (14).

[9]Schmithals, *Gnosticism in Corinth*, 117, 193–304.

[10]Ibid., 125. There have been many speculations regarding the original cultic affiliation of most members of the Corinthian community (see, for example, the discussion in Forbes, *Prophecy and Inspired Speech*, 35–38). For example, the phrase "you were led astray to dumb idols, however you may have been moved" (see 1 Cor 12:2–3; πρὸς τὰ εἴδωλα τὰ ἄφωνα ὡς ἂν ἤγεσθε ἀπαγόμενοι) has led to speculations that the Corinthians had previously been involved in some sort of ecstatic pagan cult, perhaps Dionysian; this phrase alone gives no evidence about the identity of the cult. Some have tried to explain 1 Corinthians by cobbling together the theory that the Corinthians were (pagan) ecstatics newly converted, whose women prophesied ecstatically and with wanton loose hair, whose main concern was with individualized religious experiences that looked like madness. But this interpretation assumes that Paul describes the Corinthians accurately and also relies on Orientalist stereotypes about exotic Greek and Eastern-influenced religions in antiquity.

[11]Conzelmann, *1 Corinthians*, 14–15. Thus both use scholarly categories to point to the "otherness" of the opinions against which Paul argues; "Jew," "Gnostic," "Hellenistic," and "syncretistic" are codes for "not us" and implicitly try to define Christianness in terms of what it is not. On the critique of such categories and the study of the definition of Christian identity in historiography of early Christianity, see King, *What is Gnosticism?*, and Denise Kimber Buell, "Rethinking the Relevance of Race for Early Christian Self-Definition," *HTR* 94 (2001) 449–76.

[12]Antoinette Clark Wire, *The Corinthian Women Prophets: A Reconstruction Through Paul's Rhetoric* (Minneapolis: Fortress, 1990). In support of Wire's hypothesis, see Luise Schottroff, "A Feminist Hermeneutic of 1 Corinthians," in *Escaping Eden: New Feminist Perspectives on the Bible* (ed. Harold C. Washington et al.; New York: New York University Press, 1999) 208–15.

in part working from Johannes Weiss's theory of more than ninety years earlier,[13] hypothesizes that the central issue in the Corinthian community is the ideological struggle of the "strong" and the "weak" over the body:[14] the strong are less concerned with pollution and bodily boundaries, while the weak insist upon purity.[15]

Attempts to isolate who the Corinthians are or the "factions" in which they participate are frustrated because we hear only Paul's side of the story. Paul discusses what the Corinthians are *not*, in his opinion: he challenges their self-understanding as "spiritual people." Even as Paul acknowledges the wealth and importance of spiritual gifts among the Corinthians, he ranks and prioritizes these gifts as a challenge to their own priorities. Paul effects the latter strategy not only by employing the rhetoric of unity, including the terminology of "one body" that he has borrowed from political discourse, but also—and more significantly, for this study—by his delimitation of fields of knowledge. The text seeks to "correct" the community's behavior, practice, and self-understanding by drawing the boundaries of what one can properly know or not know.

Despite these fundamental questions about 1 Corinthians and its audience, and despite a host of other important candidates like Revelation, *Shepherd of Hermas*, and the *Didache*, 1 Corinthians is nevertheless often understood to be a text of primary significance to the study of early Christian prophecy, in part because of its early date and canonical status. Scholars tend to privilege Paul's injunctions regarding prophecy and tongues in 1 Corinthians as the

---

[13]See Johannes Weiss, *A History of the Period A.D. 30–150* (vol. 1 of *Earliest Christianity*; trans. Frederick C. Grant; New York: Harper & Brothers, 1959) 323–41. The German edition appeared in 1903.

[14]Dale B. Martin, *The Corinthian Body* (New Haven: Yale University Press, 1995) esp. ch. 7: "Sex, Food, and the Pollution of the Corinthian Body."

[15]Mary Douglas's theory of group and grid as a tool informs both Wire's reconstruction of Corinthian women prophets and Martin's reconstruction of the faction of the "Strong." This theory has become a key paradigm for interpreting the Corinthian situation: high group is characterized by strong group control of the individual, while high grid signifies a shared symbolic and ritual universe. According to this theory, the Corinthian prophets veer toward the individual and toward a private system of classification of symbols. (See especially Douglas, *Natural Symbols*, ch. 4, "Group and Grid"; and Wire, *The Corinthian Women Prophets*, esp. 188–96. Martin does not use Douglas as extensively, but see his *The Corinthian Body*, 30–34.) A method gained from anthropological theory then may be used to enhance the conclusion that the Corinthians were individualistic and libertine, and that Paul is trying to rein them back into the upbuilding of community.

model of correct early Christian prophecy and to assume that Paul represents the majority of the earliest Christians' understandings of prophecy, as Elisabeth Schüssler Fiorenza demonstrates.[16] This is problematic for several reasons. First, and most obvious, Paul is a Jew, writing at a time when the term "Christian" did not even exist. 1 Corinthians provides evidence of ideas of prophecy and spiritual gifts within first-century C.E. Judaism (and Gentile converts to Judaism),[17] although of course Paul's ideas later become authoritative for early Christian communities. Second, as Schüssler Fiorenza points out, this strategy of preferring 1 Corinthians because of its early date presumes that Paul's discussion of prophecy is a more valuable tool for discussing the phenomenon in earliest Christianity, than, for example, the (to us) stranger text of Revelation—the only New Testament book which explicitly claims to be prophecy (Rev 1:3). Exposing the circular nature of such reasoning, she states: "Theologically, scholars have tended to insist on the word- and kerygma-character of early Christian prophecy, while theoretically employing the Pauline understanding of prophecy to construct the model of genuine early Christian prophecy."[18] The book of Revelation in contrast is odd, embarrassing, judgmental, and harsh; thus, some scholars have categorized it not as Christian prophecy, but as Jewish apocalyptic. Such an analysis is undergirded by "rigid differentiations between Jewish (Old Testament) and early Christian prophecy, between apocalypticism and prophecy, and between prophecy as kerygmatic event and as visionary-ecstatic expression."[19] This prejudice against Revelation can also be found in analyses that posit a single diachronic evolution of prophecy: for example, G. Friedrich sees Revelation

[16]Elisabeth Schüssler Fiorenza, *The Book of Revelation: Justice and Judgment* (Philadelphia: Fortress, 1985) 133.

[17]Although the existence of Jewish missions in the first century is much debated, I agree with those who see Paul as a Jewish missionary, and who conclude that missions were a common phenomenon within Judaism. This argument is most clearly set forth in Georgi, *The Opponents of Paul*; see also Theissen, *The Social Setting of Pauline Christianity*, 42–43. For a more recent articulation of the argument for the existence of Jewish missions, see Shelly Matthews, *First Converts: Rich Pagan Women and the Rhetoric of Mission in Early Judaism and Christianity* (Stanford, Calif.: Stanford University Press, 2001) 1–5. Regarding the inadequacy of our categories for capturing Paul's hybrid identity as "Jewgreek" or "Greekjew," see Boyarin, *A Radical Jew*, 78–79. Regarding the Corinthian community as largely Gentile, see, e.g., Werner Georg Kümmel et al., *Introduction to the New Testament* (trans. A. J. Mattill, Jr. from the 14th rev. ed. [1965]; Nashville, Tenn.: Abingdon, 1966) 200.

[18]Schüssler Fiorenza, *The Book of Revelation*, 133.

[19]Ibid.

as part of a "transition from early Christian prophecy to apocalyptic," while Paul's paranesis represents authentic prophecy.[20] Revelation is often overlooked precisely because it is a vision, a prophecy given "in the spirit," and to many of us a strange one, embraced by those deemed marginal, such as the Branch Davidians at Waco. 1 Corinthians has been given pride of place in the story of New Testament and early Christian prophecy because scholars have understood Paul as taking a stand *for* rationality and *against* madness or frenzy; or, analogically, for community building (*oikodomē*) and against individualized use of spiritual gifts; for the cross and against wisdom; for kerygma and against ecstatic glossolalia.[21] An authoritative New Testament text may reveal Christian origins in vibrant charismata, scholars want to argue, but not *too* vibrant. Hans Conzelmann, for example, states that Paul chooses the cross over wisdom and "[sets] νοῦς [mind] above ecstasy—relatively, in the same sense as he sets prophecy above speaking with tongues. The 'spirit' is subordinated to a rational, theological judgment."[22]

Why then does this study not focus on Revelation, devoting at least a chapter to it, rather than bending as it does towards Paul's powerful magnetism in early Christian tradition and the traditions of scholarly interpretation? Let me give several reasons. First, parts of Paul's discussion of prophecy in 1 Corinthians may influence some of the early third-century texts in which this study is also interested. Revelation, of course, represents a marginalized prophet of marginalized communities within the Roman empire, and its peripheral status in second- and third-century discussions and within the canon has echoed this. Second, my book focuses not so much on evidence of the phenomenon of prophecy and ecstasy, which we find in Revelation, as on

---

[20]Friedrich's view is summarized in ibid., 138–39; Schüssler Fiorenza instead understands Paul's thought as part of the larger trends of apocalyptic prophecy that can be found in the Gospels and in Revelation.

[21]Allen Hunt (*The Inspired Body: Paul, the Corinthians, and Divine Inspiration* [Macon, Ga.: Mercer University Press, 1996] 143) concludes, for example: "Paul . . . differs from many other ancient writers since he provides for the validity of rational, nonecstatic inspiration, the priority of ἀγάπη and οἰκοδομή, and a missional aspect of corporate behavior."

[22]Conzelmann, *1 Corinthians*, 237, regarding 1 Cor 14:14. Many scholars, however, insist that in 1 Corinthians Paul argues for rationality and advocates a controlled, nonecstatic prophecy and spiritual gifts. See, e.g., Forbes, *Prophecy and Inspired Speech*, 27–43, 64, 71–74.

discussions of and debates over prophecy and ecstasy.[23] Recently, scholarship has investigated 1 Corinthians as a struggle between Paul and the Corinthians (and perhaps even among the Corinthians themselves) about the variety of issues that emerge in this epistle and in those fragments of epistles found in 2 Corinthians.[24] Third, as Conzelmann's statement above shows, Paul's enormous importance within New Testament scholarship and the immense amount of attention focused on 1 Corinthians allow me to highlight some views on prophecy where they are most deeply felt and debated both in the history of interpretation and in the reconstruction of early Christianity. The stakes are high for interpreters of Paul in a way that they are not for interpreters of Revelation, since Revelation is not picked up and discussed in mainstream theological traditions with the frequency that Paul's writings are.

In the following pages, I shall argue that Paul struggled with the Corinthians over spiritual gifts, including prophecy and glossolalia, in four main ways. First, he asserted his authority by challenging the Corinthians' self-understanding as spiritual people (*pneumatikoi*) in part by using a discourse analogous to that of rationality and madness—one of wisdom and foolishness. He sought to redefine and even invert the meaning of *mōria* (folly) and *sophia*/*gnōsis* (wisdom/knowledge). Simultaneously, he constructed his own authority as father and founder of the Corinthians, and challenged the Corinthians' self-identification as *pneumatikoi*.

Second, Paul drew upon the ἓν σῶμα, or "one body," rhetoric of antiquity in order to further his argument about spiritual gifts and their role in constructing the Corinthians' religious identity and practice. His borrowings from this powerful contemporary political discourse emphasize the importance of unity, harmony, and communal benefit. Third, Paul intertwines the rhetoric of unity and one body with his discussion of spiritual gifts in 1 Corinthians 12–14.

---

[23]Some speculate, however, that Revelation itself embodies debates over prophecy and competition over prophetic groups or schools in Asia Minor. See Barbara Rossing, *The Choice Between Two Cities: Whore, Bride, and Empire in the Apocalypse* (HTS 48; Harrisburg, Pa.: Trinity Press International, 1999) 9–10; see also Paul Brooks Duff, *Who Rides the Beast? Prophetic Rivalry and the Rhetoric of Crisis in the Churches of the Apocalypse* (Oxford: Oxford University Press, 2001).

[24]This model of struggle, of course, does not assume that Paul's views are normative. As a contrast, compare the remarks of Hunt (*The Inspired Body*, 138–39), who states with regard to 1 Corinthians 15: "Paul again seeks to correct the misguided notions and behavior of the Corinthians, particularly those Corinthians who are laying claim to a unique access to the divine mind."

In this section of the letter, what seems to begin as a neutral discussion of spiritual gifts ends in the classification and ranking of charismata.

Finally, Paul further challenges the Corinthians' identity and their access to knowledge by making subtle arguments in 1 Corinthians 13 about love superseding knowledge and prophecy. This argument is undergirded by a discourse of the periodization of history. Scholars have argued that Paul's eschatology leads him to "correct" the Corinthians: while the Corinthians may have seen resurrection as a phenomenon to be achieved in the present, Paul's view of the eschaton, or end times, leads him to insist that the resurrection is a future event.[25] I argue instead that Paul's use of history within the letter is part of a larger discourse at his time: those who participate in debates over prophecy often also theorize about the spirit's role in history in order to shore up their arguments. In the following sections of this chapter, I shall address each of these four points in turn.

## Human Wisdom, Divine Folly, and the Politics of Identity: Who Are the *Pneumatikoi*?

At least a quarter of 1 Corinthians discusses "spiritual people" (πνευμα-τικοί), wisdom, and knowledge, and the relationship between Paul and other apostles and the Corinthian community (chapters 1–4). Paul's long, four-chapter beginning to the epistle is not merely an introduction or a reminder of that relationship, but a construction of it: a retelling of the relationship as Paul wants it to be seen, and his attempt to persuade his actual audience to become the model audience that he rhetorically constructs.[26] Antoinette Clark Wire points out that Paul from the beginning characterizes the Corinthians as "enriched in [Christ Jesus] with all speech and all knowledge . . . so that you are not lacking in any spiritual gift (ἐν μηδενὶ χαρίσματι) as you wait for the revealing of our Lord Jesus Christ" (1 Cor 1:5b, 7). But as the letter unfolds, it becomes clear that these things—the knowledge and speech of the Corinthians, and their

---

[25]See, for example, Wire's reading in *The Corinthian Women Prophets*, 159–96. For a similar idea taken in a different direction, see Conzelmann's argument (*1 Corinthians*, 14).

[26]See Mitchell, *Paul and the Rhetoric of Reconciliation*, 66–68; and Wire, *The Corinthian Women Prophets*, 39–40. Regarding the unusual terminology of 1 Corinthians 1–4, see Koester, *Ancient Christian Gospels*, 56: "Most striking is the frequency of the terms

spiritual gifts — are precisely what Paul wishes to challenge.[27] That wisdom and knowledge were central to the Corinthian community is a long-held scholarly view, as evidenced by the debate over Corinthian "Gnostics" mentioned above.[28] Paul constructs his own relationship with the Corinthians in terms of knowledge and its limits: "When I came to you, brethren, I did not come proclaiming to you the mystery[29] of God in lofty words or wisdom. For I decided *to know nothing* among you except Jesus Christ and him crucified" (1 Cor 2:1–2; my emphasis). And yet Paul then quickly turns, five verses later, to state that "we speak of the hidden wisdom of God in a mystery" (my translation), but only to those who are mature, or "perfect," completed (τελείοι, 2:6–7). Paul asserts that because the Corinthians know less than they think they do — that is, because they are not so epistemically advanced, he was forced to emphasize knowledge of "Christ crucified" rather than "Christ the Power and Wisdom of God."[30] In stating that "we preach Christ crucified, a stumbling block to Jews and a folly to Gentiles" (1:23), Paul critiques the Gentile Corinthian community, accusing them of finding a crucified messiah a foolish concept and of wanting to move too quickly to the idea of "Christ the Wisdom and Power of God," a teaching for the mature.[31]

---

'wise' (σόφος) and 'wisdom' (σοφία). The former occurs ten times in these four chapters of 1 Corinthians, but elsewhere in Paul only four times, the latter is used sixteen times here, but elsewhere only three times."

[27]For a different interpretation of the importance of *sophia* in 1 Corinthians, see Michael Goulder ("Σοφία in 1 Corinthians," 516–34), who sees the epistle's strong interest in wisdom as part of a Jewish debate over new halakhic interpretations of Torah and who revives F. C. Baur's thesis of "Judaizers" in the Corinthian community. For this last insight, and for an appreciative but strong critique of this argument, see Christopher Tuckett, "Jewish Christian Wisdom in 1 Corinthians?," in *Crossing the Boundaries: Essays in Biblical Interpretation in Honour of Michael D. Goulder* (ed. Stanley Porter et al.; Leiden: E. J. Brill, 1994) 201–19.

[28]Regarding *sophia* and the Corinthians, see also Helmut Koester, *Ancient Christian Gospels: Their History and Development* (Philadelphia: Trinity Press International and London: SCM Press Ltd., 1990) 55–62.

[29]Some manuscripts read μαρτύριον, "testimony," and the RSV uses this translation. The authority of the manuscripts is almost evenly split, however, and the context and use of μυστήριον a few verses later leads me to conclude that μυστήριον is the better reading in verse 2.

[30]The full force of this argument is clear by the time that Paul accuses the Corinthians of being fleshly, like infants, and not at all perfect or complete.

[31]See Elisabeth Schüssler Fiorenza, *Jesus: Miriam's Child, Sophia's Prophet: Critical Issues in Feminist Christology* (New York: Continuum, 1994) ch. 5.

Paul contrasts words of human wisdom — something which the Corinthians misguidedly value, he asserts — and true, legitimate divine power. He claims that his own message at Corinth was paradoxically powerful in its ineloquence: it was "not in plausible words of wisdom, but in demonstration of the Spirit and of power, that your faith might not rest in the wisdom of men but in the power of God" (2:4–5).[32] The incommensurability of human wisdom and divine wisdom and power undergirds much of 1 Corinthians. God's wisdom is folly in human eyes, but "the foolishness of God is wiser than humans, and the weakness of God is stronger than humans" (1:25; my translation). This sort of upside-down logic fits well with the Corinthians' situation: "For consider your call, brethren," Paul states:

> not many of you were wise according to worldly standards, not many were powerful, not many were of noble birth; but God chose what is foolish in the world to shame the wise, God chose what is weak in the world to shame the strong, God chose what is low and despised in the world, even things that are not, to bring to nothing things that are, so that no human being might boast in the presence of God. (1:26b–29)

Paul emphasizes the irony of it all: a messiah who has been humiliated and crucified and who is now God's *Sophia*, a community of low status in worldly standards which has been filled with wisdom and power through participation in the story of Christ. God prefers this upside-down universe, but Paul accuses the Corinthians — formerly low, now in God's logic brought high — of mistakenly valuing elegant speech or something that resembles a new wisdom or seems to be a new power. Paul argues that God's wisdom, which brought Christ to crucifixion, looks foolish to human eyes (that is, to the Corinthians, with their interest in power and wisdom), but even God's foolishness exceeds human wisdom (1:25). The Corinthians are not privy to this "secret and hidden wisdom of God" (2:7). The Corinthians are mistaken in thinking of themselves as wise and as complete or perfect (τελείοι) or at least moving in that direction. In fact, the Corinthians are not πνευματικοί, people of spirit, not even ψυχικοί, people of soul, but were and are σαρκικοί, people of flesh — the lowest rung (2:13–3:3). Their behavior is that of mere infants (νήπιοι).

---

[32]Schüssler Fiorenza (*Rhetoric and Ethic*, 107) writes: "The pioneering studies of Paul's rhetoric by Hans Dieter Betz and Wilhelm Wuellner have demonstrated that Paul was well skilled in formal rhetoric, despite his claim to the contrary in 1 Corinthians."

It is here that we see the discourse of rationality and madness, or, in Paul's terms, of sober wisdom and foolish misperception. Struggling with the Corinthians to maintain his authority and to shift their understanding of spiritual matters, Paul asserts that the Corinthians have it all wrong: they should be seeking the folly which marks divine wisdom, rather than the human wisdom which is folly in God's eyes. As we saw in the last chapter, Paul's contemporary, Philo, argued that during the best form of ecstasy, the divine mind enters while the human mind is expelled. The resulting behavior can seem drunken or aberrant, but is in fact a marker of a new epistemic clarity. At first, it seems that Paul will move in this direction—he does insist, after all, on the inadequacy of human wisdom compared to divine. But later in 1 Corinthians, Paul hedges against behavior that could be mistaken for madness, expressly limiting the exercise of glossolalia as a spiritual gift. He states that he is concerned that others will think the Corinthians crazy[33] if they engage in such behavior (14:22–23). Paul is not like Philo, who accepts the paradox that ecstasy simultaneously brings the clarity of divine knowledge and a human behavior which looks drunk. Instead, Paul undercuts the Corinthians in two different directions: first, he argues that spiritual gifts like glossolalia should be limited because they lead to confusion; and second, he argues that the Corinthians, despite the fact that they manifest behaviors that to others looks crazy (for someone like Philo, a possible sign of the best sort of ecstasy), only *think* that they are accessing divine knowledge.

Paul continues to challenge the Corinthians' idea of their own transformation by explaining more about knowledge and spirit: "As it is written, 'What no eye has seen, nor ear heard, nor the heart of man conceived, what God has prepared for those who love him,' God has revealed to us through the Spirit" (2:9–10a).[34] This sort of epistemic transformation makes people "mature" or "perfect." Humans are normally caught in their fleshiness or even at the level of the soul; by this state they are limited in terms of how they can grasp knowledge and what they can know. The spirit, in contrast, reveals realms of knowledge formerly unknown and perhaps normally unknowable, allowing for transformation as humans can access new realms of knowledge—knowl-

---

[33] οὐκ ἐροῦσιν ὅτι μαίνεσθε; "Will they not say that you are mad?" (1 Cor 14:23; my translation).

[34] This "strange 'quotation from scripture,'" as Helmut Koester calls it, has been much discussed because of a parallel, attributed to Jesus, which is found in *Gospel of Thomas* 17. The parallel further supports the notion of the Corinthian community's interest in *gnōsis*. See Koester, *Ancient Christian Gospels*, 58–59.

edge that is part of the divine realm, rather than the human. To explain why
the spirit is necessary for such wisdom, Paul argues from analogy: just as the
human spirit alone knows one's deepest thoughts, so also the spirit of God
alone searches "the depths of God" (2:10). Moreover, only "the spirit" can
bridge the gap between the human and the divine, and turn divine foolishness
into human wisdom, and human wisdom into divine folly. None of this, I think,
would have surprised the Corinthians. The emphasis throughout the letter
on spiritual gifts and the contestation of the Corinthians' identity as spiritual
people indicates that the Corinthians probably understood their epistemic
transformation to be linked precisely to their access to spirit and its effects.

Yet Paul criticizes the so-called spiritual people (πνευματικοί) of the
Corinthian community, who surely think that they are among the perfect or
complete. He begins at a distance, naming no names, speaking only in the
first person plural, leaving open the possibility that he and the Corinthians
are involved in the same project: "[the gifts bestowed by God] we impart
in words not taught by human wisdom but in teachings of spirit, discern-
ing spiritual things for those who are spiritual" (2:13; my translation). Paul
then makes a distinction between this πνευματικός, or spiritual person, and
a ψυχικός. The latter term will have a long history, as we shall see later.[35]
This ψυχικός "does not receive the gifts of the Spirit . . . ,[36] for they are folly
to him, and he is not able to understand them because they are spiritually
discerned" (2:14). The spiritual person, in contrast, judges all things, and
can be judged by no one.

Paul's critique becomes more incisive as he recounts his history with the
community, stating that he could not address them as πνευματικοί, but had
to approach them as σαρκικοί — people of the flesh. This was not only true
in the past; they are "still of the flesh" (3:3).[37] Paul attributes this low anthropological state to the Corinthians' habit of associating themselves with one
particular (human) apostle or another ("I am of Apollos"; "I am of Paul").[38]

---

[35]In a Stoic world view, as we shall see in Tertullian, the state of being a spiritual person
is understood to be secondary and accidental, not natural to the human condition, which
received a soul at its origin, but not an additional, divine or demonic spirit. 1 Corinthians
alone of Paul's letters contains the term ψυχικός, which probably indicates Paul's adoption
of Corinthian terminology.

[36]Note that "of God" is present only in inferior manuscripts.

[37]ἔτι γὰρ σαρκικοί ἐστε. Paul characterizes their strife as κατὰ ἄνθρωπον, "human."

[38]Koester (*Ancient Christian Gospels*, 62) suggests that "a Corinthian faction" may have
"understood particular apostles as their mystagogues from whom they received sayings
which revealed life-giving wisdom." Stephen Pogoloff (*Logos and Sophia: The Rhetorical*

Paul relativizes his own position and authority in the community, and also that of Apollos: God is the active principle, the apostles rendered equal as equally active servants of this active God. The Corinthian community is depicted as passive—it is "God's field, God's building," on which Paul and others toil (3:5–9).[39] Later, Paul will overturn this image of his equality with Apollos, asserting the primacy of his own relationship with the community. Here, however, Paul renders the Corinthians literally as constructions of his and Apollos's labors. It is the Corinthians' improper activity, their assertion of religious genealogy from Paul or Apollos or another apostle, and their struggle to define their religious identities that, according to Paul, are evidence of their low anthropological status as σαρκικοί.

In a way, it is the Corinthians' false sense of wisdom and knowledge that has led them to folly, according to Paul: "If any one among you thinks that he is wise in this age, let him become a fool that he may become wise. For the wisdom of this world is folly with God" (3:18–19). And Paul soon again upends the spiritual triumph of the Corinthians by using what may be their joyful terms of spiritual wealth to foreground a description of his misery. They are filled, rich; they rule as kings (4:8); there is some sort of ongoing transformation in the community. Although they were once despised and weak, they now enjoy some sort of power. Paul's ironic speech[40] emphasizes how he in contrast suffers for Christ in labor, in persecution, in slander, hunger, and homelessness, while the Corinthians are strong, honored, "wise in Christ" (4:10). This irony is capped off by Paul's insistence that he is the father of the community: "For I became your father in Christ Jesus through the gospel. I urge you, then, be imitators of me" (4:15b–16). His insistence on this status and on imitation is an endpoint in the evolution of his argu-

---

*Situation of 1 Corinthians* [SBLDS 134; Atlanta, Ga.: Scholars Press, 1992] esp. chs. 4–5) argues that rhetoric is related to social status, and that the Corinthians were using the status of rhetors such as Paul and Apollos to fuel divisions in the community. I disagree with this hypothesis, even as I agree with Pogoloff's articulation of a connection between rhetorical skill and status.

[39]This metaphor of building is quickly rendered anew into the image of the Corinthians as "God's temple," a holy place, in which God's spirit dwells: "Do you not know that you are God's temple and that God's Spirit dwells in you?" This question may have surprised: of course the Corinthians, whom Paul early on characterizes as "enriched in [Christ Jesus] with all speech and all knowledge . . . so that you are not lacking in any spiritual gift" (1:5, 7), are aware of God's spirit, which grants speech, knowledge, and spiritual gifts.

[40]For a more extensive discussion, see Karl Plank, *Paul and the Irony of Affliction* (Atlanta, Ga.: Scholars Press, 1987).

ment: first, he insisted on the equality of his status and Apollos's, but here he constructs his relationship with the Corinthian community as that of a father with his "beloved children," a shift from his usual kinship rhetoric of brotherhood.[41] The insistence on mimesis is part of a discourse of power and persuasion, whereby Paul demotes the current Corinthian identity as wrong-headed, and promotes himself as the authority and even as a model for constructing an alternative identity.[42]

In 1 Corinthians 1–4, Paul does not explicitly say that the Corinthians *cannot* attain the wisdom of God. His discussion of the spirit of God in 2:9–16, however, asserts that there is a deep gap between the human and the divine. Only the spirit of God comprehends the thoughts of God, just as one only knows one's own thoughts through one's spirit. It is indeed possible, says Paul, to possess the spirit of God, but the critique that follows indicates that although the Corinthians think that they have it, they do not, in Paul's eyes. "Now we have received not the spirit of the world, but the Spirit which is from God, that we might understand the gifts bestowed on us by God" (2:12),[43] Paul states earlier in the letter, but his tone changes in chapters 12–14, as he makes an argument about how the Corinthians should understand those gifts: "Now concerning spiritual gifts, brethren, I do not want you to be uninformed" (12:1).[44] Paul wants to assert that the Corinthians do not have a correct understanding of *pneumatika*, and perhaps then do not really have the spirit of God.

---

[41]See R. F. Collins ("Reflections on 1 Corinthians as a Hellenistic Letter," in *The Corinthian Correspondence* [ed. R. Bieringer; BETL 125; Leuven: Leuven University Press, 1996] 47–53) on 1 Corinthians as a letter of admonition that establishes a paternal tone, as well as a piece of deliberative rhetoric. Schüssler Fiorenza ("Rhetorical Situation," 397) states, "while I agree with Dahl that the rhetoric of 1 Corinthians clearly intends to *establish* 'the authority of Paul *as* the founder and father of the entire church at Corinth,' I would argue that it does not reestablish, but introduces such unique authority claims." See also idem, *Rhetoric and Ethic*, 119.

[42]Elizabeth A. Castelli, *Imitating Paul: A Discourse of Power* (Louisville, Ky.: Westminster/ John Knox, 1991) 23–33.

[43]ἡμεῖς δὲ οὐ τὸ πνεῦμα τοῦ κόσμου ἐλάβομεν ἀλλὰ τὸ πνεῦμα τὸ ἐκ τοῦ θεοῦ, ἵνα εἰδῶμεν τὰ ὑπὸ τοῦ θεοῦ χαρισθέντα ἡμῖν.

[44]The debates over the gender of πνευματικῶν will not be rehearsed here. See Conzelmann's convincing argument that it is neuter (*1 Corinthians*, 204).

## One Body

Paul begins his letter by questioning the Corinthians' identity as *pneumatikoi*. Paul later attempts to shape the identity of the Corinthians in another way: by utilizing the common contemporary political rhetoric of "one body," which emphasizes community harmony and mutual benefit. In 1 Corinthians 1–4, Paul asserted that human wisdom is foolishness, and that divine wisdom, revealed by the spirit, is the thing to seek, the thing that makes one truly a spiritual person and truly "perfect." Yet in chapters 12–14, in a discussion of *pneumatika* ("spiritual things") and charismata,[45] Paul argues that there is no real access to full, perfect, divine wisdom, either. Paul inserts his argument about community—the rhetoric of "one body"—even as he makes a larger point about epistemology and community identity: certain kinds of knowledge are inaccessible in the present, and complete epistemic transformation—perfection, or access to full and divine knowledge, or a resurrected life—is impossible in the here and now.

Paul introduces the topic with the statement, "Now concerning spiritual gifts, brethren, I do not want you to be uninformed" (12:1).[46] This statement was probably quite a shock to the Corinthian community: with their interest in wisdom and knowledge, the Corinthians likely understood themselves to be quite well informed about spiritual gifts.[47] Indeed, as Helmut Koester argues, it is likely that the Corinthians' own vocabulary may dictate much of the letter's lexicon, since many terms in the letter do not appear frequently elsewhere in Paul's correspondence.[48] And the Corinthians, with their interest in *pneumatika*, are on the cutting edge of an emerging medical and philosophical debate in the first and second centuries. From the fourth to the first centuries B.C.E., terms etymologically related to *pneumatika* are found approximately thirty-six times. In the first century C.E. we find at least one hundred and four uses of the term, and in the second century C.E., a shocking nine hundred and ninety uses.[49] Nevertheless, even as Paul likely mimics

---

[45]Both terms are used in 1 Cor 12:1–4.

[46]See Schüssler Fiorenza, *Rhetoric and Ethic*, 122; see also Wire, *The Corinthian Women Prophets*, 159–96.

[47]See Wire, *The Corinthian Women Prophets*, 136–37.

[48]Koester, *Ancient Christian Gospels*, 55.

[49]This topic of the discursive explosion of terms marking spirit is the topic of an ongoing research project. This search was conducted using the *Thesaurus Linguae Graecae* CD-ROM

the Corinthians' own interest in and discussions of *pneumatika* and their participation in a broader cultural fascination with the topic (a fascination which will later be fed by debates over 1 Corinthians), he asserts that they do not understand spiritual gifts particularly well. He seeks to re-order and rank spiritual gifts and thus to reconfigure the importance of knowledge in the Corinthian community.

Paul embeds his ranking of spiritual gifts in a discussion of the body. 1 Corinthians uses the term σῶμα in two primary ways. The first is the σῶμα as the individual body which can be transformed. The second is an image of "one body" which derives from the deliberative political discourse of the day. 1 Corinthians is full of advice on the discipline and control of the individual body in relation to the "one body" of the ἐκκλησία; indeed, 1 Corinthians deliberately constructs the individual over and against the community, and insists that the inscribed audience (that is, the audience as constructed by the author) is concerned with the former, and Paul with the latter. Concerns about the body are first articulated in detail in chapter 6.[50] Paul "corrects" the Corinthian slogan "I am free to do anything"[51] (usually translated "all things are lawful for me"), suggesting that this idea leads to immorality in the community. "The body is not meant for immorality but for the Lord, and the Lord for the body" (6:13), he insists.[52] A series of correc-

---

D (Irvine, Calif.: University of California, 1992). The search term was πνευματικ-. Not all second-century references to the term are quotations or interpretations of Paul; many derive from discussions in medical literature.

[50]Concerns about regulating the body are first expressed in ch. 5, with discussion of "the man who is living with his father's wife." Note however that the term σῶμα is not used here; rather: "you are to deliver this man to Satan for the destruction of the flesh, that his spirit may be saved . . ." (5:5).

[51]Helmut Koester, *History and Literature of Early Christianity* (vol. 2 of *Introduction to the New Testament*; 2d ed.; New York: de Gruyter, 2000) 2:127. Stanley Stowers ("Paul on the Use and Abuse of Reason," in *Greeks, Romans, and Christians: Essays in Honor of Abraham J. Malherbe* [ed. David Balch et al.; Minneapolis: Fortress, 1990] 263) argues that this "seems to be a well-attested version of the Stoic paradox 'Only the wise man is truly free.'"

[52]With the phrase "your bodies are members of Christ," we see the beginnings of the terms which Paul will echo again in 1 Corinthians 12–14. Paul asserts that by associating oneself with a prostitute, one drags Christ's members into the bargain. Moreover, Paul uses Genesis's "the two shall become one flesh" to articulate a contrast: the one who "joins himself to a prostitute becomes one body (ἐν σῶμα) with her," while the one "who is united to the Lord becomes one spirit with him" (1 Cor 6:16, 17). Paul concludes with an elusive but strong statement: "Shun immorality. Every other sin which a man commits is outside the

tions of individual bodily practices (some directed toward men, some toward women, and some toward both)—sex with one's step-mother (5:1–5), visiting prostitutes (6:15–20), abstaining from sexual activity (chapter 7),[53] eating food "sacrificed to idols" (chapter 8), women's veiling in prayer and prophecy (11: 1–17)—are undergirded by the notion that one's body is not one's own, but is part of the one body of the community. A person's body is defined by the body politic to which it is subject, and in which it participates, whether that be the ἐκκλησία, the household, or the state. Talking about the body is a means of talking about hierarchy, ordering, and boundaries. As Elizabeth Castelli states, 1 Corinthians uses the image of "one body" to manage a variety of bodies, not only constructing boundaries with regard to food or sex, but also delimiting the possibilities for the body as a site of power and expression.[54]

1 Corinthians 15 is also interested in the individual's body, but only insofar as it relates to the more general question of what happens to the body in the resurrection.[55] The chapter begins with Paul's reference to a tradition that, as he signals, precedes him: the story of Jesus Christ, buried and raised, appearing to many, grounds Paul's argument about resurrection. For Paul the body of Christ—the crucifixion and resurrection—becomes a way of thinking about one's own and the communal body.

---

body; but the immoral man sins against his own body" (1 Cor 6:18). This sin, moreover, is not something which only damages one's own body; it damages the property of another. Paul eases the Corinthians into the shocking news: "Do you not know that your [pl.] body is a temple of the Holy Spirit within you, which you have from God?" (6:19). Paul has already used this image in a corporate sense, in 1 Cor 3:16 ("Do you not know that you [pl.] are God's temple and that God's spirit dwells in you?"). The more provocative argument comes in 1 Cor 6:19–20: "You are not your own. You were bought with a price. So glorify God in your [pl.] body" (ἢ οὐκ οἴδατε ὅτι τὸ σῶμα ὑμῶν ναὸς τοῦ ἐν ὑμῖν ἁγίου πνεύματος ἐστιν οὗ ἔχετε ἀπὸ θεοῦ, καὶ οὐκ ἐστὲ ἑαυτῶν; ἠγοράσθητε γὰρ τιμῆς· δοξάσατε δὴ τὸν θεὸν ἐν τῷ σώματι ὑμῶν).

[53]The Corinthians may have been pursuing an ascetic path, not marrying and not engaging in sexual activity. See Schüssler Fiorenza, *Rhetoric and Ethic*, 120; and Wire, *Corinthian Women Prophets*, 181–96.

[54]Castelli, "Interpretations of Power," 209–12.

[55]The odd, tacked-on quality of 1 Corinthians 15, and its introduction of what seems to be a new topic, has puzzled many scholars. Conzelmann asserts that "Chap. 15 is a self-contained treatise on the resurrection of the dead," and understands Paul to be here offering "theology in the form of exposition of the creed" (250). Margaret Mitchell's *Paul and the Rhetoric of Reconciliation* sets out with the hypothesis that 1 Corinthians as a whole is a unified work of deliberative rhetoric; in doing so she demonstrates that 1 Corinthians 15

Chapter 15 indicates that the Corinthians may have understood resurrection to have already occurred through the act of baptism and thus may have been acting out a transformed and liberated life in the present.[56] Paul then uses the typology of Adam and Christ to reinforce the order of things: Christ is raised, the firstfruits, but then "each in his own order" (v. 23) is raised; this order does not occur in the present time, but is deferred to the future. This contrast between Adam and Christ and between present and future is part of Paul's elaboration of a system of oppositions, which contrasts the perishable to the imperishable, dishonor to glory, weakness to power, the physical to the spiritual, the earthly to the heavenly, and the σῶμα ψυχικόν to the σῶμα πνευματικόν. Paul places the spiritual body in a different epistemological and ontological realm, one that is not attainable in the present.[57] To put it in terms that we shall see later in Tertullian, what is natural to a human is to be ψυχικός; one is only secondarily πνευματικός, and then, according to Paul in 1 Corinthians, never fully so, as one can be after one is raised from the dead. This is consistent with his attempts to delimit or to bound the realms of knowledge to which the Corinthian community has access in the present through his ranking of leadership roles and charismata, and his downgrading of glossolalia.

In 1 Corinthians, Paul discusses the body in a second way: as ἓν σῶμα—the one, unified body of the community. While 1 Corinthians 15's discussion of the resurrected body of individuals may seem far afield from the image of ἓν σῶμα, the two are interconnected. Paul closes 1 Corinthians with his

---

is an intrinsic part of the argument, the final of the πίστεις, or proofs, that Paul offers to convince his audience.

[56]See Wire, *Corinthian Women Prophets*, ch. 8, "Women Risen to New Life in Christ: 1 Corinthians 15–16"; and Martin, *The Corinthian Body*, ch. 5, "The Resurrected Body."

[57]We also find the idea that the human—"we all"—is transformed "from glory to glory" (2 Cor 3:8). This theme is picked up in Origen and in Gregory of Nyssa's mention of the angelic body or angelic nature that can be attained even on earth through practices of holiness; this view can be found in Gregory's *On Virginity*, in his *Commentary on the Song of Songs*, and his *Life of Macrina*. See also Jean Daniélou, *From Glory to Glory: Texts from Gregory of Nyssa's Mystical Writings* (trans. Herbert Musurillo; New York: Scribner, 1961).

Of the anthropological terms that Paul tends to use—σῶμα, σάρξ, and πνεῦμα—σῶμα alone is fluid in category, able to cross from one side of the binary to another. For example, in Phil 3:10–21, Paul depicts the body ripe for metamorphosis. He concludes in verses 20–21: "Our citizenship is in the heavens, from which we also await a savior, the Lord Jesus Christ. He will transform our body of humiliation to be similar in form to his body of glory, through the active power which also enables him even to subject all things to himself" (my translation).

discussion of the resurrected, spiritual body; this body, deferred to the future, echoes Paul's earlier assertions about the one body and *pneumatika* in 1 Cor 12: 12–30. As many scholars have pointed out, most carefully Margaret Mitchell, Paul's use of ἓν σῶμα derives from the deliberative rhetoric of political union, in particular the rhetoric of concord (*homonoia*)[58] and from philosophical (especially Stoic) rhetoric.[59] The image of one body is regularly used to argue for unity in community, and Paul uses it here to corral the various somatic practices of the Corinthian community—whether celibacy or sleeping with a prostitute or speaking in tongues—and to construct the Corinthian identity.[60] This image is, as Elizabeth Castelli argues, an apparently benign one: it presents a picture of cooperation and mutual need, of a community knit together so intimately that no division is possible if it is to be healthy, well, alive. But this image also functions, as she argues, to erase difference and to insist upon unity and lack of debate as proper behaviors.[61] This image of one body and its concomitant erasure of difference controls the discussion of spiritual gifts.

Paul begins chapter 12 with a general list of spiritual gifts. But before he turns to rank these gifts in 12:28—a ranking the Corinthians probably found surprising—he speaks first of the community baptized into Christ as a body. The many are one, Paul insists, just as the members of the body are separately named and defined, yet do not exist apart from the body, and need each other to function properly: "For by one Spirit we were all baptized into one body—Jews or Greeks, slaves or free—and all were made to drink of one Spirit" (12:13).[62] This brief reference to the pre-Pauline baptismal formula

---

[58]Mitchell, *Paul and the Rhetoric of Reconciliation*, 157–64, passim. As part of his argument about the strong and the rich, Dale Martin (*The Corinthian Body*, 92–96) argues that Paul here upends normal uses of this topos by emphasizing the value of the weaker members of the body.

[59]Conzelmann, *1 Corinthians*, 214.

[60]As Mitchell (*Paul and the Rhetoric of Reconciliation*, 300) explains: "This means that Paul in 1 Cor presents a viewpoint on the church as *a real political body* (even the local church) to which some Greco-Roman political lore, especially the call for concord, is directly applicable"; "1 Corinthians is throughout filled with terms and topoi which were of general commerce in the Imperial period for urging divided groups to become reunified" (296).

[61]Castelli, "Interpretations of Power," 212.

[62]Helmut Koester (*History and Literature of Early Christianity*, 2:127) comments that the themes of baptism, words of wisdom, knowledge, and mystery recur especially in the debate with the "strong people." For radically different interpretations of Paul's image of one body and baptism, see Boyarin (*A Radical Jew*), who argues that Paul's attempts to erase

more fully preserved in Gal 3:28,[63] along with other references to baptism in 1 Corinthians,[64] indicates that baptism is an important ritual for many in the Corinthian community. Paul here appeals to the ritual and glosses its meaning: baptism signifies the ingathering of different ethnicities and social statuses—and we may note the absence of gender in 1 Cor 12:13[65]—into one unified body, which has a different set of restrictions and demands.

Along with the rhetoric of one body, Paul employs the language of "general benefit" to persuade the audience: all spiritual gifts must be for the general benefit (πρὸς τὸ συμφέρον, 12:7). Margaret Mitchell has discussed the way in which arguments about advantage and disadvantage are typical of deliberative rhetoric; Paul in 1 Corinthians borrows another topos of unity and harmony typical in Hellenistic deliberative rhetoric to encourage his idea of community life.[66] Paul's statement that all spiritual gifts are from the same spirit (12:11), moreover, further underscores his emphasis on unity and sameness.

The image of "one body" and the idea of communal benefit are powerful tools of deliberative rhetoric, and present an argument that few would want to dispute. Who wants to be the rebelling organ? Who wants to damage the common body? The image subtly reinscribes order and hierarchy, when read in the broader context of 1 Corinthians, and when we are reminded of the reason

---

difference and ethnicity are part of a radical egalitarianism which deconstructs ethnicity in the ancient world, and Castelli (*Imitating Paul*), who, in contrast, is deeply suspicious of the language of unity and one body, which she sees as an argument that seeks to obliterate difference and construct a tyranny of the same.

[63] Schüssler Fiorenza, "Rhetorical Situation," 397, for example.

[64] See the emphasis on baptism and identity in 1 Corinthians 1 and 10 (allegorically stated) and the mention of baptism on behalf of the dead in 1 Cor 15:19. Schüssler Fiorenza ("Rhetorical Situation," 399) posits that baptism is central to 1 Corinthians: "The whole letter documents this baptismal self-understanding of the many who were nothing in the eyes of the world before their call, but who now have freedom, knowledge, wisdom, riches, and power over their own bodies and life in their new kinship-community." If Paul is from a relatively high social and educational stratum of society, his experience would have been quite different: "While for them their call meant freedom and new possibilities not open to them as poor, slave and even freeborn women in 'the eyes of the world,' for Paul and those of equal social status, their call implied relinquishment of authority and status, it entailed hardship, powerlessness, and foolishness 'in the eyes of the world'" (400).

[65] The lack of reference to gender here—from Gal 3:28 we expect "neither male and female"—may arise from tensions with women in the community, as evidenced in 1 Corinthians 11. See Wire, *Corinthian Women Prophets*, 137–38. Regarding Gal 3:28 and the Corinthian community, see also Schüssler Fiorenza, *Rhetoric and Ethic*, 120.

[66] See Mitchell, *Paul and the Rhetoric of Reconciliation*, 25–39; see also Conzelmann, *1 Corinthians*, 211 (esp. n. 8) for various similar texts.

this image was introduced—as a framework for the discussion of *pneumatika* in 1 Corinthians 12–14.[67] The image of one body with its members functioning harmoniously for the benefit of the whole also rhetorically controls the religious practices connected to spiritual gifts in the Corinthian community.

## Ranking *Pneumatika*

Chapters 12–14 work together as a rhetorical and conceptual unit to discuss phenomena of the spirit in the Corinthian community.[68] In 1 Corinthians 12–14, Paul first discusses the topic in general, then offers a kind of excursus in 1 Corinthians 13 which explicates and hones his criticism of the gifts of prophecy and tongues. He returns again with more specificity to issues of community practice and spiritual gifts in chapter 14. While chapters 12–14 represent a rhetorical unit, the discussion of prophecy, one of the spiritual gifts, in fact began with Paul's discussion of veiling in 1 Corinthians 11. 1 Cor 11:1–16 constructs a system of organization, order, and hierarchy for the community as it prays and prophesies: God is the head of Christ, who is the head of man, who is the head of woman. Paul may deliberately disaggregate his assertions regarding women, men, prophecy, and prayer from his focus on *pneumatika* in the next chapter, because his conclusions were controversial. Wire argues that Paul here and elsewhere subordinates women who were prophesying and thus gaining power within the community.[69]

---

[67]Castelli, "Interpretations of Power," 212.

[68]Several scholars have defended the unity of 1 Corinthians 12–14. Joop Smit ("Argument and Genre of 1 Corinthians 12–14," 211–30), among others, has identified 1 Corinthians 12–14 as a textual unity, and he has argued powerfully for how this section of the epistle partakes in the deliberative rhetoric of the larger piece, and is a self-contained unity of deliberative rhetoric, following rules of composition. Thus the theme of one body launched especially in 1 Corinthians 12 is rhetorically interconnected with the theme of *pneumatika* throughout these chapters. See also Castelli, "Interpretations of Power," 211–30; and Conzelmann, *1 Corinthians*, 204 (περί introduces a new topic in the "style of answer to questions"). Margaret Mitchell (*Paul and the Rhetoric of Reconciliation*, 258–83) instead sets apart 11:2–14:40 as Paul's third section of proof of the Corinthians' factionalism. See esp. 258 n. 402 for a list of scholars who support the idea of 11:2–14:40 as a coherent section. Schüssler Fiorenza ("Rhetorical Situation," 395) sees 1 Cor 11:2–14:40 as part of a ring composition. It is my opinion that by introducing the topic in chapter 11, and only marking it fully in chapter 12, the text deliberately sets off from the rhetorically unified chapters 12–14 the (uncomfortable) issue of gender and praying and prophesying in chapter 11:1–16, thus marking as insignificant the issue of women and prophecy for the proper discussion of *pneumatika*.

[69]Wire, *The Corinthian Women Prophets*, 116–34.

While the controversial issue of women and prophecy in chapter 11 is rhetorically marginalized from the discussion of *pneumatika* in chapters 12–14, in chapter 12 Paul discusses spiritual gifts in terms of the topos of one body. This interposition of the theme of one communal body in the midst of his corrective discussion of spiritual gifts downplays Paul's ranking of gifts (the ranking is distanced from his introduction of the topic)[70] and appeals to the reader or hearer's sense of community. Paul's emphasis in chapter 12 on the common benefit and on one body is part of his attempt to reorder and marginalize those spiritual gifts which are connected to wisdom and knowledge, and which the Corinthians most value. Paul emphasizes unity over diversity again and again. In 1 Cor 12:4, the variety of spiritual gifts is distilled to the same spirit; diversity again leads back to a unified source. Verse 7, too, uses rhetoric typical of political discourses on harmony and unity: "To each is given the manifestation of the Spirit for the common good" (ἐκάστῳ δὲ δίδοται ἡ φανέρωσις τοῦ πνεύματος πρὸς τὸ συμφέρον). The individualism of "to each" is directed toward the communal good of τὸ συμφέρον. Paul insists that spiritual gifts are all effected "by one and the same Spirit, who apportions to each one individually as it wills" (πάντα δὲ ταῦτα ἐνεργεῖ τὸ ἓν καὶ τὸ αὐτὸ πνεῦμα διαιροῦν ἰδίᾳ ἑκάστῳ καθὼς βούλεται, 12:11; my translation).

This emphasis on unity frames Paul's discussion list of spiritual gifts in 1 Cor 12:8–10. The list is not just a random configuration of the gifts which occurred to Paul at the moment, but is carefully crafted. Verse 8 ("To one is given through the Spirit the utterance of wisdom; and to another the utterance of knowledge according to the same Spirit") picks up themes particularly important to the Corinthians, as evidenced by the extensive discussion of wisdom and knowledge in chapters 1–4. The list then wends its way through various gifts, concluding with those which worry Paul most: "to another prophecy, to another the ability to distinguish between spirits, to another various kinds of tongues, to another the interpretation of tongues" (12:10).

As mentioned in the last chapter, the general list of spiritual gifts in verses 8–10 is made more specific by the ranking proffered in 12:28: "And God has

---

[70]Joop Smit ("Argument and Genre of 1 Corinthians 12–14," 213–14) states, "In 1 Corinthians 12–14 Paul clearly intends to call the Corinthians to order in the question of glossolalia." He goes on to discuss the riskiness of this plan, given that the Corinthians seem to value glossolalia highly, and concludes that Paul uses the rhetorical technique of *insinuato*, and avoids broaching the topic directly.

appointed in the church first apostles, second prophets, third teachers, then workers of miracles, then healers, helpers, administrators, speakers in various kinds of tongues." As Smit, among others, has remarked, the ordering of *pneumatika* in 12:28 erodes the emphasis on wisdom and knowledge — and concomitantly glossolalia and prophecy, charismata which the Corinthians held dear.[71] Paul has to admit the importance of prophets, but subordinates them to apostles; he also disaggregates prophecy from glossolalia, and ranks the latter last. And while 1 Cor 12:14–26 argues for the significance of every member of the body, both the "weaker" and those given more "honor," this argument is undercut by the numbering set forth in verse 28.

In 1 Cor 14:1, Paul picks up the themes of the previous chapters and continues to work out his arguments about spiritual gifts, especially prophecy and glossolalia. "Make love your aim," Paul insists, referring back to the contents of chapter 13; "and earnestly desire the spiritual gifts," reminding his readers/hearers of chapter 12, "especially that you may prophesy." This last phrase is what Paul has been driving at: a highlighting of prophecy over and against tongues. This division may indeed have been invented by Paul; it is possible that the Corinthian community had not categorized and ranked the *pneumatika* received at baptism, or, alternatively, had thought of the phenomenon of tongues and prophecy as interlinked. Paul encourages the Corinthians — and modern readers — to understand glossolalia as an individualistic phenomenon, the indulgence of some personal mysticism that burns out quickly and benefits no one, in the end.[72] Yet Paul is cautious about his own argument, sometimes backpedaling and conceding the significance of tongues. Here and again in verses 18–19, he breaks the rhythm of his argument, speaking in the first person singular, in order to retreat and concede the significance of tongues: "Now I want you all to speak in tongues, but even more to prophesy" (14:5). Even so, the construction of a hierarchy of spiritual gifts becomes even more clear: "The one who prophesies is better than the one who speaks in tongues, unless someone should interpret, so that the church may be edified." Prophecy is described as a tool for the building up of the assembly.

[71]Ibid., 219: "In that enumeration 'services of Christ', the apostolate in the first place, take precedence over 'charismata of the Spirit', of which glossolalia comes last."

[72]For example, Conzelmann (*1 Corinthians*, 235) states regarding 1 Cor 14:3: "Here, too, we have to think of the Corinthians' individualism as the butt of Paul's attack."

In setting up prophecy as a gift over and against tongues in chapter 14, Paul constructs a schema which then cascades into other distinctions and definitions to support his point. Paul starts with his definitions: "For one who speaks in a tongue speaks not to humans but to God; for no one understands, but s/he speaks mysteries in the spirit. But the one who prophesies speaks upbuilding and comfort and consolation for the people" (14:2–3; my translation).

From here the division between tongues and prophecy deepens as Paul refers to οἰκοδομή, "upbuilding"; this word and its verbal form are used in deliberative rhetoric to argue about the good of the state or community: the benefit of the many over the one, recalling the discussion of one body found earlier in the letter. The use of the term becomes only more intense in 1 Cor 14:4, which characterizes the one who speaks in a tongue as building up him- or herself (ἑαυτὸν οἰκοδομεῖ) while the one who prophesies is building up the assembly or church (ἐκκλησίαν οἰκοδομεῖ). Paul's key term here, οἰκοδομή, and his emphasis on the assembly (ἐκκλησία) hearken back to the discussions of "one body" found earlier in the letter. In 1 Cor 14:6–13, Paul pairs, links, and highly values "benefit" and intelligibility.[73]

Speaking in tongues is characterized as unbeneficial to community, "unless I bring you some revelation or knowledge or prophecy or teaching" (ἐὰν ἔλθω πρὸς ὑμᾶς γλώσσαις λαλῶν, τί ὑμᾶς ὠφελήσω ἐὰν μὴ ὑμῖν λαλήσω ἢ ἐν ἀποκαλύψει ἢ ἐν γνώσει ἢ ἐν προφητείᾳ ἢ [ἐν] διδαχῇ;). Paul here elaborates the elements of his initial distinction—tongues versus prophecy.[74]

In 1 Corinthians 14, Paul uses the concept of one body and of building up community in order to prescribe "correct" ritual activity in assembly.

Paul offers a series of arguments which deconstruct the importance of tongues. These arguments hinge on the concepts of οἰκοδομή and intelligibility. In 1 Corinthians 14, by his own admission, Paul seeks to rein in tongues, which are a primary means of accessing the divine and divine knowledge:

[73]Conzelmann (ibid., 233) is right that the argument is not one about rationality, as it is in other texts which we shall read; it is about intelligibility.

[74]To elaborate the necessity of intelligibility (εὔσημος λόγος, v. 9) Paul uses the example of musical instruments, drawing on a common trope in discussions of prophecy/ecstasy in late antiquity. This metaphor elaborates how a god interacts with a human in the moment of prophecy or ecstasy: like an instrument, the human is "played" by the god or by a spirit. (Philo uses this image in *Her.* 266.) But while in other texts this image emphasizes the passivity of the prophet, Paul's use of this trope emphasizes the need for intelligibility, clarity, distinction between tones. For him, this image bolsters his argument for order and clarity over and against disorder—"For God is not a God of confusion" (1 Cor 14:33a).

"For one who speaks in a tongue speaks not to humans but to God; for no one understands, but s/he speaks mysteries in the spirit" (14:2; my translation). Yet Paul admits in 1 Corinthians 14 that he too speaks in tongues. He thus asserts that he can match the high status of any Corinthian who exhibits glossolalia,[75] but chooses not to. By the time of the writing of 2 Corinthians 12, Paul feels forced to argue again on the Corinthians' terms, especially over and against the "superapostles" with their spiritual gifts. Thus Paul circuitously talks about his own "visions and revelations" (2 Cor 12:1). In his famous "fool's speech," Paul insists that the Corinthians' resistance to him has compelled him to enter into a sort of performance competition where he must demonstrate that he too has experienced rich charismatic experiences.[76]

Throughout chapters 12–14 we see Paul taxonomizing spiritual gifts. He ranks and prioritizes *pneumatika* even as he uses available political rhetoric about unity and harmony, emphasizing the metaphor of one body and many members, and urging the audience to strive for the common benefit. Although Paul's taxonomy of spiritual gifts does not immediately resemble the three- and four-fold lists of ecstasy, madness, and dreams that we investigated in chapter 1, I would argue that it echoes both their form and their purpose. As Conzelmann states, the argument here is "no longer a *critique* of πνευματικά, but their *classification*."[77] In the next section, we shall see how 1 Corinthians 13, with its emphasis on love over and against prophecy and tongues, uses a discourse of history to strengthen further Paul's argument.

## 1 Corinthians 13: Love Trumps Wisdom

At the end of chapter 12, Paul ranked various *pneumatika*, and concluded with the injunction: "earnestly desire the higher gifts" (12:31a).[78] The ranking begins with clear enumerations: first apostles, second prophets, third teachers. The rest of the gifts are then listed as a group, but the placement of "speakers in various kinds of tongues" at the end of the list

[75]Regarding speaking in tongues as a marker of high status in the Corinthian community, see Martin, *Corinthian Body*, 87–88.

[76]Georgi, *Opponents of Paul*, 244–45. Paul uses the verb ἀναγκάζω to signal this compulsion: "I have been a fool! You forced me to it. For I ought to have been commended by you" (2 Cor 12:11; Γέγονα ἄφρων, ὑμεῖς με ἠναγκάσατε. ἐγὼ γὰρ ὤφειλον ὑφ' ὑμῶν συνίστασθαι· οὐδὲν γὰρ ὑστέρησα τῶν ὑπερλίαν ἀποστόλων εἰ καὶ οὐδέν εἰμι).

[77]Conzelmann, *1 Corinthians*, 233; see also 209.

[78]Conzelmann (ibid., 215) hears a "remarkably antagonistic" tone in this verse.

is no accident (12:28),[79] for Paul goes on to deal with the topic of tongues in a roundabout way in chapter 13, and again very directly, as we have seen, in chapter 14.

Chapter 13 seems like a digression because some of these materials are pre-Pauline, a kind of aretalogy of love derived from Jewish wisdom traditions.[80] For the purposes of my argument, the origin of these materials is less significant than the question of how Paul uses this part of his epistle within his larger argument; with this question foregrounded, it becomes clear that the contents of chapter 13 are intimately linked to the rest of Paul's argument. Not unlike the rhythm of chapter 12, where we saw Paul begin with the topic of *pneumatika*, shift to the powerful image of the one body of Christ, and then shift back to *pneumatika*, giving his own ranking, we see in chapters 12–14 the larger rhythm of direct discussion of *pneumatika*, a shift in chapter 13 to a personal (note the use of the first person singular) argument and a compelling aretalogy for love, and then back to a more incisive and "corrective" discussion of the spiritual person in chapter 14.

1 Corinthians 13 seeks to constrain realms of knowledge by challenging certain spiritual gifts important to the Corinthians, contrasting them with love, and by developing a historiography that limits the epistemic possibilities of the present exercise of spiritual gifts. Chapter 13 sets forth three principal, intertwined arguments. First, Paul puts the spiritual gifts most valued in the Corinthian community into a larger perspective, and so downgrades some of them. Second, he subordinates wisdom to love and offers an aretalogy of love instead of the aretalogies of wisdom which may have been important to the Corinthians.[81] Third, he posits an as-yet insurmountable gap between the human and the divine,[82] contrasting what is possible in the present with

[79]See also Mitchell, *Paul and the Rhetoric of Reconciliation*, 270.

[80]Margaret Mitchell (ibid., 57–58) rightly points out that love is only the subject of six verses, and that Paul speaks in the first person singular throughout much of this passage. Conzelmann (*1 Corinthians*, 218–19, esp. 219 n. 14), in contrast, sees 1 Corinthians 13 as a "self-contained unity"; he points to the variety of stylistic forms within 1 Corinthians 13 which are different from Paul's writing, and he emphasizes (in the excursus on 219–20) the many parallels that would lead one to conclude that this chapter is in the style of Jewish wisdom literature, a kind of aretalogy of love.

[81]An opposition between love and knowledge is already found in 1 Cor 8:1.

[82]Forbes (*Prophecy and Inspired Speech*, 138–39) states, "In chapter 14, Paul again seeks to correct the misguided notions and behavior of the Corinthians, particularly those Corinthians who are laying claim to a unique access to the divine mind." He also asserts

what will be seen at some later time (as some scholars would argue, in the eschaton). While chapter 13 has sometimes been discussed in terms of apocalyptic and eschatology, these categories in my opinion obfuscate rather than clarify. Rather than trying to systematize Paul's understanding of the world by comparing this chapter with chapter 7's opinions on marriage, or by looking back at 1 Thessalonians, this chapter makes the most sense if it is read where it stands, and in terms of a larger goal of downplaying knowledge and wisdom and their manifestations in prophecy and tongues. Paul here argues for that one can know the divine only in a limited way, not the least because human means of knowing the divine, such as prophecy, are limited. Not only is human knowledge folly, as Paul has argued so strongly in chapters 1–4; so also is thinking that one has any sort of clear knowledge of the divine. Knowledge is not yet τέλειος—perfect or complete.

As Conzelmann rightly points out, chapter 13 begins by citing values significant at Corinth, but "these recognized values are then relativized."[83] "If I speak in tongues of humans, and of angels, but have not love, I have become a loud gong or a clashing cymbal. And if I have [the gift of] prophecy, and understand all mysteries and all knowledge, and if I have all faith so that I move mountains, but I do not have love, I am nothing" (13:1–2; my translation). At the very beginning of the subsection of 1 Corinthians 13 (which was introduced by 12:31b's ironic "and I will show you a still more excellent way"),[84] Paul comes back to tongues, prophecy, and wisdom and knowledge as the main points of discussion. His inclusion of other gifts/practices is treated in a similar fashion to his list of spiritual gifts in chapter 12: faith, giving away everything, giving up one's body—these are quickly dropped in order that Paul might get at what most concerns him (and the Corinthians) throughout the epistle: prophecy, tongues, and knowledge.[85] Paul emphasizes that these

---

that this claim probably "coincided with an overvaluation of the spiritual gift of speaking in tongues." Although I thoroughly disagree with Forbes, he represents a certain trend in interpreting the relationship between Paul and the Corinthians.

[83]Conzelmann, *1 Corinthians*, 221.

[84]Joop Smit ("Two Puzzles: 1 Corinthians 12.31 and 13.3: A Rhetorical Solution," *NTS* 39 [1993] 246–64, esp. 250–55) makes a fascinating argument about the connection between 12:31b and ch. 13. Smit concludes that 12:31b is an ironic and hyperbolic statement rooted in his response to the Corinthians' competition for *pneumatika*.

[85]Conzelmann (*1 Corinthians*, 222) argues that in 1 Cor 13:2, "Paul follows the Corinthian order of merit in the spiritual gifts, which he will reverse in chapter 14."

three things that the Corinthians value most will all pass away, while "love never ends" (1 Cor 13:8). Returning to the theme of perfection (τὸ τέλειον) raised in chapter 2, where Paul contrasted the perfect or mature person with the faults of the Corinthians, Paul insists, "Our knowledge is imperfect and our prophecy is imperfect; but when the perfect comes, the imperfect will pass away" (1 Cor 13:9–10). Using metaphors of human development and of a dim mirror, 1 Corinthians 13 emphasizes the immaturity and partialness of any sort of present knowledge and wisdom.

Verses 4–8a may represent a pre-Pauline aretalogy of love, but even if this material is pre-Pauline, Paul's selection and use of it is significant. Paul uses this praise of love to relativize the importance of wisdom in the Corinthian community. Aretalogies of love are known from Jewish and pagan sources, but aretalogies of wisdom are found more frequently. The Corinthians may even have had their own aretalogy of wisdom. Paul's praise of love in chapter 13 deliberately displaces and controls the Corinthians' interest in wisdom, as chapters 1–4 had done before.

By offering an argument that holds up love in the face of wisdom, and relativizes the importance of knowledge, tongues, and prophecy in the Corinthian community, Paul uses a subtle discourse of history's periodization, restricting and critiquing the Corinthians' ideas about what can and cannot be known in the present and through the presently available spiritual gifts. Paul severely limits the significance of spiritual gifts which bridge the gap between the human and divine. Verses 8b–13 solidly place the phenomena of tongues and prophecy and knowledge onto the transitory side of the divide. These things are not eternal, fixed: they will be abolished or rendered inoperative (καταργέω); they will cease. They are associated with the partial rather than the complete and perfect (v. 10); they are ranked developmentally with the child, not the adult, and the "childish things" are similarly abolished. Verse 12 harshly exposes the inadequacy of human knowledge: "For now we see by means of a mirror, as by a riddle, but then face to face; now we know partially, but then we will know even as we are also known."[86] The riddling unclarity and distortion of polished-metal mirrors in antiquity is a metaphor for the warping and inaccuracy of all present knowledge. Tongues and prophecy only barely mediate this higher knowledge; even tongues and prophecy, Paul insists, are only partial glimpses of the divine.

[86]My translation. βλέπομεν γὰρ ἄρτι δι᾽ ἐσόπτρου ἐν αἰνίγματι, τότε δὲ πρόσωπον πρὸς πρόσωπον· ἄρτι γινώσκω ἐκ μέρους, τότε δὲ ἐπιγνώσομαι καθὼς καὶ ἐπεγνώσθην.

## Conclusions

In 1 Corinthians, issues of identity, authority, and epistemology are tangled up within a debate over spiritual gifts. Paul challenges the Corinthians' self-identification as *pneumatikoi*; he establishes his authority by setting up his role as founder and father of the community; and, concomitantly, he suggests that there are limits to what can be known in the present, and that prophecy, tongues, and other spiritual gifts, valuable as they are, are limited in the knowledge of the divine that they produce.

Paul uses a discourse of madness and rationality—articulated as foolishness and wisdom—to make his point in 1 Corinthians. Stanley Stowers rejects as misguided the question "What does Paul's letter have to say about reason?" but still concludes that 1 Corinthians does have something to do with reason and with a struggle over knowledge between Paul and the Corinthians.[87] Stowers's insights point us in the right direction: away from reason per se, and towards issues of epistemology. Indeed, Paul does not use the concept of reason in the way that scholars often claim he does. 1 Corinthians has sometimes been read as a text in which Paul argues for rationality, for nonecstatic prophecy and spiritual gifts, and for control, over and against the Corinthians' irrationality, foolishness, and ecstasies. We have already seen that Conzelmann characterizes 1 Corinthians as the struggle of the mind over ecstasy or rational judgment over spirit.[88] Scholars have reached this conclusion from various angles. Allen Hunt concludes, for example, that "Paul . . . differs from many other ancient writers since he provides for the validity of rational, nonecstatic inspiration, the priority of ἀγάπη and οἰκοδομή."[89] Hunt believes that Paul corrects the understanding of the search for the divine mind current in antiquity; unlike other Greco-Roman religions, which see this as an individuated search marked by irrationality in mystical ascent, Paul insists that the Corinthians must place this search within a communal and rational framework.[90] Similarly, David Hill reveals a little more of what is at stake

---

[87]Stowers, "Paul on the Use and Abuse of Reason," 253.

[88]Conzelmann, *1 Corinthians*, 237.

[89]Hunt, *Inspired Body*, 143.

[90]Christopher Forbes' *Prophecy and Inspired Speech* reveals another interesting attempt to place Paul squarely within a "rational" camp. Forbes surveys the work of scholars such as Luke Timothy Johnson, M. Eugene Boring, U. B. Müller, Catherine Kroeger and Richard Kroeger, and Morton Smith, all of whom roughly work from the hypothesis that glossolalia represents a Hellenistic phenomenon against which Paul wants to guard. Smith, for instance,

for modern interpreters—namely, a Paul who directs the Corinthians away from glossolalia which occurs in a frenzy or ecstasy, who implicitly stands on the side of rationality: "The condition of ecstasy in which it [glossolalia] was uttered must have been subdued; it could not have been an abandoned frenzy. At most it could have been a state in which speech was automatic, i.e. not controlled by the conscious mind. However, our view is—and many scholars would assent—that for Paul prophecy or inspired speech was not uttered in any kind of ecstatic condition at all."[91]

---

sees glossolalia as connected to magical practice, while Kroeger and Kroeger, like many others, read 1 Corinthians 12–14 in light of characterizations of the maenads, drunkenness, and ecstasies of Dionysian cult during the same time period (27–43, esp. 35–36). All these are tarred with the brush of irrationality. Forbes argues rightly that we cannot read 1 Corinthians solely or even primarily as an anti-Hellenistic response. But he makes an interesting and wrong-headed argument in yet another attempt to place glossolalia within a "rational" framework. Reading the scene of Pentecost in Acts 2 alongside 1 Corinthians 12–14, Forbes argues that Luke and Paul agree in their definition of glossolalia: "I am confident that Paul, like Luke, understands glossolalia as the miraculous ability to speak unlearned human and (possibly) divine or angelic languages" (64). Forbes's method is both historicizing and harmonizing. This argument presumes that Luke presents a more "primitive" term to describe the phenomenon ("to speak in other tongues," λαλεῖν ἑτέραις γλώσσαις, over and against Paul's "to speak in tongues," λαλεῖν γλώσσαις); it also presumes that the account in Acts 2 gives us a window on historical reality (71–74). Forbes dismisses years of scholarship that point to Luke's broad purpose throughout Acts to emphasize the multiethnic appeal of Christianity, and to set visionary experiences within a rhetorical framework that emphasizes the reasonableness—represented by the logic of human language—of the encounter between the human and divine in ecstasy.

[91]Hill, *New Testament Prophecy*, 212. Thomas Gillespie (*The First Theologians: A Study in Early Christian Prophecy* [Grand Rapids, Mich.: Eerdmans, 1994] 32) takes a different approach, hypothesizing that early Christian prophets were theologians: "according to the apostle Paul, the early Christian prophets were interpreting theologically the inherent implications of the kerygma when they were prophesying. We will seek to recover on alternative grounds, therefore, the intuitive insight of Käsemann that the prophets were the hermeneuts of the gospel and as such the first theologians of the church." His conclusions provide an example for Schüssler Fiorenza's critique, cited at the beginning of this chapter, that a focus on Paul and prophecy often is linked to a scholarly concern with word and kerygma. Gillespie takes Bultmann's and Käsemann's insights about prophecy as part of a larger set of activities of interpretation and teaching in early Christian communities, and carries them too far in trying to apply them to 1 Corinthians. For more discussion of early Christian prophecy, see M. Eugene Boring, *The Continuing Voice of Jesus: Christian Prophecy and the Gospel Tradition* (Louisville, Ky.: Westminster/John Knox, 1991) ch. 1; this volume is a revised edition of Boring's 1982 *Sayings of the Risen Jesus*. Boring's own working definition of early Christian prophecy is problematic: "The early Christian prophet was an immediately

Even if Paul is influenced by Stoic thought,[92] in 1 Corinthians he is not interested in *logos*.[93] He does not argue for rationality, as scholars like Hill or Hunt claim. In fact, Paul argues for the opposite: he claims to stand on the side of folly, and challenges human pretensions to wisdom. He toys with the very definitions of folly and wisdom or knowledge. Paul does not introduce the dichotomy of subdued versus frenzied or conscious versus unconscious, as these scholars claim. Indeed, his approach to tongues and prophecy is very complex, sometimes acknowledging the importance of tongues, sometimes resisting and downgrading glossolalia. Paul's argument is launched in a very specific rhetorical situation, and is not meant to be a broad philosophical pronouncement or the foundation for a systematic theology. The dichotomy which Paul sets up between wisdom/knowledge and folly cascades into other analogous distinctions: prophecy versus tongues, community versus individual benefit, intelligibility versus unintelligibility. These distinctions are directed against Corinthian practices and against their interest in developing an identity as spiritual, completed persons. Paul's championing of divine folly and his downgrading of human wisdom are part of a discourse of madness and rationality, deployed in a context of struggle.

Paul also uses a discourse of the periodization of history in the midst of his struggle with the Corinthians over prophecy and spiritual gifts. Especially in 1 Corinthians 13, he argues that prophecy and tongues, mysteries and knowledge, are merely passing phenomena. Present knowledge is dim and imperfect; only in the future will knowledge be full and complete. Paul here uses precisely the adjective that he earlier wielded against the Corinthians, challenging the idea—whether their claim or his accusation, we cannot know—that they are perfect or complete (τελείοι). Complete knowledge, Paul argues, is deferred until the future. As we shall see in the following chapters, Tertullian and the Anti-Phrygian too use a discourse of the periodization of history, but in very different ways: Tertullian insists that the time of

---

inspired spokesperson for the risen Jesus, who received intelligible messages that he or she felt impelled to deliver to the Christian community or, as a representative of the community, to the general public" (38).

[92]E.g., Conzelmann, *1 Corinthians*, 10. Conzelmann maintains that there is no close connection between Paul and Stoicism, but rather that Paul draws upon Stoic ideas and terminology because these are part of the popular philosophical milieu.

[93]See, for example, Paul's argument in Romans 1. On Paul as a critic of Stoicism, see also Stowers, "Paul on the Use and Abuse of Reason," 263, 286.

greatest spiritual gifts and prophecy is the present; the Anti-Phrygian insists that this time is long past.[94]

The model of struggle used in this study reveals that Paul's discussion of spiritual gifts in 1 Corinthians provides no evidence of a blast of spiritual gifts at the origin of Christianity, but something far more complex: struggle and ambivalence over spiritual gifts at a time when Christianity as such did not yet exist. Paul's discussion of prophecy, tongues, and intelligibility is not disinterested speculation about epistemology, but evidence of a debate that has concrete implications for community practice. Paul seeks to control the Corinthians' spiritual practices and to redefine their community identity by providing a new picture of what is epistemically possible in the present. He describes himself as founder and father of the community, and in so doing authorizes himself to correct the Corinthians. While the Corinthians through spiritual gifts establish their identity as *pneumatikoi*, Paul upends their self-understanding, insisting that their spiritual gifts must be reordered, and that the Corinthians are not perfect or complete or even spiritual. Paul posits a current epistemic chasm between realms of human knowledge and realms of divine knowledge so deep that humans only dimly see the possibility of being spiritual, so deep that folly and wisdom are inverted.[95] Tertullian, as we shall see in the next chapter, sees no such epistemic chasm, and argues passionately that humans enjoy a range of epistemic possibilities.

---

[94]See my "'Now I Know in Part': Historiography and Epistemology in Early Christian Debates about Prophecy," in *Walk in the Ways of Wisdom: Essays in Honor of Elisabeth Schüssler Fiorenza* (ed. Melanie Johnson-DeBaufre, Cynthia Kittredge, and Shelly Matthews; Valley Forge, Pa.: Trinity Press International, 2003).

[95]Paul in 2 Corinthians, however, faces a more urgent rhetorical situation, and retreats from the divide that he proposes in 1 Corinthians. As discussed above, 2 Corinthians 12 indicates that he grudgingly will engage in discussions of the interpenetrability of the divine and human realms.

CHAPTER 3

# Tertullian and the Soul's Condition

While 1 Corinthians allowed us only fragmentary glimpses at a first-century C.E. struggle over prophecy, Tertullian's *De anima* is a regular *Wunderkammer*, a textual cabinet of curiosities and a rich collection of data from early-third-century C.E. Carthage. It contains shreds of philosophical debate, stories of what happened during someone's sleep, legends of the body at death, tales from Tertullian's own community, and Tertullian's ruminations on his own sleep and dreams. These are grounded in Tertullian's "conversation" not only with many philosophical and religious thinkers of his time and before, but also in the physician Soranus's own *De anima*, upon which Tertullian relies heavily. We recall from chapter 1 that Tertullian's taxonomy of dreams discussed in detail one peculiar form of dream, the kind that is somehow not willed by the soul; it surpasses "opinion and interpretation and power of exposition" and is "distinct, . . . properly belonging to ecstasy and its mode" (*An.* 47.4). This understanding of dreams and ecstasy emerges out of Tertullian's complex ideas about the human and the soul, his ruminations on anthropology found in *De anima*.

This chapter discusses the rhetorical structure of *De anima* and untangles the complexities of the anthropology that Tertullian expounds. Among Tertullian's many works, *De anima* gives us the richest picture of his idea of the soul, its substance in relation to the divine and creation, its propensity for and ability to experience ecstasy or prophecy, and its potential to access knowledge. This treatise is psychology in the strictest sense of the word's etymology: Tertullian is concerned with describing the soul and its *logos*, in opposition to what he considers to be other Christians' erroneous views. Unlike Paul, Tertullian is not so much concerned with drawing epistemic boundaries as he is with blasting through them. Philo made room within Middle Platonism for an interconnection between prophecy, ecstasy, and madness; Plato himself had made such a move in the *Phaedrus*. With Tertullian, we shall see an author who claims to despise Platonism, yet understands *amentia* or madness to occur during prophecy, and sets forth an understanding of the soul and its epistemic capabilities entirely different from the texts we have encountered thus far.

An extensive discussion of Tertullian's understanding of the soul is necessary for several reasons. First, it would be easy to misunderstand passages in *De anima* (and thus perhaps to mischaracterize the New Prophecy in Carthage) if the larger project of *De anima* were not clear. Indeed, some scholars have mined the text for evidence of Tertullian's "Montanism," using certain passages to prove their points, without considering the complex framework within which Tertullian launches his *exempla*. Second, in the absence of Tertullian's lost treatise *De ecstasi*, the majority of his comments about prophecy and ecstasy are found in *De anima*. Third, an extensive discussion of Tertullian's understanding of the soul helps to make sense of his use of the term *amentia*, madness. Although madness is often used rhetorically in a polemical fashion, to construct one group's identity over and against another's, this is not the case with Tertullian, for the most part. Why this is true is tied to his understanding of the soul, and if we do not immerse ourselves in his arcane, detailed, but nonetheless fascinating explanation of what the soul is and how it works, we will be unable to understand his views on prophecy, madness, and ecstasy.

Finally, in this chapter and the next I pursue the argument that, in debates over prophecy and ecstasy, three things are at stake: authority, epistemology, and Christian identity. Tertullian's *De anima* might seem to be merely another long-winded treatise on the soul. It is this, and more: a carefully rhetorically constructed argument about the nature of the soul and its epistemic capabilities, especially in ecstasy and dreams, and a long argument against other available Christian Platonizing understandings of the soul. Tertullian thus defines "correct" Christian identity in *De anima*. At the same time, he constructs his own authoritative voice both by the breadth of his philosophical discussion, and, paradoxically, by his rhetorical stance that he is unphilosophical, a pure Christian, distanced from the frivolities and delusions of Platonizing thought. In the next chapter, we shall see even more clearly how Tertullian's discourse of madness and his discourse of the periodization of history bolster his epistemology and serve to foster his definition of Christian identity.

## Locating Tertullian

Much of Tertullian's work is read through the lens of dicey biographical information. Timothy Barnes begins his book on Tertullian by listing (and then deconstructing) what other scholars generally claim are the common "facts" of the matter: Tertullian was born around 155 C.E. in Carthage, the son of a Roman centurion; he studied law in Rome and converted to Christianity in approximately 193 C.E. He became a priest, joined the Montanists, wrote ever more curmudgeonly tomes against the Romans and other Christian groups, and died between 230 and 240 C.E.[1] Scholars thus often read Tertullian's work through one or more of three lenses: he is a church official and his works should be understood as part of his attempt to shore up his own ecclesiastical authority; he is a practiced jurist and his works are rooted in a legal style or logic; as he aged, and in his so-called Montanist period, his work became increasingly marginal, extreme, crazy, and even heretical.

The only account of Tertullian's life is that given by Jerome. His thumbnail sketch states that "Tertullian the presbyter is ranked first of the Latin writers after Victor and Apollonius," that he was from "Carthage, where his father was a proconsular centurion," that he was impetuous in temperament, and that "because of the envy and reproaches of the clerics of the Roman church, he had lapsed into Montanism, and he makes mention of the new prophecy in many books."[2] But Jerome's information is flimsy. While it is true that some of Tertullian's writings are in sermon form or address specific issues of church practice (for example, *On Baptism, On Prayer, On the Veiling of Virgins*), Tertullian himself nowhere states that he is a priest, although it would have been to his advantage to do so in order to establish his authority.[3] Nor is it certain that Tertullian was a jurist; while this idea is based in part upon the correct observation that Tertullian's writings reflect some knowledge of legal matters and are sophisticated in their rhetoric, it wrongly elides Tertul-

[1]Timothy David Barnes, *Tertullian: A Historical and Literary Study* (Oxford: Clarendon, 1971) 1–2.

[2]*Vir. ill.*, cited from Jerome, *On Illustrious Men* (trans. Thomas P. Halton; FoC 100; Washington, D.C.: Catholic University of America, 1999) 74.

[3]Barnes, *Tertullian*, 11. Waszink (171–72), in discussing *An.* 9, agrees that Tertullian was not a priest. Johannes Quasten (*Patrology* [4 vols; Westminster, Md.: Newman, 1964] 2: 246–47), however, argues that he was. I use the Latin edition and commentary of Jan H. Waszink, cited above on p. 52 n. 52, and abbreviated as "Waszink."

lian with a figure by the same name, whose juridical opinions are quoted in the *Digest* and the *Codex Justinianus*.[4]

Tertullian was, however, a well-educated man, writing the majority of his works in Latin, but some in Greek. Carthage, moreover, was a center of learning at this time.[5] Authors tend to credit Tertullian with a special role in the renaissance of Latin literature: for Robert Sider, Tertullian represents a marriage of Christian heritage and classical rhetoric;[6] for Timothy Barnes, it was Tertullian's "powerful example that inspired Minucius Felix, Cyprian, Arnobius and Lactantius. . . . Tertullian had shown that a Christian could write elegant Latin."[7]

In reaction to those who dismiss Tertullian, Barnes is particularly enthusiastic about Tertullian and his influence. Some tend to ignore Tertullian, thinking he is a dull hack, an example of Roman pragmatism and an unsubtle Latin degradation of philosophy into sophism. It is true that Tertullian is sometimes given short shrift, and depicted as an intellectual lightweight who merely borrows from florilegia. More recent scholarship has recognized that Tertullian should be understood in terms of the education and rhetoric of his day. Barnes champions Tertullian for his erudition and clarifies how Tertullian's Christian Stoicism arises from and contributes to a sophisticated philosophical discussion at the time.[8] Use of handbooks and florilegia was common in this period, and Tertullian demonstrates a deep knowledge of some authors, a knowledge not merely attained from scanning a collection

---

[4]Barnes (*Tertullian*, 21) convincingly demonstrates the weakness of the idea that Tertullian was a lawyer: for example, Eusebius's construction of Tertullian as a famous lawyer among the Romans, presenting his *Apology* in Rome, serves Eusebius's rhetorical purposes quite well, and is probably unreliable. See also D. I. Rankin, "Was Tertullian a Jurist?," *Stud. Pat.* 31 (1997) 335–42. After a careful review of scholarly argumentation on the topic, Rankin concludes that Tertullian's use of legal terminology and argumentation does indicate that he was well trained in law, but that he was not a lawyer strictly speaking; at most he was an advocate (*rhetor, causidicus*).

[5]Apuleius is Tertullian's contemporary, and was writing in Carthage as well as in Rome; Barnes (*Tertullian*, 194) points out that some of Apuleius's speeches were written for a Carthaginian audience and presuppose much knowledge of Latin and Greek. The schools of Carthage outlasted Roman rule, and in 534 C.E., Justinian restored salaries for four chairs at the school in Carthage (195).

[6]Robert Dick Sider, *Ancient Rhetoric and the Art of Tertullian* (Oxford: Oxford University Press, 1971) 9.

[7]Barnes, *Tertullian*, 194.

[8]Ibid., chs. 13–14.

of quotations.[9] Sider carefully demonstrates how Tertullian's writings reveal both a deep understanding of classical rhetoric and a willingness to innovate.

Sider's detailed explanation of the practices of contemporary handbooks of rhetoric—the formal structures of speeches and treatises, and to the syllogisms and *exempla* which so characterize legal argumentation of the day—help us to understand Tertullian's tendency to amass a profusion of arguments as part of a complex tradition of thinking and writing, rather than as a strange amalgamation of proofs, some weaker and some stronger.[10] Jan H. Waszink, too, frequently argues against Heinrich Karpp that a given argument in *De anima* is Tertullian's own, and not merely filched from Soranus's text of the same name.[11]

Criticism of Tertullian applies not only to his rhetoric and writing; it gets more personal. Frend suggests that Tertullian is "combative" in his old age, and "puritanical" and rigid.[12] Some hint that he has gone terribly wrong in his rejection of Platonism and Platonizing Christianity.[13] Labriolle praises his genius but speaks wistfully of the contribution that he could have made to "the Church" rather than Montanism.[14] Trevett champions his erudition and then continues:

---

[9]Ibid., esp. 200; see also 201–5.

[10]Sider (*Ancient Rhetoric*, 3) begins with a question that rightly assumes the coherence of Tertullian's thought: "How far would a thorough investigation of the classical patterns of rhetorical argument in Tertullian's writings explain his workmanship and illuminate his mind?"

[11]Even if all agree that Tertullian's *De anima* is heavily dependent upon Soranus's. See, e.g., Waszink, 131; see also "Introduction," 34, where Waszink explicitly argues against Karpp's idea that whole chapters are lifted from other sources; Waszink deems Tertullian too "obstinate and original" for this.

[12]W. H. C. Frend, *The Rise of Christianity* (Philadelphia: Fortress, 1984) 349.

[13]See, e.g., the title to ch. 6 in the Roberts-Donaldson edition of the writings of the Ante-Nicene Fathers: "The arguments of the Platonists for the soul's incorporeality, opposed, perhaps frivolously" (*Tertullian* [trans. Peter Holms; ANF 3; repr. Grand Rapids, Mich.: Eerdmans, 1989] 185). Elizabeth A. Clark has commented insightfully on the political and religious tendencies of the editors of the Ante-Nicene Fathers series ("Footnotes. A More Curious History," paper presented at the Fourteenth International Conference of Patristics, Oxford University, Oxford, 18–22 August 2003).

[14]De Labriolle, "Introduction," *Les sources de l'histoire du Montanisme*, lxxviii: "Talent incisive et passionné, d'une dialectique inexorable, d'une erudition extrêmement riche, il déspensa ses dons les plus rares à la défense du Paraclet méconnu, et il n'hésita pas à compromettre par cette apologie le meilleur du prestige que lui avaient acquis les immenses service rendus à l'Église."

But what a troubled and troublesome man too. Pierre Labriolle in *History and Literature of Christianity from Tertullian to Boethius* wrote of "tempestuous genius" and "a passionate attachment to his own private judgment." An "explosive personality," wrote Klawiter and in Fredouille's major study in 1972 there emerged a restless man of his time, never satisfied, spurred on by *curiositas* as far as that stubborn "Tertullianism" with which his life ended. . . . Many similar things have been written. I have pondered most that memorable judgment of Nisters in his *charakterlogischer Versuch*, made in 1950, namely that Tertullian was not quite a psychopath, though paranoid! He may be right.[15]

Barnes, in contrast, concludes: "Tertullian recovers his credit as a learned man. He knew a forgotten period of Latin literature. Why then deny him equal acquaintance with more fashionable authors? And if his curiosity extended so far, why deny or play down his knowledge of Greek literature? His erudition does not always show, because he was intent on effective use in argument rather than on empty display."[16] Tertullian arouses a strange passion in his modern-day readers.

Scholars often try to date Tertullian's works according to his pre-Montanist and post-Montanist phases, based on the idea that at some point he "converted" to Montanism. I assume a different model, based on the ideas of struggle and negotiation of identity and authority in early Christianity. It is clear that Tertullian considered himself to be aligned with the "new prophets" (*Pud.* 21.7), given his many references to spiritual gifts and prophecy, revelations from the Paraclete, and even to oracles of the well-known prophet Prisc(ill)a (*Res.* 11.2; *Exh. cast.* 10.5). This does not mean, however, that he converted or that he understood himself or that others understood him to be anything other than a true Christian, attentive to God's revelation. Rather, the New Prophecy was one of many forms of Christianity available in Carthage at his time.[17]

[15]Trevett, *Montanism*, 68.

[16]Barnes, *Tertullian*, 204.

[17]See Tabbernee, *Montanist Inscriptions and Testimonia*, 54–55: "Despite the traditional view to the contrary, there is no evidence that Tertullian, or anyone else for that matter, left the official church in Carthage to join a Montanist group in that city. In fact there is nothing to suggest that such a separate Montanist congregation existed in Carthage during [the early third century]."

Tertullian's work is erudite, using sophisticated techniques of rhetoric. We do not know, however, if he was a jurist or a church official, and evidence indicates that he probably was neither. Moreover, the model of his "conversion" to Montanism, itself a troubled category, does not help us to determine with any more clarity who Tertullian was.[18] The text of *De anima*, however, allows us a glimpse of Tertullian's complex self-construction—his depiction of himself as a Christian, as an authoritative philosophical thinker, and, simultaneously, as deeply antiphilosophical.

## Tertullian the Philosopher, Tertullian the Antiphilosopher

Tertullian's antiphilosophical statements are part of his elaboration of a Stoic Christian worldview over and against various opponents, especially those with a more Platonizing vision. They are also part of his construction of his own identity over and against other philosophers, Christian and non-Christian, of the time. As Barnes explains, a bit hyperbolically, "Philosophy and theology, it must be concluded, are subordinate to oratory—which accounts for the effectiveness of Tertullian's writings. 'What has Athens to do with Jerusalem?' he once exclaimed 'or what has the Academy in common with the church?' Almost every word he wrote gave the lie to the

---

[18]Scholarly discussions of Tertullian's "conversion" to Montanism are problematic, assuming as they do that Christianity or orthodoxy is one thing, and the New Prophecy another. Barnes (*Tertullian*, 43) traces the chronology of Tertullian's works, assuming such a conversion, and having developed criteria which are "distinctive of Montanist beliefs." These criteria are questionable and the method is, of course, somewhat tautological. Some of the more questionable of these criteria are as follows: the commendation of ecstasy; the mention of spiritual gifts possessed only by the Montanists (with no explanation of this); the description of the Holy Spirit as *Paracletus*; the use of *nos* or *noster* to "describe things or persons particularly Montanist"—again, with no definition of "Montanist"; and the abuse of Catholics as *psychici* (43–44). Barnes does not question the categories of orthodoxy and heresy, which were not established, but being manufactured at the time as part of Christian struggles over identity and authority. Frend (*Rise of Christianity*, 349–50) assumes the validity of an orthodox-heresy divide in his statement that Tertullian "lashed out at the lax but orthodox members of the church in Carthage." R. F. Evans ("On the Problem of Church and Empire in Tertullian's Apologeticum," *Stud. Pat.* 14.3 [1976] 21–36) also remarks that "the significant shifts in Tertullian's thought are shifts which mark his removal to Montanism" (29), although he argues that this is not the cause of tensions in the Apology: rather, in this text Tertullian deliberately suppresses some of his disagreements with other Christians. Against the idea of Tertullian's conversion, see Trevett, *Montanism*, 68–69.

answer he implies."[19] It is true that despite Tertullian's protestations against philosophy—his purported rejection of Athens and Plato's Academy and its legacy—he is steeped in philosophical argumentation and addresses a vast range of philosophical hot topics, from the origin of the world to the fate of the human soul. At the same time, Tertullian eschews or embraces philosophical debates according to their usefulness for establishing his authority as an author and thinker, on the one hand, or for their usefulness for constructing the identity of Christian community, on the other.

At the beginning of *De anima*, Tertullian points to the dangers and falsehood of philosophy, complaining that "it is better *not* to know what is not revealed by God, than to know by humans what someone has him or herself presumed to know" (*An.* 1.6; my emphasis). He also insists that "it is certain that nothing should be received which does not agree (*conspiret*) with the genuine provision of prophecy which has also sprung forth in this very age" (*An.* 2.3).[20] Christian identity, Tertullian claims, is rooted in a rejection of certain realms of knowledge:

> The Christian, in a few words, works out this topic [of the soul] from his/her knowledge. Therefore things which are certain are always [discussed] in few words, and it is not permitted to seek there more than what is permitted to be discovered. For the apostle prohibits infinite questioning. Moreover, it is not permitted to discover more than what is learned from God; indeed what is learned from God is all.[21]

Tertullian sounds antiphilosophical and even anti-intellectual. Yet his argument that all knowledge should be checked according to the (deliberately rather fuzzy) category of that which God teaches is not necessarily unphilosophical. Rather, Tertullian's thought is directed against elements of Platonic philosophy and is undergirded by elements of Stoic philosophy,

---

[19]Barnes, *Tertullian*, 210. On Tertullian's arguments in *De anima* as philosophical, see Robert H. Ayers, *Language, Logic, and Reason in the Church Fathers: A Study of Tertullian, Augustine, and Aquinas* (Hildesheim, Germany: Georg Olms, 1979) 27.

[20]"certos nihil recipiendum quod non conspiret germanae et ipso iam aevo pronatae propheticae paraturae." *An.* 2.3; Waszink, 3. The use of *conspiret* may be a deliberate pun.

[21]"Christiano autem paucis ad scientiam huius rei opus est. Nam et certa semper in paucis, et amplius illi quaerere non licet quam quod inveniri licet; infinitas enim quaestiones apostolus prohibet. Porro non amplius inveniri licet quam quod a deo discitur; quod autem a deo discitur, totum est." *An.* 2.7; Waszink, 4.

which continually tries to align human action and opinion with the divine reason with which the universe is imbued.[22] Tertullian's antispeculative rhetoric constructs his Christian opponents as infinite questioners, who are aligned with Greek philosophy instead of divine truth, and who try to rush past the proper bounds of knowledge.

Even as he claims to reject certain realms of knowledge, Tertullian accepts others. Tertullian alludes to the New Prophecy—to his mind, part of God's providential plan—as another standard against which knowledge should be judged; this knowledge must agree with the prophecies of Tertullian's age. While lambasting philosophy in *De anima*, accusing philosophers of perverting and destroying truth, Tertullian subtly and not-so-subtly roots his epistemology in Stoic philosophy and in his adherence to the New Prophecy, and he constructs both his Christian identity and his authority as resisting the imperialism of Greek philosophy and its role as the common coin of education and intellectual sophistication in the Greco-Roman world.

Tertullian reworks the Greek-barbarian divide as part of his stance on philosophy, championing the Judean and the Galilean, or Jerusalem rather than Athens, even as he uses Greek philosophy.[23] This strategy points to how a group's identity is rhetorically constructed through geographical/ethnic tropes that at the same time refer to fields of knowledge. Tertullian appropriates the rhetoric of "barbarian" and "Greek" according to his needs. In the first paragraphs of *Adversus Marcionem* (1.1), for example, Tertullian describes the barbarians who live around the Euxine Sea, wandering around half-naked and eating their parents, and then goes on to say that Pontus, Marcion's birthplace, is even more barbaric than this.[24] This over-the-top rhetoric and

---

[22]The "God of the Stoics is neither an Olympian nor a Dionysus. He is a god who lives among men and reasonable beings and who arranged everything in the universe for their benefit. His power penetrates everything, and his providence overlooks not even the slightest detail" (Émile Bréhier, *The Hellenistic and Roman Age* [trans. Wade Baskin; Chicago: University of Chicago Press, 1965] 35).

[23]Epiphanius's source, as we shall see in ch. 5, below, and Tertullian, as we see in this chapter and will see in the next, demonstrate most clearly the ways in which the debate about prophecy and ecstasy configures boundaries, boundaries both of knowledge and of Christian identity. Epiphanius's source constructs Maximilla, Montanus, and those who participate in the New Prophecy as "other" by linking them to the barbarian.

[24]The best example of this strategy is found in the *Address of Tatian to the Greeks*, which begins, "Do not maintain a totally hostile attitude to foreigners, men of Greece, nor resent their beliefs. For which of your own practices did not have a foreign origin [ἀπὸ βαρβάρων]?" (1.1; ET *Tatian* Oratio ad Graecos *and Fragments* [ed. and trans. Molly Whittaker; Oxford:

heavy-handed othering of the barbarian (and of course especially of Marcion) contrast with Tertullian's admission in *De anima* that the sources of authority and knowledge for Christianity did not spring up in Greece, the intellectual center of empire: "The divine teaching offends, I suppose, since it comes from Judea rather than Greece. Christ also erred in sending forth fishermen rather than Sophists for proclamation [of this teaching]!" (*An.* 3.3). In this he riffs on one of his favorite themes and most pervasive rhetorical tropes, more famously stated in his *Prescription Against Heretics*:

> What, then, is there between Athens and Jerusalem? What between the academy and the church? What between heretics and Christians? Our education comes from the portico of Solomon, who himself also taught that God must be sought in simplicity of heart. Let those who bring forth a Stoic and Platonic and Christian dialectic be exposed![25]

---

Clarendon, 1982] 3). Tatian upends the label of barbarian by stating, on the one hand, that the Greeks derived much from the "barbarians" in the first place, and, on the other, that Greek identity and language are not so pure, and not so monolithic. Tatian discusses different ways of speaking among the Aeolians, the Ionians, the Dorians, those from Attica: "When there is so much dissension, where there should not be, I do not know whom to call a Greek. Moreover, most absurd of all, you have given honour to alien expressions and at times by your use of foreign words have contaminated your own language, This was the reason why we abandoned your school of wisdom, even though I was myself very distinguished in it" (1.3; ET Whittaker 5). In no way does the term "Greek" imply a thoroughbred and pure identity or realm of knowledge, asserts Tatian.

In the present, we see a similar discursive manipulation of labels and identity in postcolonial theory. Gayatri Spivak, recognizing as she does the hybrid identities of postcolonial subjects today, nonetheless coined the term "strategic essentialism." She suggests that sometimes, for pragmatic reasons, groups may argue as if they had essential identities based on gender or ethnicity. Tertullian does something like this in his positioning of himself as unphilosophical— that is, he takes back a provincial identity, emphasizing his geographical and philosophical distance from intellectual metropolitan centers. See Bart Moore-Gilbert, *Postcolonial Theory: Contexts, Practices, Politics* (London: Verso, 1997) 198. Regarding the dangers of the term "hybridity," which originated in nineteenth-century discourses about race and difference, see Robert Young, *Colonial Desire: Hybridity in Theory, Culture, and Race* (London: Routledge, 1995) 1–28.

[25]"Quid ergo Athenis et Hierosolymis? quid academiae et ecclesiae? quid haereticis et christianis? Nostra institutio de porticu Solomonis est qui et ipse tradiderat Dominum in simplicitate cordis esse quaerendum. Viderint qui Stoicum et Platonicum et dialecticum christianismum protulerunt." *Praescr.* 7.9–10; text in Tertullian, *Opera* (2 vols.; CCSL 1–2; Turnholt, Belgium: Brepols, 1954). This edition is hereafter referred to by the abbreviation CCSL, followed by volume and part number; the present citation is from CCSL I.I.193.

The geographical terms employed in these two passages stand in analogical relationship to barbarian and Greek, and rhetorically they function as metonyms for the knowledges and cultures associated with these regions. Tertullian shifts rhetorical strategies, sometimes mocking the barbarians and their knowledge, and sometimes siding with the barbarian. He is a sophisticated *bricoleur*, sampling Stoic, Platonic, and other philosophical thought together with scriptures and with legends, with stories from church and stories from pregnant women; his work is a compendium of *exempla*, drawn from all walks of life. His rhetoric shifts depending on his audience, and in *De anima* he works to shift the sources of authority and of knowledge away from Greece, the symbolic intellectual center of empire, to locales further east, and to maintain that his intellectual pedigree is simpler—and more simple-minded—but also purer, than that of Greek philosophy. Thus, arguments which seem to be about geography and community identity—Who are one's intellectual forebears? From where do they come?—are also arguments about the legitimacy of various kinds of knowledge. In *De anima*, the philosophers are labeled the "patriarchs of the heretics" (3.1). Yet, in the very same text, Tertullian draws on everything from Soranus's medical writings to Plato to Stoic philosophy to entymology—even speculating on spirit and the windpipes of bugs. But ultimately in *De anima*, Tertullian trumps Athens and Greek philosophy as the center of knowledge by relocating any knowledge of truth from human regions to divine realms. He states: "For who can know truth without God? Who can understand God without Christ? Who has sought out Christ without the Holy Spirit? Who has conformed to the Holy Spirit without faith, by the sacrament? Socrates was led about easily by a different sort of spirit" (*An.* 1.4). In this short set of questions, Tertullian crescendoes toward another epistemology, rhetorically constructing a higher ground of knowing. Something like Socrates' *daimon* hardly compares to the truth governed by God.[26]

In *De anima*, Tertullian locates his knowledge somewhere entirely different and superior to "Greece," claiming to shatter the intellectual hegemony of philosophy produced and used at the intellectual center of the empire. He asserts that it is better to be ignorant than to learn something apart from God (*An.* 1.6), all the while using and refuting Plato and other philosophers throughout *De anima*. His comfort with championing no-knowledge and his rhetorical construction of himself as just another non-Greek nonphi-

[26]He also talks about the "wisdom of the school of Heaven" (*An.* 1.6).

losopher who appreciates knowledge from the margins of empire make less surprising *De anima*'s complex take on madness and ecstasy. By rhetorically marginalizing the intellectual center, he has cracked open the possibility of a broad range of valuable sources of knowledge.

This rhetorical strategy also provides a way for Tertullian to differentiate himself from others in the intramural Christian debate. Given Tertullian's own adherence to many ideas from Stoic and Platonic philosophy, his arguments against Greek philosophy do not indicate the excision of Stoic and Platonic philosophy from his work, but rather serve Tertullian's rhetorical purposes. According to Tertullian, his "opponents" are philosophers under the spell of Greek intellectual hegemony and, more specifically, of Platonism. There is Marcion, who split off the creator/demiurge from the true God—a move that occurs at a time of philosophical speculations about creation influenced by Platonism and certain traditions of scriptural interpretation. There are follow-ers of Valentinus, whom Tertullian describes as having constructed a complex system of emanations and semideities,[27] again an idea that was being worked out and debated within the Middle Platonism of Tertullian's day. Waszink points out that Tertullian calls Plato the *condimentarius haereticorum* (the supplier or pimp of the heretics); even so, or perhaps for this very reason, he cites Plato more than all other philosophers.[28] But Tertullian doesn't limit himself to Platonism; Stoicism, too, falls under his critique. In *De anima* as well as *Adversus Hermogenem*, Tertullian argues against Hermogenes, who, in his opinion, compromises the uniqueness of God by describing God and Matter as coexisting. Tertullian makes the charge specific to Hermogenes' association with philosophy: "he turned away from Christians to philosophers, from the church into the Academy and the Portico, whence he took [from the Stoics] to put matter (at the same level) with God" (*Herm.* 1.3).

Tertullian's intentional construction of himself and his ideas over and against philosophy (*An.* 2.4) is part of a larger strategy that has to do not only with the construction of group boundaries, and his staking a claim to true Christian identity, but also with his presentation of his epistemol-ogy as simple, straightforward, and reliant upon divine truth. Tertullian's antiphilosophical stance is part of the rhetorical construction of truth and true wisdom—and, concomitantly, unity of opinion—over and against the diversity of philosophical or heretical beliefs.[29] Tertullian often argues that

[27]See also Irenaeus's overblown critique of the Valentinians in *Haer.* 1.1–9, 11.
[28]Waszink, "Introduction," 34; quotation is from *An.* 23.5.
[29]See *An.* 2; *Val.* 4. For this theme more generally, see King, *What is Gnosticism?*.

truth is original and primary; heresy came only after it (*Marc.* 1; *Praescr.* 31–32, 35). He reinforces the authenticity and truth of his own knowledge and trumps philosophers by appealing to "God's documents," while at the very same time conceding that borrowing from his philosopher-opponents is sometimes necessary.[30] Tertullian lampoons the complex theological and philosophical debates of his time in order to construct his Christian opponents as *philosophers*, not Christians, and especially as Platonic philosophers, who partake in an esoteric philosophical theology that compromises the unity and ontological uniqueness of the divine.[31] Tertullian's construction of himself as antiphilosophical is part and parcel of this strategy.

Tertullian enjoys the best of both worlds, wielding appeals to God's teachings to authorize his conclusions, and at other times appealing to catalogues of famous philosophers to shore up his arguments. *De anima*, with its theories of the soul and its capacity for knowledge, is born from the convergence of medicine and philosophy in antiquity, and especially in Stoicism;[32] indeed, Tertullian's main source for *De anima* is the physician Soranus's text known by the same name.[33] In Hellenistic and Roman thought, philosophy and medicine were linked, as Martha Nussbaum argues, because of the idea that both provided a *therapeia*, a cure: one for the body, and one for the soul; these cures could and should bring health to the state, to the body politic, as well.[34] Stoic philosophy, insisting upon "ideas of rational self-government and universal citizenship," maintained that any "patient"—no matter the patient's class, gender, status, whether s/he suffered a philosophical or a medi-

---

[30]"ad dei litteras"; *An.* 2.5; Waszink, 4. See also E. Osborn's article, "Was Tertullian a Philosopher?" (*Stud. Pat.* 31 [1997] 322–34) in which he points out that Tertullian's use of paradox is not antiphilosophical, but stands within the tradition of Stoic philosophy (326–28).

[31]Frend (*Rise of Christianity*, 349) argues, "Indeed, it was he more than anyone who emphasized the cleavage between the two [Athens and Jerusalem, the Academy and the Church], and if he took a part of his pagan intellectual inheritance with him into Christianity, he did so not to build bridges, but to turn that heritage against its adherents, and to make more effective and more telling his defense of the Christian sect." I agree that Tertullian adopts so-called pagan philosophy and turns it against its adherents, but I would argue that his "opponents" are also (and even mainly) Christians. The struggle is intramural.

[32]Bréhier, *The Hellenistic and Roman Age*, 32; Nussbaum, "Extirpation of the Passions," 129. Plato anatomizes his understanding of the cosmos in the *Timaeus*.

[33]On Tertullian's *De anima* and its use of Soranus, see Waszink, "Introduction," 21–37. Soranus was influenced by Stoic philosophy (25); he was part of the methodist sect of medical practice and theory. See Oswei Temkin's introduction to his translation, *Soranus' Gynecology* (1956; Baltimore, Md.: Johns Hopkins University Press, 1991).

[34]Nussbaum, *Therapy of Desire*, 341.

cal complaint—could and needed to provide the data regarding the ordinary beliefs and the personal situations that were the cause or the symptoms of the trouble.[35] Reason, *logos*, would be the remedy for all such symptoms and false beliefs.[36] Thus, Stoic works overflow with concrete information and vivid *exempla* from experience, which we also find in Tertullian's works. Tertullian's *exempla* partake in a Stoic epistemology which respects the situatedness of knowledge, on the one hand, and which attempts to work through and root out murkiness and inconsistency in practical reasoning, on the other.[37]

The Stoic goal of a cure, a *therapeia*, emphasizes the importance of disclosing the knowledge one gains through experience and sense perception. Tertullian's commitment to Stoic epistemology thus allows him to place great emphasis on sense perception as a guide to the discovery of reality and truth, and allows him to use a variety of sources to prove his points. Crudely stated, Platonic epistemology assumes a gap between true reality (the Ideas or Forms) and what humans experience through sense perception. To attain this true reality, humans must shear off the distractions of sense perception and strive noetically—through the mind alone—to perceive the true Forms of things. As we recall, Plato's fourth and best ecstasy in the *Phaedrus* presented something like this, even if the soul's highest flight away from the body and sense perception involved madness. Tertullian himself characterizes Platonism in this way:

> Furthermore, [Plato] asserts that he who knows most of all by means of the mind by consequence knows in a superior way (*supersapere*),[38] neither reporting by means of vision nor drawing in any sense perception in any way to the soul, but using the mind itself entirely for the purpose of considering that he should lay hold of things which are real, if he is cut off principally from the eyes and the ears, which is to say, from the entire body, as the body throws into disorder and does not allow minds to possess truth and good judgment when it is conjoined to them. . . .

---

[35]Ibid., 46, 317–18; Bréhier, *The Hellenistic and Roman Age*, 64: "The early Stoics had as their aim not what we might call ethical progress but, as Clement of Alexandria expresses it, an inner transmutation that changes the whole man into pure reason and the citizen of the city into a citizen of the world." See Clement of Alexandria, *Strom.* 4.6.

[36]Nussbaum, *Therapy of Desire*, 49.

[37]Ibid., 348–49.

[38]Lewis and Short (s.v. *supersapio*) define *supersapio* incorrectly (and oddly) by reference to this text alone: "to possess very good taste Tert. *Anim.* 18." See notes on this passage by Waszink, 256. Waszink maintains that Tertullian is here quoting sections from Plato's *Phaedo*.

For Plato wants [to argue about] the existence of certain invisible, incorporeal, supermundial substances, divine and eternal, which he called Ideas, that is, Forms, the *exempla* and origins of manifestations of these natural things, and connected to the corporeal senses. The former are indeed true, but these latter things are images of them. Don't the heretical seeds of Gnostics and Valentinians shine forth? For here they seize upon the distinction of corporeal senses from intellectual powers.[39]

In contrast, Stoic thought (especially Tertullian's version of it) generally insists that humans can come to understand the world through sense perception. Stoic philosophy, which often argues for the unity of the soul, over and against the Platonists' tripartite soul, does not necessarily place the mind above sense perception as a source of knowledge. Tertullian is annoyed by Platonists' claims to "super knowledge." For Stoics, experience more broadly defined is epistemically valuable.[40]

---

[39]"2. Itaque rursus illum ergo ait supersapere qui mente maxime sapiat, neque visionem proponens neque ullum eiusmodi sensum attrahens animo, sed ipsa mente sincera utens in recogitando ad capiendum sincerum quodque rerum, si egressum potissimum ab oculis et auribus et, quod dicendum sit, a toto corpore ut turbante et non permittente animae possidere veritatem atque prudentiam, quando communicat. . . . 3. Vult enim Plato esse quasdam substantias invisibiles incorporales supermundiales, divinas et aeternas, quas appellat ideas, id est formas, exempla et causas naturalium istorum manifestorum et subiacentium corporalibus sensibus, et illas quidem esse veritates, haec autem imagines earum. 4. Relucentne iam haeretica semina Gnosticorum et Valentinianorum? Hinc enim arripiunt differentiam corporalium sensuum et intellectualium virium." *An.* 18.2–4; Waszink, 24.

[40]Bréhier, *The Hellenistic and Roman Age*, 37: "The object is no longer to eliminate the immediate, sensible datum but on the contrary to see Reason take shape; nor is there any progression from the sensible to the rational since there is no difference between one and the other. . . . In Platonism the intelligible is beyond the sensible while for the Stoics it is in the sensible things that Reason acquires the plenitude of its reality." The Stoic Chrysippus even asserts that the passions (παθή) themselves are strong and informed judgments which must be evaluated, but which nevertheless tell us something true about the world around us. See also Nussbaum's characterization of (some) Hellenistic thinkers (*Therapy of Desire*, 38): "Passions may be 'irrational' in the sense that the beliefs on which they rest may be false, or unjustified, or both. They are not irrational in the sense of having nothing to do with argument and reasoning." Regarding Chrysippus, Nussbaum ("Extirpation of the Passions," 137–38) states: "And if judgments are *all* that the passions are, if there is no part of them that lies outside the rational faculty, then a rational art that sufficiently modifies judgments, seeking out the correct ones and installing them in place of the false, will actually be sufficient for curing human beings of the ills that are caused by the passions."

Thus, the range of sources to which Tertullian refers in order to support his arguments and to render them authoritative is extensive. He does not limit himself to philosophy and scripture, although in *De anima* these are by far the mainstays of his argument. In his authorial self-construction as a great rhetorician and as someone who eschews philosophy in the search for truth, he allows himself to wander broadly and to bulldoze the reader with evidence from many *exempla*.[41] He refers to stories circulating in the Christian community; for example, when he refutes the idea that the soul can return to the body, he admits that he argues against a popular story of a young woman who had died, but during her graveside service moved her arms to a position of prayer, and then moved them back again. He also challenges the stories of bodies that politely shifted themselves in their graves to accommodate others' burials (*An.* 51). He cites the experiences of pregnant women in order to support his idea that the fetus, too, has a soul (*An.* 25). He even argues based upon his own dreaming, saying that fasting before sleep, rather than stimulating dreams, only makes him unaware that he dreamt at all (*An.* 48). Tertullian also refers to the ecstatic experiences of members of his community as valuable proof for his argument that all women, including virgins, should be veiled (*Virg.* 17), and for his contention that the soul is corporeal (*An.* 9)—an important case to be discussed below.

Tertullian's use of diverse *exempla*, some philosophical and others appealing to experience or scripture or legend, is made possible not only because of his rhetorical stance over and against philosophy, but also because he can appeal to some of the tenets of Stoic epistemology to bolster the legitimacy of introducing a broad range of data into his argument.[42] Indeed, as I have argued in the introduction to this book, we must dispense with our contemporary disciplinary divisions between medicine, philosophy, psychology, theology,

---

[41]See Sider, *Ancient Rhetoric*, 7–8: "Pétré shows that his use of *exempla* is based on the rules of the rhetorical schools and this fact explains many curious features of his work. It explains, for example, the frequent use of lists of *exempla*, especially the historical *exempla*. Tertullian's wide knowledge of history and philosophy is due less probably to broad reading than to the custom in the rhetorical schools of learning lists of examples, particularly historical examples."

[42]Barnes (*Tertullian*, 196, 213–14, 219) and Sider (*Ancient Rhetoric*, 7–8) are careful to emphasize that the use of florilegia and of a diversity of *exempla* is evidence not of Tertullian's shallowness, but of his sophisticated use of established rhetoric techniques. Barnes discusses Tertullian's use of collections of *exempla*, a common practice of the time, and states that Tertullian's rhetorical style and erudition are a manifestation of the Second Sophistic movement in Carthage.

and the like when we investigate the discussion of ecstasy and prophecy in antiquity. Tertullian borrows from and is part of a rich interplay of materials within the debate over prophecy. We turn now to *De anima* to see how Tertullian uses philosophical materials and proposes a broad epistemology as he investigates the soul.

## De anima

The study of prophecy and ecstasy in Tertullian, and of *De anima* in particular, is complicated by the fact that several key books are not preserved. My study might be much different if the seven books *On Ecstasy*, which Tertullian wrote after he completed *De anima*,[43] or Soranus's *On the Soul*, from which Tertullian borrowed extensively, were preserved. Moreover, Tertullian's *De anima* is a companion treatise to *De censu animae*, which was an extensive argument with Hermogenes regarding his views on the origin of the soul. This book, too, is lost to us.

*De anima* was written toward the end of Tertullian's life, between 210 and 213 C.E.[44] Although Barnes, Waszink, and others have studied the classical rhetorical techniques employed in *De anima*, no clear consensus exists about its genre. Barnes argues that although "its structure is conventionally analyzed as if it were discursive philosophy," it should be analyzed as a speech since it partakes in the traditional rhetorical structures of a speech delineated by Cicero's *De inventione* and other rhetorical handbooks.[45] This is consistent with the fact that formal education at this time and place most often took the form of an education in rhetoric,[46] and that Tertullian himself is clearly a product of such education, as demonstrated by the style and construction of argumentation in this work and others.

---

[43]Waszink, "Introduction," 5.

[44]Ibid., 5–6. Tertullian's allusion to Perpetua (*An*. 55), who was martyred 7 March 203 C.E., sets a *terminus post quem*. Two manuscripts of *De anima* are extant, and two sixteenth-century editions are also valuable authorities (Waszink, "Introduction," 1–4).

[45]Barnes, *Tertullian*, 206. It is curious that Waszink offers no real discussion of the genre of *De anima*. In his *Ancient Rhetoric and the Art of Tertullian*, Ron Sider refers to *De anima* only once in detail (and only one other time in a note; see 84–85, 103 n. 1) and he offers no theories about its overall genre.

[46]George Kennedy, *A New History of Classical Rhetoric* (Princeton, N.J.: Princeton University Press, 1994) 173.

In classical oratory, three kinds of rhetoric are often delineated: epide-
ictic or demonstrative, deliberative, and judicial.[47] The first often takes the
form of panegyric; the second is intended to convince an audience toward
a certain path for the future, as Paul did in 1 Corinthians. The third, judicial
or forensic rhetoric, attempts to persuade an audience of one's point of view
on present or past matters. This, the rhetor asserts, is how things are, or how
they happened. I would argue that Tertullian's *De anima*, while clearly an
extended working out of philosophical arguments about the soul, is also an
example of judicial rhetoric. Barnes asserts that *De anima* is a speech and
organizes its sections into the traditional sections of a speech.[48] Tertullian's
larger purpose is to persuade an audience that his view on the soul is the
correct one, as if he were in a court demonstrating his point, putting on
trial Hermogenes' and others' "philosophical" ideas about the soul. Indeed,
Tertullian's strange, small piece titled *Testimony of the Soul* is explicitly
a piece of judicial rhetoric, which uses the literary device of depicting a
courtroom setting where the soul is called to the stand as a neutral witness
to defend the truth of Christianity.[49]

   The identity of the audience for *De anima*'s judicial rhetoric is even more
elusive than that of the much-debated original audience for 1 Corinthians, for
example. Tertullian admits at the beginning of *De anima* that this work is a
grab bag, a riposte to all the philosophical notions regarding the soul that he
has not already covered in his sustained arguments against Hermogenes in
*Adversus Hermogenem* and *De censu animae*. Moreover, because Tertullian
wrote in Latin, at a time when most cutting-edge philosophical-theological
discussion was conducted in Greek, and because of his affiliation with the
New Prophecy, his ideas were not picked up extensively by later authors,
making it almost impossible to track a history of reception, much less a history of interpretation.[50] This makes it difficult for us to understand the actual
audiences of his work, and the history of his ideas.

---

[47]Quintilian here follows Aristotle's taxonomy. George Kennedy, *Quintilian* (New York:
Twayne Publishers, 1969) 59.

[48]Barnes, *Tertullian*, 206.

[49]Simon Price, "Latin Christian Apologetics: Minucius Felix, Tertullian, and Cyprian," *Apologetics in the Roman Empire: Pagans, Jews, and Christians* (ed. Mark Edwards et al.; Oxford: Oxford
University Press, 1999) 110.

[50]Waszink ("Introduction," 48–49) discusses the fact that Tertullian had only a slight
influence on later authors. He attributes this to his opinion that *De anima* is not a "well-
thought-out system of psychology" and because of its polemical intentions. He also assumes

We do know, however, that *De anima* is intimately tied to a broader project: it is the third step of an argument with Hermogenes, and thus must be read with *Adversus Hermogenem* in mind, and fortunately this text is extant. Tertullian had proceeded from *Adversus Hermogenem*, which deals with creation, to *De censu animae*, another treatise against Hermogenes, which continues the logic of arguments about origins by arguing about the soul's origin.[51] As Tertullian explains, "I discussed with Hermogenes only the original essence of the soul, since he assumed this to be produced from matter rather than to be established from the breath of God. Now I will strive to contend with the philosophers as I turn to the remaining questions."[52] Thus *De anima*'s first section (chapters 1–3) explains that Tertullian has already done philosophical battle with Hermogenes and is now turning outward to contend with philosophy more generally. As Waszink asserts, *De anima* also presupposes the reader's familiarity with *De censu animae*, referring to its arguments nine times.[53] *De anima* thus claims its place in a trilogy of philosophical treatises launched against opponents.

Although throughout *De anima* we find heavy and explicit reliance on contemporary Stoic philosophy, *Against Hermogenes* begins with a disavowal of the Stoics. Tertullian cannot support their cosmology: "[Hermogenes] turned away from Christians to philosophers, from the church into the academy and the portico, whence he undertook [from the Stoics] to put matter (at the same level) with God, as if it had always existed, neither born nor made, neither having beginning at all nor end, from which matter God afterwards created all things" (*Herm.* 1.3).[54] This initial argument turns into a prolonged treatise

---

that the idea of the corporeality of the soul, taken from pagan physicians, "must soon have repelled Christian readers." According to Waszink, Jerome knew of *De anima*, as did Fulgentius, Prudentius, and Augustine, but it influenced only Vicentius Victor.

[51]Waszink ("Introduction," 7) states that Tertullian assumes that his readers are familiar with *De censu animae*, and implies that they need to be familiar with this text in order to understand *De anima*. Waszink also speculates about the content of *De censu animae* (12–14).

[52]"De solo censu animae congressus Hermogeni, quatenus et istum ex materiae potius suggestu quam ex dei flatu constitisse praesumpsit, nunc ad reliquas conversus quaestiones plurimum videbor cum philosophis dimicaturus." *An.* 1.1; Waszink, 1.

[53]Waszink, "Introduction," 7.

[54]Tertullian is not alone in his concern about the uniqueness of God's role as creator (a concern that is discussed further in *Adversus Marcionem*), or in his insistence that God is absolutely other—not only from the world which God brings into being and which God will return to nothingness (*Herm.* 34), but also from matter, and all that preceded the beginning of time and the creation of the world. See also Philo, *Opif.* 5.21. John Dillon (*The Middle*

in defense of God's uniqueness and priority to Matter; Tertullian spins his argument of *creatio ex nihilo*: God is first and all, coeternal with nothing.[55]

The *exordium* of *De anima* sets forth the problem: in this new work, Tertullian is tying up remaining arguments from his debates with Hermogenes on the soul.[56] The *exordium* is also a perfect place for the speaker or author's self-construction to begin, especially when orally delivered in a court of law, or, in this case, when employing elements of judicial or forensic rhetoric.[57] Its contents have already been discussed: Tertullian constructs himself and his epistemology over and against philosophical speculation of the day. He, in contrast to these complex philosophers, wishes simply to discuss the soul as the breath of God. Creation in general and the creation of the human in particular form the immediate conceptual and literary backdrop of Tertullian's discussion of the soul. Although there are many sometimes tortuous arguments in *De anima*, some Tertullian's own and many taken from doxographies of the time,[58] Tertullian emphasizes again and again only a few main points about the soul.

---

*Platonists 80 B.C. to A.D. 220* [1977; rev. ed.; New York: Cornell University Press, 1996] 158) concludes that it cannot be proven that Philo held to a concept of *creatio ex nihilo*. Irenaeus, too, shares a concern about God and matter co-existing (*Haer.* 5.4, passim). For a later debate about God and matter, see Athanasius, *On the Incarnation of the Word* 2.

[55]See Tertullian, *Herm.* 17, for the subordination of Wisdom, who is understood to be "God's Spirit." See also his conclusion where the Word is secondary to Wisdom: "For the prophets and apostles did not hand on the tradition that God made the world by merely appearing and drawing near to matter, nor were these things named matter at all, but at first Wisdom was established, the beginning of his ways, in his works. Then the heavens were established by his Word (*sermone*)" (45). See also Philo, *Opif.* 2.8–9.

[56]See Barnes, *Tertullian*, 206. Although Waszink's analysis of the structure of *De anima* ("Introduction," 15) does not specifically identify chapters 1–3 as the *exordium*, he too sets these apart from the next section. Given Waszink's meticulous work on *De anima*, it is surprising that he does not analyze its structure according to the tools of classical rhetoric.

[57]Kennedy (*Quintilian*, 65) discusses the fact that in Latin oratory, the *exordium* in judicial rhetoric allowed a speaker to establish his/her identity over and against that of the client. This differs from the Greek system, where the client often represented him- or herself.

[58]Waszink ("Introduction," 28) can conclude "with Diels . . . that the very rich doxographical material contained in *De anima* derives from Soranus"; that is, Soranus's *On the Soul* consisted in part of long recitations of other philosophers' ideas on the soul, and Tertullian borrowed from these, as well as from the *exempla* which Soranus used. Not all materials are from Soranus, however. See ibid. (28–34) for a discussion of Soranus's and Tertullian's uses of doxographies.

## *The* status animae *(De anima 4–22)*

The first full section of *De anima* (chapters 4–22) concerns the *status animae*. This can be translated as "the condition of the soul."[59] But by the first century C.E., *status* is a technical rhetorical term used to talk about an issue which arises from a conflict: it is the central issue of an argument.[60] Perhaps Tertullian engages in wordplay: What is the central issue of the text? The condition of the soul. The thesis of *De censu animae* inaugurates the discussion of the *status animae*: "we claimed that the soul is from the breath of God, and not from matter" ("ex dei flatu, non ex materia vindicamus"; *An.* 3.4; Waszink, 5). The soul, since it originates with the breath of God, has a beginning: it is born and made, unlike Plato's concept of the soul (*An.* 4). Against Plato's notion of the soul, Tertullian argues along with the Stoics (and here particularly with Soranus, no doubt)[61] that the soul is corporeal: "they state almost as we do that the spirit is soul, which among them closely resembles the breath and spirit; nevertheless they easily persuade (us) that the soul is a body" ("qui spiritum praedicantes animam paene nobiscum, qua proxima inter se flatus et spiritus, tamen corpus animam facile persuadebunt"; *An.* 5.2; Waszink, 6).

The rapid-fire juxtaposition of *spiritus*, *anima*, and *flatus* is unpacked slightly later in *De anima*; here what is most surprising is the equation of *anima* and *corpus*. This bodied soul is a heavy argument, bending other issues toward its gravity. It confounds Platonic arguments regarding body and animation. Platonists argue, according to Tertullian, that the soul is not a body "because it is not moved from any direction by the pattern of corporeal things" ("quae non corporalium forma ex aliqua regione moveatur"; *An.* 6.1; Waszink, 7). This is because the soul is not moved from outside (which would make it a nonanimate body) since it is by definition animate, nor is it moved

---

[59]Waszink translates "essence," but "physical state or condition" is a more appropriate translation (*Oxford Latin Dictionary*, s.v. *status*).

[60]According to Kennedy (*Quintilian*, 51), in Greek, the term was *stasis*, and in earlier Latin oratory, it was *constitutio*. Quintilian used the term *status* to encompass this idea. Kennedy explains the term this way: "*stasis* is not the first conflict of opinion . . . , but the issue which arises from the first conflict: 'you did it'; 'I didn't'; the issue in fact, 'did he do it?' In practice an individual speech may contain more than one issue: 'it was just to do it, but in fact I didn't.'" The *status* is thus the "basic issue in the case."

[61]Waszink, "Introduction," 22–44. See also Bréhier, *The Hellenistic and Roman Age*, 45: "only bodies exist . . . for what exists is what is capable of acting or being acted upon, and only bodies have this capacity."

from within, since the soul has the power to move the body.[62] The bodied soul also gives motion to the body; it is, "as it were, a little figure moving the surface, impelling internally" ("velut sigillario motu superficiem intus agitante"; *An.* 6.3; Waszink, 7). This corporeal soul is visible: according to the vision of a woman in the church, it has a bodily shape, "delicate and light and of an airy color" ("tenera et lucida et aerii coloris, et forma per omnia humana"; *An.* 9.4; Waszink, 11). This concept of the soul mixes the Platonic binary of visible-invisible and corporeal-incorporeal. Tertullian complexifies things by arguing from Rev 6:9 that the bodied soul is invisible to the flesh, but visible to the spirit, as the souls of the martyrs under the altar were seen by John when he was "in the spirit" (*An.* 8.5).

Although Waszink argues that the main point of Tertullian's entire treatise is that the soul is a body,[63] the scales are in fact tipped elsewhere. This section on the *status animae* is primarily concerned with supporting the Stoic idea that the soul is simple and uncompounded over and against the more widespread Platonizing scheme of a tripartite soul. In chapters 4–22, and again in chapters 23–41, where he offers an argument on the birth and development of the soul to continue his arguments about the *status animae*, Tertullian works through the rhetorical features of the proof and *reprehensio* of the text.[64] The proofs and refutations of opposing arguments are juxtaposed with alacrity in *De anima*; Tertullian weaves these two traditionally separate rhetorical sections together in order to strengthen and guide his argument. Indeed, refutation of an opposing argument often propels him into the next set of ideas, all connected (if loosely) to his main theme. This *propositio*[65] about the uniform and undivided soul is enunciated in *An.* 10.1: "The condition of

---

[62]Tertullian clarifies: "hence, suppose the soul is moved by something else, by external means: moreover, we demonstrate elsewhere that the soul is moved even by another when it is prophesying, when it is mad, surely by something external." ("Dehinc si corporis est moveri extrinsecus ab aliquo, ostendimus autem supra moveri animam et ab alio, cum vaticinatur, cum furit, utique extrinsecus"; *An.* 6.3; Waszink, 7.)

[63]Waszink ("Introduction," 48) states that Tertullian's chief thesis is corporeality of soul, which is taken from pagan physicians. Barnes (*Tertullian*, 207), too, argues that the *propositio* of *De anima* is found in 5.6: "Igitur corpus anima, quae nisi corporalis corpus non derelinquet" (Waszink, 7).

[64]Regarding Quintilian's model, see Kennedy, *Quintilian*, 65–72. Regarding Tertullian's use of rhetoric, see Ayers, *Language, Logic, and Reason*, 9–10.

[65]According to Quintilian, the five parts of a speech are the exordium, the narration, the proof, the refutation, and the peroration. Note that Quintilian maintained that the *propositio* and *partitio* are subdivisions of the proof. See Kennedy, *Quintilian*, 64, who is citing Quintilian, *Inst. or.* 3.9.1.

the faith determines that the soul is uncompounded, along with Plato; it is of only one form."[66] It is interesting to note that in this important statement Tertullian claims to argue *alongside* Plato, when Plato describes a tripartite soul in the *Timaeus*. *De anima* is particularly confusing because Tertullian claims to agree with Plato that the soul is tripartite, yet Tertullian also argues violently against this idea. Tertullian shores up his authority by appealing to Plato, at the same time that elsewhere in *De anima* he enhances the integrity of his own stance and argument by disagreeing with Plato.

This assertion of the unity and uniformity of the soul allows Tertullian to defend several other ideas that he considers important. Tertullian is concerned to argue that the mind (νοῦς, *mens, animus*; see 12.1) is not superior to the soul, nor is it separate or different from it. It is "nothing other than what we understand to be the inborn and innate supplier of the soul and proper to it by birth";[67] there is no distinction between the mind and the soul; "the mind is a function" or "performer" of the substance which it shares with the soul.[68] Tertullian does, however, ask which is superior, and decides that the soul is superior, since the mind works for it ("in officium naturale substantiae deputetur"; *An.* 13.1; Waszink, 17). Although Tertullian makes an argument that the soul has a ruling part, an ἡγεμονικόν, he locates this in the heart (*An.* 15).[69] This championing of a unitary soul has important implications for social organization and for authority, as we shall see, since the mind is not granted primacy of place.

Tertullian maintains with the Stoics that the soul is not only unitary but also entirely rational.[70] He rejects Plato's division of the soul, yet simultaneously (and oddly) accepts the notion of a desiderative/appetitive portion of the soul, since this idea helps to explain the soul's "fall" from its original rationality into

[66]"Pertinet ad statum fidei simplicem animam determinare secundum Platonem, id est uniformem." *An.* 10.1; Waszink, 12.

[67]"Non aliud quid intellegimus quam suggestum animae ingenitum et insitum et nativitus proprium." *An.* 12.1; Waszink, 16.

[68]"Nos autem animum ita dicimus animae concretum, non ut substantia alium, sed ut substantiae officium." *An.* 12.6; Waszink, 17. Quain's translation (206) is misleading: "the mind is a faculty of the soul."

[69]This conclusion is again in keeping with his Stoic inclinations, since Stoicism generally considered the part of the soul in which representation, assent, and inclination happen to be the ἡγεμονικόν. It is pictured as a fiery breath seated in the heart. See Bréhier, *The Hellenistic and Roman Age*, 55.

[70]But see Nussbaum, "Extirpation," for other possibilities in Stoic thought.

appetite and irrationality. He accomplishes this logical gymnastic by insisting that some elements are natural to the soul, and some are not. Thus he moves from the statement that "Plato's twofold division of the soul into rational and irrational is consistent with [our] faith," and argues that "we must believe the rational element to be natural, because from the beginning, [this element] of the soul was engendered by its author, who is clearly rational."[71] Where he differs from Plato is in the ontological makeup of the soul: the irrational is a later phenomenon, or, puzzlingly and contradictorily, it isn't even irrational at all. The irrational element accrued later, with the serpent, as an *accidens*, according to Tertullian; in so arguing, he defends both God and the human as naturally good and rational, and maintains the essential unity of the soul. He then shifts his argument to explain that even if the irrational element were part of the nature of the soul, it too would be derived from God, but then—and here the argument is confused—it would not in fact be irrational, because "the irrational is an alien principle" to God.[72] It is here—and nowhere else in *De anima*—that Tertullian brings in Christ as a model.[73] The triad of qualities—rational (*rationale*), indignant (θυμικόν), and desirous (ἐπιθυμητικόν)[74]—was present in Christ, but in an entirely reasonable way (*rationaliter*): he was reasonably angry with the scribes and Pharisees, and he reasonably desired to eat the Passover with his disciples. Thus, too, in humans, these can be reasonable qualities: someone can desire to be bishop, or be indignant as Paul was at a lack of "discipline and order" (*An.* 16.6).[75]

---

[71]"Est et illud ad fidem pertinens, quod Plato bifariam partitur animam, per rationale et inrationale. . . . Naturale enim rationale credendum est, quod animae a primordio sit ingenitum, a rationali videlicet auctore." *An.* 16.1; Waszink, 20.

[72]*An.* 16.2. See Bréhier, *The Hellenistic and Roman Age*, 36–37.

[73]We might expect Tertullian to model the soul upon Christ: often, anthropology is deduced from the "perfect man," since early Christian writers often understand Christ to be the perfect *imago dei* to which humans should attain. (See, e.g., Irenaeus, *Haer.* 5.16.2, about the resemblance of humans to the Word of God, and human loss of similitude to the invisible Word, after whose image the human was created.) Tertullian, however, is consistently more interested in the human than in Christ: *De carne Christi*, for example, is driven by Tertullian's desire to explain how it is reasonable that the flesh of humans in general can be resurrected.

[74]Tertullian glosses the Latin *indignativum* and *concupiscentivum* with Greek terms.

[75]This idea of the rationality of anger and of desire may be derived in part from the Stoic idea of the transformation of the passions into the *eupatheia*. Desire (ἐπιθυμία), fear (φόβος), pleasure (ἡδονή), and distress or grief (λυπή) are "contrary to Nature, being irrational motions of the soul, based on false opinions (δόξαι), and the Sage should have nothing to do with them" (Dillon, *Middle Platonists*, 77; see Nussbaum, "Extirpation of the Passions," 159, on how they connect with temporality). They should not be moderated, as the Academic-Peripatetics believe,

These arguments reflect a sophisticated play with Stoic and Middle Platonic philosophy. Tertullian is toying with Plato's discussion of the soul in the *Timaeus*, which contrasts the rational and immortal principle of the soul with its mortal form, which is full of the passions. One lower portion of the soul is located in the chest and has to do with "courage and spirit" (*Tim.* 70A);[76] and one is located below the diaphragm. This is "the part of the soul which has appetites (τὸ ἐπιθυμητικόν) for both food and drink and which has need for such other things on account of the nature of the body"; it is "tied up there, like a wild creature which needs to be joined in order to be nourished, if the mortal race is going to exist somehow" (*Tim.* 70E). In Christ, Tertullian marries the common Stoic notion of the soul, with its unity and rationality,[77] and the Platonic tripartite soul. In Christ, what appear to be passions are caught up and redeemed in the rational; his passions are, as the Stoic Chrysippus might argue, rational, but more importantly, they are not passions at all, but are correct judgments (δόξαι).[78]

Tertullian's second main set of arguments continues this line of thought. He argues that the intellectual faculty is not superior to the faculty of sense perception, a hierarchy he ascribes to the "Gnostics and Valentinians," who, he claims, inherited it from Plato. Tertullian fully admits that "it is because of these views that we have in a former passage [chapter 12] stated as preliminary fact that the mind is nothing else than an apparatus or instrument of the soul, and that the spirit is no other faculty, separate from the soul, but is the soul itself exercised in respiration" (*An.* 18.5). The intellectual faculty and the faculty of sense perception are of equal value: "For how can the intellect be given preference over sense perception, by which the intellect is instructed

---

but should be entirely extirpated. Philo presents *eupatheia* which match all four passions: χάρα (joy) instead of ἡδονή, βούλησις (will) instead of ἐπιθυμία, εὐλαβεία (caution) instead of φόβος, δέγμος (conscience) instead of λυπή (Dillon, *Middle Platonists*, 151).

[76]The Greek edition of Plato is that of Burnet in *Platonis Opera* and the translations are mine, unless otherwise noted. For a full reference to Burnet, see above p. 33 n. 10.

[77]But note that some Stoics, such as Posidonius, returned to the idea of a tripartite soul; see Nussbaum (*Therapy of Desire*, 373–74) for a measured discussion of Stoic ideas of the unity and rationality of the soul as their conclusion—as something to be demonstrated, rather than a given starting point.

[78]For Stoics, sense perception leads to judgment (δόξα), which is "an assent to an appearance" (Nussbaum, *Therapy of Desire*, 374). That assent can then be either correct or incorrect, but should be based upon a reasonable judgment. See ibid., 374–84. Tertullian does not point to a Christ who moderates his passions, but in line with Stoic insistence on the extirpation of the passions, presents a dispassionate and utterly rational Christ.

for the purpose of acquiring true knowledge?"[79] Even sense perception which provides slightly inaccurate information, such as the eye which thinks it sees an oar that bends under water, has a perfectly good cause; the error is not due to our senses.[80] Although Tertullian admits that sensible objects are inferior to spiritual ones, he differentiates between what is perceived and the faculty of perception, and places the faculty of the intellect and that of sense perception on the same level.

Tertullian's third main point in this section regarding the condition (and unity) of the soul is nicely mirrored in the first and penultimate chapters (11 and 21). Using Gen 2:21–24 and the image of Adam's ecstasy, Tertullian insists that humans—Adam's offspring—are not *naturally* spiritual (*spiritalis*, πνευματικός); prophecy and ecstasy are a secondary and accidental phenomenon. We recall from chapter 1 that Tertullian holds that Adam is not naturally spiritual, even if he did prophesy "the great mystery of Christ and the church" in his statement that Eve is "bone of my bone, and flesh of my flesh" (Gen 2:23–24). His prophecy was secondary: "this . . . only came on him afterwards, when God infused into him the madness (*amentia*), or spiritual force, which constitutes prophecy."[81] The surprising use of *amentia* here will be discussed later; now it is sufficient to note that in both chapters 11 and 21 Tertullian uses the story of Adam in Genesis 2 to combat the idea that the soul is multiform, and that humans are ontologically fixed or assigned one of three immutable natures, a viewpoint he characterizes as the "Valentinian trinity" ("trinitas Valentiniana"; *An.* 21.1). Tertullian wants instead to assert the possibility of change through the "power of the grace of God" which gives free will. Thus no human is limited to being either spiritual, carnal, or psychical.

Tertullian's *Against the Valentinians* allows us to see more of what was at stake in this debate over the human soul's relation to the spiritual. Tertullian characterizes Valentinian thought as creating ontological distinctions between

[79]"Quomodo enim praeferatur sensui intellectus, a quo informatur ad cogitionem veritatum?" *An.* 18.11; Waszink, 26.

[80]*An.* 17.8. He launches this argument against the Platonists (*An.* 17); on the reliability of the senses in Stoic literature, see Bréhier, *The Hellenistic and Roman Age*, 38–44: "The Stoic theory of knowledge consists precisely in making sensation the key to certainty and wisdom." A faithful image is apprehended and judged by the soul, which assents to its truth.

[81]"Hoc postea obvenit, cum in illum deus amentiam immisit, spiritalem vim, qua constat prophetia." *An.* 21.2; Waszink, 29–30. See also *An.* 11.4: "accidentiam spiritus passus est: cecidit enim ecstasis super illum, sancti spiritus vis operatrix prophetiae" (Waszink, 15).

humans: humans have different capacities to reach goodness and to attain a spiritual state.[82] Tertullian explains:

> They profess that in the beginning there was a triform nature — nevertheless united in Adam; then they divide [it] into unique properties of a class. In this way they obtain an occasion for distinctions from the posterity of Adam himself, for a tripartite (division), too, for different morals: Cain and Abel and Seth. From these fonts, in a way, of the human race, they derive just as many arguments regarding nature and moral sense: clay (*choicum*), a condition of degeneracy, they associate with Cain; they match the animal (*animale*), determined to be a median hope, to Abel; the spiritual (*spiritale*), surely a condition that is preordained, they hoard up for Seth. Thus also they divide souls themselves into two by their property, good or bad, according to the condition of clay from Cain or the animal from Adam. The spiritual they bring forth from Seth by accident, therefore not by nature but grace.[83]

This representation of Valentinian thought is hardly fair,[84] but Tertullian's point becomes clear from his representation of his constructed opponent. Tertullian insists that if the human soul appears to be tripartite, this is not natural, but arises from the "mutability of its accidental circumstances." This

---

[82]Of course this point is much contested, and I here refer to Tertullian's argument about "Valentinians" to highlight his construction of his opponents, not to advocate for any definition of Valentinus's thought or that of his students. Regarding this debate, see also Luise Schottroff, "Animae naturaliter salvandae: Zum Problem der himmlischen Herkunft des Gnostikers," in *Christentum und Gnōsis* (ed. Walther Eltester; Berlin: Alfred Töpelmann, 1969) 65–97; see also Einar Thomassen's proposal (*Le Traite tripartite (NH I, 5)* [Bibliothèque Copte de Nag Hammadi Section texts 19; Quebec: Presses de l'Université Laval, 1989] 39) that the *Tripartite Tractate* maps ethnicity onto ontology, as different ethnicities (Greek and barbarian, as well as Hebrew) have different ontological status. See *Tri. Trac.* 118–22.

[83]"Triformem naturam primordio professi et tamen inunitam in Adam, inde iam diuidunt per singulares generum proprietates, nacti occasionem distinctionis huiusmodi ex posteritate ipsius Adae, moralibus quoque differentiis tripertita, Cain et Abel <et> Seth. <Hos> fontes quodammodo generis humani in totidem deriuant argumenta naturae atque sententiae: choicum, saluti degeneratum, ad Cain redigunt, animale, mediae spei deliberatum, ad Abel componunt, spiritale, certae saluti praeiudicatum, in Seth recondunt. Sic et animas ipsas duplici proprietate discernunt, bonas et malas, secundum choicum statum ex Cain et animalem ex Abel. Spiritalem ex Seth de obuenientia superducunt iam non naturam sed indulgentiam." *Adv. Val.* 29.1–3; CCSL II.II.773. This kind of anthropology is found in the treatise *Hypostasis of the Archons*, but see also the *Tri. Trac.*, esp. 104–8 and 118–22.

[84]See Schottroff, "Animae naturaliter salvandae"; and Michel Desjardins, *Sin in Valentinianism* (Atlanta, Ga.: Scholars Press, 1990).

perspective allows for equality among all humans, and levels the spiritual playing field: because all are descended from Adam and thus all have the soul which is God's *afflatus*, Tertullian can argue that all have the same unitary and good soul, and any evil or spiritual influence is not natural to it, but an *accidens*.[85] Tertullian rhetorically situates his understanding of the soul and its spiritual capacities in opposition to Platonizing Christians. He concludes this section of *De anima* by summarizing: "We define the soul as born from the breath of God, immortal, corporeal, formed, simple in substance, aware of itself, advancing in various ways, free in its decisions, subject to accidents, changeable in disposition, rational, ruling, divinely inspired, overflowing from one."[86]

## The Birth and Development of the Soul *(De anima 23–41)*

Where one would expect a peroration, or a concluding statement to the argument about the *status animae*,[87] the reader finds instead the start of a new but related theme. Tertullian's second full section addresses the question of where souls come from, and explores from this different angle the issue of the soul's substance. He overturns Plato's notion of an unborn soul, formerly with God in the heavens, which learns through reminiscence (μαθήσεις ἀναμνήσεις);[88] this theory of Plato's, he insists, has catered to "heretics" such as Carpocrates, Apelles, and Valentinus (*An.* 23). Rather, Tertullian argues from experience and from his theories that the soul is born and passible, but also immortal and a "diluted divinity" ("dilutioris divinitatis"; *An.* 24.2, Waszink 32).

If the soul is unborn and is just like God (as Tertullian claims that Plato argues) the soul should suffer no passions and should experience no loss of memory. But although natural knowledge never fails—even Queen Berenike's pet lion, fed with cakes, *really* wants to eat flesh—memory does fail. Because

---

[85]This too is related to underlying Stoic ideas. Nussbaum (*Therapy of Desire*, 352) explains, "This optimism in Stoicism is connected . . . with the fact that they refuse to trace human misery to any natural or inherent evil; instead, it is produced by ignorance, confusion, and weakness of thought."

[86]"Definimus animam dei flatu natam, immortalem, corporalem, effigiatam, substantia simplicem, de suo sapientem, varie procedentem, liberam arbitrii, accidentis obnoxiam, per ingenia mutabilem, rationalem, dominatricem, divinatricem, ex una redundantem." *An.* 22.2; Waszink, 31.

[87]Barnes, *Tertullian*, 207.

[88]Tertullian interjects the Greek here. See Waszink, 32.

of this, Tertullian launches into a "confutation of the Platonic doctrine of reminiscence."[89] The soul's ability to prophesy and the human capacity to remember that prophecy become part of Tertullian's argument:

> Plato himself also offers many proofs that witness the power of foreknowledge of the soul. . . . But everyone has felt in him- or herself the soul foretelling either omens or dangers or the increase of joys. If the body does not obstruct the power of foretelling, neither does it thwart memory, in my opinion. In this theory, souls indeed both forget and remember because of the body.[90]

Tertullian argues against the Platonic excuse that memory fails because of the soul's entrapment in the body; he insists that Plato cannot coherently argue that the body is the site—literally, the reason, the *ratio* (*An.* 24.10)—of both forgetfulness and remembrance. Setting aside the dubious coherence of Tertullian's own argument here—it is one of the weaker among the four arguments he launches against Plato's unborn soul—we see that Tertullian implies that divination and foresight are natural to the soul, common activities that are not hindered by the body.

As we have seen in chapter 1, Gen 2:21 is a site of interpretive debate and great interest among those discussing prophecy and ecstasy, whether Philo, Tertullian, or the Anti-Phrygian, because of the significance of arguments about creation and human origins. Tertullian also exhibits this interest in creation in his construction of an analogy between Adam's creation and every human's origin. Tertullian insists that when a living being is conceived, the soul and the body are formed simultaneously. There is no priority: "both are conceived and bound together at the same time."[91] Just as in natural, chaste

---

[89]Waszink's title for the section (p. 303); see his clear explanation of the various elements of the argument.

[90]"Multa item documenta teste ipso Platone divinationem animae probaverunt. . . . Sed nec quisquam hominum non et ipse aliquando praesagam animam suam sentit, aut ominis aut periculi aut gaudii augurem. Si divinationi non obstrepit corpus, nec memoriae, opinor, officiet. In eodem certe corpore et obliviscuntur animae et recordantur." *An.* 24.10; Waszink, 34. In fact, as we have seen in ch. 1, above, Plato states that divination occurs precisely when intelligence is "fettered"; this flash of insight into the future is stimulated by the appetitive soul, with its lusts for bodily things, which is then being frightened by the smooth reflective surface of the liver.

[91]He argues against Stoics and Platonists, who think that the soul is a separate formation, inhaled at one's first breath, and exhaled at one's last, by appealing to various sources, including women's experiences during pregnancy (for snide remarks about men's unwillingness to

sexual relations (as Tertullian bills them), the soul supplies the desire and
the body the gratification, so in the case of Adam two things were involved:
wet clay and the breath of God, and thus also two substances flow forth in
conception, which result in the body and the soul (*An.* 27).[92] At the time of
conception, the soul also receives its sex: "the soul is sown in the uterus
equally with the flesh, equally with it the sex is also obtained, so equally
that neither substance can be held as the cause of the sex" (*An.* 36.2). Thus
sex cannot be attributed only to the soul or only to the body.[93]

Tertullian ends this section on the birth and the growth of the soul by
explaining that "every soul, then, by birth, is imagined to be in Adam until
it is reckoned to be in Christ; impure until it is reckoned in Christ" (*An.*
40.1). He is careful to point out that while this sinfulness contributes to the
shame of the clay-like substance of which humans are made, this substance
is only an instrument, not guilty on its own account: by nature, it is neutral,
and it only takes part in the operations or effects of most sins. It is an ac-
complice to the soul, which is the primary offender. Tertullian addresses the
discrepancy between this first "nature" and the wrongs that humans do. He
thus speaks of a second nature, which is almost original to the first.[94] "What
comes from God is not extinguished but overshadowed" (*An.* 41.2) because
of this second evil nature; thus while all souls are part of the same genus,
some humans are good and others bad. Baptism is the second birth whereby
this corruption is taken away.

---

discuss pregnancy with women, see *An.* 25.3), and to various scriptures, including the story
of the baby leaping in Elizabeth's womb when she sees Mary (*An.* 27). When a human is
conceived, the soul and the body are formed simultaneously.

[92]Sections 28–35 contain a long argument against metempsychosis, the details of which
need not concern us here. Waszink also points out that the discussion of transmigration is a
digression (419).

[93]Tertullian argues implicitly against the sexless souls posited by many Christian writers
and explicitly against Apelles' idea that the soul has priority, and impresses its sex/gender
upon the body. Tertullian does, however, argue from creation that the male is more complete
and formed first, and that Eve (and by extension, females in general) received God's *afflatus*
through Adam. For various early Christian views on the sex/gender of the soul, see the
discussion in Waszink, 420.

[94]"Malum igitur animae, praeter quod ex obventu spiritus nequam superstruitur, ex originis
vitio antecedit, naturale quodammodo." *An.* 41.1; Waszink, 57. According to Nussbaum
(*Therapy of Desire*, 333), "the Stoics, like Aristotle, strongly deny that there is in human beings
any innate or original evil: when they go wrong, it is on account of false belief, and this is why
correct teaching can play such a valuable ethical role."

## The Soul at Death and in Sleep (De anima 42–58)

Having dealt in his second section with the birth and development of the soul, Tertullian now moves to complete his treatise by introducing endings: death, and sleep as type of what happens to the soul in death. The subject of death is introduced in section 42, but Tertullian immediately moves in sections 43–49 to a long excursus on sleep. (This section also discusses ecstasy, which I shall pass over now and discuss in the next chapter.) Tertullian states that death is the end of knowledge from the senses and the dissolution of the body.[95] Because the soul is immortal and thus indivisible, Tertullian argues against the common belief that the soul escapes the body slowly, bit by bit, at death, and that some particle of the soul remains in the body.[96]

Death is not natural, but is the fault of sin, and so all death is violent since it cleaves the soul from the body, two companion substances which had been together since conception (*An.* 52). Here again Tertullian emphasizes the harmony of body and soul, arguing that death is always an alien expulsion of the soul. Tertullian maintains a positive anthropology of the body, arguing that it is not a prison, as Plato says, but the temple of God, as scripture indicates. Nevertheless, he asserts that the soul is purified by its departure from the flesh (*An.* 53). He implicitly argues against the idea that the soul disintegrates after death.[97] Rather, "in liberty it recovers divinity" ("in divinitatem ipsa libertate resipiscit"; *An.* 53.6; Waszink, 72).

Where does the soul go when it leaves the body at death?[98] Tertullian describes Hades, at the interior of the earth, where all souls await their pun-

---

[95]This passage occurs in the context of an argument against Epicurus, who thought that death was irrelevant: "Is it not absurd that it is said that such a power is irrelevant to a human being, when death is experienced by humans as a dissolution of the body and an annihilation of sense perception?" ("Quodsi hominis est pati mortem dissolutricem corporis et peremptricem sensus, quam ineptum, ut tanta vis ad hominem non pertinere dicatur!" *An.* 42.1; Waszink, 58).

[96]See also *An.* 53. As I mentioned earlier, Tertullian even discusses the fascinating story of a young woman who, after death, moved her hands into a position of prayer during her graveside service and then moved them back afterwards: such activity should be ascribed to God, not to any "remainders of the soul" (*An.* 51.7).

[97]Views held by Epicurus and Lucretius, and found in Plato's *Phaedo*, according to Waszink, 539–40.

[98]Barnes (*Tertullian*, 208) understands this question and its answer to be a peroration that closes the entire work; its subject is the issue of rewards and punishments in the afterlife which closes the entire work.

ishment or their ascension to the kingdom of heaven, except for the souls
of the martyrs, which are already under the altar in Paradise, as John saw
(*An.* 55, referring to Rev 6:9). Refuting the common idea that some souls,
especially those who die young, are detained on earth, Tertullian argues that
demons—the same demons who dwelt in them when they were alive (*An.*
57)—act as if they were these souls and communicate with and mislead the
living. Pythonic spirits which claim to represent the dead or Saul's consulta-
tion of the "soul" of Samuel are not what they seem to be: the soul cannot be
dragged to Hades by evil spirits (*An.* 57). These souls in Hades are passible,
even without the body of flesh: they suffer punishment and joy in Hades as
they await the judgment of God (*An.* 58). Tertullian's one cited source of
authority for this viewpoint is the Paraclete (*An.* 58.8). Tertullian ends his
treatise neatly, having moved from a discussion of the birth and development
of the soul to conclusions regarding its judgment and death.

## Conclusions

Tertullian constructs himself and his theological insights over and against
opponents whom he characterizes as Platonist and philosophers, despite
the fact that he himself uses Plato as much as, if not more than, he abjures
him. Tertullian participates and is deeply invested in the philosophical debates of the time. Tertullian's construction of himself as antiphilosophical
bolsters his authority; he locates himself on the side of true knowledge,
which is characterized by simplicity, straightforward thinking, God's revelation, and truth, and distances himself from any "syncretism" between
Platonizing philosophy and Christianity. Through his championing of
Jerusalem and Judea and his critical words about Athens, he constructs
his own Christian identity over and against the hegemony of Hellenistic
philosophy and culture.
    The modified Stoic epistemology which undergirds Tertullian's thought
allows him the framework for developing a very different anthropology and
epistemology than the thinkers we have previously encountered. Plato and
Philo clearly understood the mind to be the highest portion of the human
soul. Plato describes the highest *mania* as the ascent of the mind toward
the heavens; Philo describes the expulsion of the mind at the highest point
of ecstasy. Like Plato and Philo, Tertullian comfortably employs the term
*amentia* to talk about ecstasy and its epistemic benefits. Yet Tertullian works
with a completely different idea of the human and the human soul, one that

constantly subverts and displaces the primacy of the mind.[99] Tertullian argues for a different anthropology and epistemology, insisting that the human being is constructed in such a way that the soul has no division, and that the mind is merely a faculty of the soul. Tertullian continually relativizes the importance of the mind by insisting that it is not the ruling portion of the soul but is one of many significant faculties. This unity of the bodied soul is the main thesis of Tertullian's *De anima*.

Tertullian insists that sense perception—knowledge collected by means of the body—is as valuable as knowledge collected by means of the intellect alone. While he admits that objects of sense perception, in their material state, inevitably are of lesser quality than objects of intellectual perception, he maintains that the intellectual faculty has no priority over the faculty of sense perception, and that indeed sense perception sometimes provides the mind with materials with which to think and abstract.

Tertullian collapses or hybridizes many of the binaries that we have seen in Middle Platonism. Instead of placing body opposite soul, and arguing for the priority of the soul, Tertullian strenuously insists on the importance of both. He argues that the soul is not unborn: that is, the soul has not transmigrated from one rational being into another. Rather, the soul is created simultaneously with the body, so that there is no priority of one over the other. He also argues that the soul is corporeal. Even if the bodied soul is different from the material body proper, this strange thesis (which, as we recall, Barnes and Waszink thought was the *propositio* of the entire piece) certainly challenges the binaries of Middle Platonism, which most often set body in a different and opposite category to soul.

This chapter detailed Tertullian's theories about the soul in order to provide a context for the next chapter, which discusses Tertullian's ideas about the soul's capacity for prophecy and ecstasy, and why it is that he uses *amentia*, "madness," as an easy synonym for the ecstasy that he approves. In *De anima*, Tertullian sets forth a revolutionary anthropology and epistemology. In the chapter that follows, we shall investigate more fully what this theory of the soul and its epistemic capabilities has to do with Tertullian's ideas about prophecy and ecstasy.

---

[99]See also Jacqueline Amat, *Songes et visions: L'au-delà dans la literature latine tardive* (Paris: Études Augustiniennes, 1985) 94.

# CHAPTER 4

# Ecstasy as Madness: Tertullian and the Competition over Spiritual Gifts

Tertullian challenges Marcion to a fight over Christian identity with the taunt, "Let him produce some psalm, some vision, some speech, insofar as it is spiritual, in ecstasy—that is, in madness (*amentia*)."[1] The weapons of the fight consist of spiritual gifts and, in Tertullian's opinion, Marcion will lose the battle. Concerns over spiritual gifts and the status of being a spiritual person (*pneumatikos* or, in the Latin, *spiritalis*) do not end with 1 Corinthians. They continue into the early third century, when Tertullian presents himself as a champion of authentic spirit and a challenger of Christians who claim—or so he characterizes them—that the spirit is only accessible to a few who are ontologically fixed as "spiritual people."

Because Tertullian's epistemology and his idea of the soul are so complex and distinctive, the previous chapter explored the details of his *De anima* and demonstrated that Tertullian uses Stoic and Platonic concepts when they serve his purposes. He also trumps them, however, by claiming that he is not a philosopher, but a Christian working out ideas based in revelation. At times borrowing from several philosophical traditions, and at times rejecting them entirely, Tertullian authorizes his theories with a wide variety of evidence, including experience, medical texts, women's bodies, and Christian legends. He establishes his identity as a Christian over and against those "philosophers" such as Hermogenes or Valentinus. Tertullian gives authority to his

---

[1] *Marc.* 5.8.12.

arguments in part by claiming that his views are true because they come from God, not philosophy.

Tertullian's anthropological speculations and ideas about prophecy, ecstasy, and dreams are part of the intramural name-calling and construction of identity among early Christian communities. This chapter argues that two foundational aspects of Tertullian's thinking allow us to understand his spirited use of epithets such as *psychici* ("soul-people"; we recall Paul's use of the same term in Greek) and his championing of a term like *amentia* ("madness") in his debates with other Christians. First, Tertullian constructs a broad epistemology, insisting that the mind does not have privileged access to the divine; sense perception too is a significant means for knowledge. The mind and sense perception function together as part of a unified and bodied soul; *amentia*, instead of being an embarrassing aberration or a moment of mental absence in the smooth stream of normal knowledge, is a privileged moment of epistemic access. Second, Tertullian's periodization of history supports his comments about spiritual gifts and prophecy. He understands the present period to be that of the Paraclete or Spirit, a unique time of spiritual activity in history. Just as Paul's rhetoric about spiritual gifts, especially prophecy and glossolalia, was bolstered by a discourse of periodizing history, so also Tertullian's understanding of prophecy and the Paraclete is embedded within his own argument about history and the spirit.

This chapter makes its argument about Tertullian's epistemology and periodization of history in three sections that explore interconnected strands of Tertullian's participation in the early-third-century struggle over prophecy and spirit. The first section investigates Tertullian's theories about dreams and ecstasy in *De anima* and the epistemological implications of these theories. The second section explores texts, similar to the vignette above, that represent Tertullian's battles with other Christian communities over ecstasy, *amentia*, and the identity of true Christians as "spiritual people." The third section makes sense of Tertullian's theories of the soul, his discussion of *amentia*, and his battles with other Christians by exploring his discourse of a periodization of history—his ideas about the place of the spirit and its gifts within history.

## The Soul and the Spirit

The previous chapter's discussion showed that, in Tertullian's anthropology, everything cascades from two main theses: the soul is simple or unified, and the soul is born or created. These two seemingly dry points are in fact controversial conclusions rooted in complex philosophical argumentation and launched against other contemporary theories about the soul. By arguing that the soul is unified and simple, Tertullian resists those who claim that it is made up of multiple parts, and that the mind is the highest segment of the soul. By arguing that the soul is born or created, Tertullian upholds the idea that God's status as eternal and uncreated is unique, and at the same time he resists Plato's idea of the immortal soul that returns again and again. While the human soul shares attributes of divinity (namely, immortality), God is fundamentally other than the human. These two principles undergird *De anima*'s attempts to explain what the human soul is and how it is susceptible to prophecy, *ecstasis*, and *amentia*.

### *"For What Was Spiritual in Adam?"*

Tertullian argues that evil and good spirits can attach themselves to human souls. An evil spirit is usually linked to a child from birth, since the midwife often calls upon Juno, Lucina, Diana, and others in the rites which accompany birth, and then the child is again susceptible to evil spirits in the important (non-Christian) ritual moments which punctuate his or her life. A *daimon* followed Socrates himself from his childhood on (*An.* 39)—one of the Christian apologists' favorite critiques of the poster boy of Greco-Roman philosophy. In an earlier section (*An.* 28) Tertullian has even provided a taxonomy of evil spirits: they can be katabolic (spirits that cause fits), paredral (attendant spirits), or pythonic (spirits of divination). In addition to the evil spirit that falls upon the soul at birth, there is an "antecedent . . . evil" that is "in some way natural," existing at the soul's origins (*An.* 41.1).[2] Baptism is the second birth, on which occasion the Holy Spirit pushes away the evil spirit that might have associated itself with one's soul.[3]

Yet Tertullian wants to distinguish carefully between spirit and soul. He argues that soul is simple and uncompounded, and any contact that it has

---

[2]Tertullian here is careful to avoid the argument that there is something naturally evil within the human: the sin of Adam accrued later. But while Tertullian avoids the idea of original sin, he does insist that Adam's sin befalls all humans.

[3]See also *An.* 35.5–6: "spirit and power" are external gifts of God, while "soul and body" are natural properties. This issue arises as Tertullian addresses the question of whether John the Baptist was a reincarnation of Elijah, since he came in the "spirit and power" of Elijah (Luke 1:17).

with a spirit is accidental to its nature. But Tertullian struggles to clarify semantics: the human soul and the *afflatus* or breath of God are the same, the soul and spirit(s) (either demonic or divine, or even the Holy Spirit) are fundamentally different.[4] When *spiritus* is understood to be the *afflatus* of God, one can say that the soul is *spiritus*. But two different and separable components do not exist within the human (*An.* 10–11): the soul is spirit "because it respires (*spirat*) and not because it is strictly a 'spirit.'"[5] Thus, the soul is also different from the spiritual; it is not naturally spiritual, when "spirit" refers to an external force, something demonic or divine that is not natural to the state of being human. Tertullian argues against the "heretics," who, according to him, "introduce into the soul some spiritual seed" (*An.* 11.3) from Sophia. Similarly, he argues, in terms now familiar to us from discussions in chapters 1 and 3, against those who assert that Adam is naturally a "spiritual" human:[6]

> Certainly, even if Adam immediately prophesied that great mystery with regard to Christ and the church—"Now this is bone of my bones and flesh of my flesh; for this reason a man leaves his father and mother and clings to his wife, and the two become one flesh"—[this is because] he experienced an accident of the spirit, for an ecstasy fell upon him, a power of the holy spirit, effecting prophecy.[7]

[4]Here he stands alongside Irenaeus (*Haer.* 5, especially 5.6) and against some later anthropologies, such as that of Athanasius, which maintain a tripartite natural anthropology: the mind, soul, and flesh are what make up the human. On Athanasius's anthropology, see Khaled Anatolios, *Athanasius: The Coherence of His Thought* (New York: Routledge, 1998) 61–62; but note Anatolios's caveat: Athanasius offers no systematic teaching on anthropology.

[5]"Hoc dum animae vindicamus, quam uniformem et simplicem agnoscimus, spiritum necesse est certa condicione dicamus, non status nomine, sed actus, nec substantiae titulo, sed operae, quia spirat, non quia spiritus proprie est. Nam et flare spirare est. Ita et animam, quam flatum ex proprietate defendimus, spiritum nunc ex necessitate pronuntiamus." *An.* 11.1; Waszink, 14. But see *An.* 11.6: "Therefore, if neither the spirit of God nor of a demon is sown in the soul at birth, it exists by itself before either spirit befalls it. If it is alone, it is simple and uniform in substance, and therefore it breathes (*spirantem*) not from another, but because of the condition of its own substance."

[6]First, he first directs his argument against philosophers/medical theorists who argue from the idea that gnats, ants, and moths have no windpipes (!), thus providing ground for the theory that breath and soul are different things (*An.* 10). (Tertullian argues that the windpipes and other organs are merely too small for us to see or perceive.)

[7]"Nam etsi Adam statim prophetavit magnum illud sacramentum in Christum et ecclesiam: hoc nunc os ex ossibus meis et caro ex carne mea; propter hoc relinquet homo patrem et matrem et agglutinabit se mulieri suae, et erunt duo in unam carnem, accidentiam spiritus passus est: cecidit enim ecstasis super illum, sancti spiritus vis operatrix prophetiae." *An.* 11.4; Waszink, 15.

In this discussion of Adam, Tertullian argues about both epistemology and identity, engaging in a larger discourse that privileges origins as a site for argument and proof. Humans are like the first human, Adam: not naturally spiritual, but naturally having a soul. While others (he says) use the story of Adam to claim that some souls are naturally imbued with spirit, and thus have access to different realms of knowledge, Tertullian instead argues that all humans are equally created as souls (that is, as the breath of God).[8] He levels the playing field, limiting special or unique claims to spiritual knowledge or unique Christian identity. Although the soul is made up of *spiritus*, of the breath of God, it is not spiritual; the spirit and the soul are different things, and the spiritual is subsequent to the natural.

We are familiar with Tertullian's contention that the spiritual is accidental or secondary from the first chapter's analysis of Tertullian's taxonomy of ecstasy. Both Tertullian and the Anti-Phrygian base their arguments upon Adam's ecstasy in Gen 2:21, but Tertullian concludes that although Adam prophesied after this ecstasy, this prophecy is not due to Adam's naturally being a spiritual person, but to an *accidens* of the Holy Spirit.[9] In the passage above, Tertullian makes equivalent the terms *accidens, ecstasis, sancti spiritus vis*, and *operatrix prophetiae*. This ecstasy is accidental, secondary, and at the same time it is a power of the Holy Spirit which effects prophecy. In the phrase *accidentiam spiritus passus est*, Tertullian clearly asserts that the spiritual is secondary to a human's nature.

Tertullian repeats this argument in a slightly different way in *De anima* 21. Here, Tertullian again argues that Adam's soul—a soul paradigmatic for all humans, who are Adam's offspring—was uniform and simple. He directs this argument against those who say the soul is multiform, and against the Valentinians (or rather, against his caricature of them), who declare the soul is tripartite (*An.* 21.1).[10] "For what was spiritual in him?" Tertullian asks (*An.* 21.2), then referring to Adam's prophecy regarding the "great mystery of Christ and the church" in Gen 2:23–24. Tertullian states, in almost the same words that we find in *De anima* 11, that "this came upon him later, when God introduced *amentia* upon him, a spiritual power which is prophecy" ("hoc

---

[8]Paul's dichotomization of the natural (i.e., σῶμα ψυχικόν) and the spiritual in 1 Corinthians 15 is employed as an *exemplum* to support Tertullian's claim (*An.* 11.3) that the spiritual is something over and above what happened to humans at creation.

[9]Émile Bréhier, *The Hellenic Age* (trans. Joseph Thomas; History of Philosophy; Chicago: University of Chicago Press, 1963) 160.

[10]See also pp. 106, 109–10, 119–22, above.

postea obvenit, cum in illum deus amentiam immisit, spiritalem vim, qua constat prophetia"; *An.* 21.2, Waszink, 29-30). Here we find stated even more clearly that prophecy, the power of the spirit, and *amentia*, often translated as "madness" or "rapture," are equivalent.[11]

## Amentia

What is this *amentia*, which is a spiritual power equivalent to prophecy? Some scholars translate the term dramatically as "madness," and thus argue that Tertullian is radical and liminal in his use of the term.[12] Tertullian here casually uses *amentia* as a synonym for prophecy or ecstasy. It is indeed curious, in the face of the Anti-Phrygian's calumny against madness or unsound minds, which we shall see in the next chapter, and in the context of Paul's manipulation of the term "folly" in 1 Corinthians, that Tertullian would employ the term *amentia* without thought for the weight it would carry in the context of the larger discourse on madness and rationality.

Indeed, Tertullian knows that *amentia* can refer to a negative sort of madness. A scan of Tertullian's work[13] reveals several examples of *amentia* as problematic mental disturbance: he uses *amentia* to refer to the madness caused by certain waters[14] or to the folly of an opponent's accusation.[15] Tertullian knows the negative connotations that can adhere to the term *amentia*, yet, in debates over prophecy, he uses the term simply as a Latin equivalent to his frequent transliteration of *ecstasis* from the Greek. It is my contention that he also uses the term *amentia* deliberately and provocatively in order to make a broader point about epistemology, and in order to challenge others' Christian identity.

[11]See also Waszink, 484–85: "In other passages Tert. does not shrink from calling ecstasy an *amentia.*"

[12]"1. The state of being out of one's mind, madness; 2. Violent excitement, frenzy; poetic inspiration; 3. Senselessness, extreme folly, infatuation." Lewis and Short, *Oxford Latin Dictionary*, s.v. *amentia.*

[13]This scan was conducted using the search term "ament-" in Tertullian on the online *Patrologia Latina Database* (4th ed.; Alexandria, Va.: Chadwick-Healey, 1995).

[14]"et lymphatos et hydrophobos vocant, quos aquae necaverunt, aut amentia vel formidine exercuerunt." *Bapt.* 5.4; CCSL I.I.281.

[15]"Quod etsi diceremus, quacunque ratione muniremus sententiam nostrum, dum ne tanta amentia qua putauit, tanquam ipsam carnem Christi opinemur ut peccatricem euacuatam in ipso." *Carn. Chr.* 16.1; CCSL II.II.902.

In *De anima*, Tertullian's use of the term madness, or *amentia*, squares with one of his fundamental propositions regarding the soul: its unity. In *De anima* 18, Tertullian addresses the issue using a form of *demento*, a cognate of *amentia*.[16] In this passage, Tertullian collapses the categories of mind and of body or sense perception: "Isn't it true that to feel is to understand and to understand is to feel? For, what is sensation if not the perception of the thing itself?"[17] "Things which are different should be separate from one another"[18] in their functions, he states. Yet while many philosophers would see the soul and mind as different, Tertullian argues that they cannot be clearly distinguished. The soul senses, perceives, understands; the mind grasps corporeal things in a sensual and intellectual way, feeling, thinking, and perceiving all at once (*An.* 18.8). His point is this: since the functions of the mind and the soul of a human cannot be separated, the mind and soul are not different or separable. "Indeed," Tertullian argues,

> you would have to consider the mind to depart from the soul, if at any time, it were thus accomplished that we should not know that we saw something or heard it, because it—that is, the mind—was elsewhere with its active power. Moreover, I contend by all means that the soul itself would not see or hear, because it—that is, the mind—was elsewhere with its active power. Therefore also when a person is insane (*dementit*), his or her soul is insane (*dementit*). The mind does not wander, but is its co-sufferer; the soul is the one principally overthrown in the first place.[19] How is this proven? Because when the soul departs, the mind is not found in a person; therefore the mind follows the soul wherever [it goes].[20]

[16]Perhaps this is because no verbal form of *amens* exists (my thanks to Ellen Aitken, who pointed this out). In order to argue that the soul is corporeal, he mentions: "Have we not shown in another work (Quain [190 n. 2] conjectures that this is *De censu animae*) that the soul is moved by another when it rages and predicts things, and, therefore, that it is moved from without?" ("Ostendimus autem supra moveri animam et ab alio, cum vaticinatur, cum furit, utique extrinsecus"; *An.* 6.3; Waszink, 7). The raging soul (*cum furit*) is also the predictive soul (*cum vaticinatur*); prophecy and madness are connected as the soul is moved from without.

[17]"Non enim et sentire intelligere est et intelligere sentire est? Aut quid erit sensus, nisi eius rei quae sentitur intellectus?" *An.* 18.7; Waszink, 25.

[18]"Quae enim distant, abesse invicem debent, cum suis muneribus operantur." *An.* 18.8; Waszink, 25.

[19]Waszink's commentary, 264–65, was especially helpful as I prepared this translation.

[20]"Putabis quidem abesse animum ab anima, si quando, nam ita effici ut nesciamus vidisse quid vel audisse, quia alibi fuerit animus. Adeo contendam immo ipsam animam nec vidisse nec audisse, quia alibi fuerit cum sua vi, id est animo. Nam et cum dementit homo, anima

Insanity proves Tertullian's point (or so he claims): the mind doesn't depart, but co-suffers with the soul.

Tertullian proceeds from a general case which is impossible—the soul which sees and hears without *knowing* it—to a more pertinent example—the co-suffering mind and soul of one who is insane. What is at stake here is Tertullian's notion of the unified soul. If the mind and the soul are separable, then the soul is not unitary. Moreover, a mind separable from the soul implies a Platonic framework (in which the highest part of the soul is intellectual, and this part is purest, and most like the divine; the νοῦς /*mens* is the *hegemonikon* of the soul), and thus an enormous shift in epistemology. Platonic and Middle Platonic epistemology generally assumes the capacity of the trained mind to apprehend—or at least to strive to apprehend—metaphysical realities that are not apprehensible by sense perception; in fact, sense perception frequently misleads, or distracts from these abstractions. Tertullian, because of his Stoic influences and because of his commitment to the idea that prophecy is widely available, rather than being accessible only to the few who are noetically trained, works against this anthropology and epistemology.

Tertullian, like Artemidorus and others in antiquity, speculates on the nature and mechanics of sleep and dreams, and in doing so, theorizes more about *amentia*. As we saw in chapter 1, Tertullian asserts that sleep is reasonable, a temporary suspension of the senses' activities. The soul does not rest; immortal, it is always active. And just as in insanity the mind does not shear off from the soul, so also the soul does not separate from the body during sleep, despite the legend of Hermotimus; it cannot be true, Tertullian asserts, that when his body was burned while he slept, his soul returned to find no habitation (*An.* 44).

Although Tertullian argues that sleep and dreams are reasonable, and that the soul does not escape during sleep, at the same time, he talks about *amentia*, or madness, that occurs during dreams, as we recall from chapter 1. He argues in *An.* 45.3 that the natural form of dreaming consists of this: sleep brings rest to the body, but ecstasy or *amentia* upon the soul, which thus does not rest.[21] He also tries to explain how much humans are "in power" in this liminal, if natural, state of sleep. A new word arises in this discus-

---

dementit non peregrinante, sed conpatiente tunc animo—ceterum animae principaliter casus est. Hoc unde firmatur? Quod anima digressa nec animus in homine inveniatur; ita illam ubique sequitur." *An.* 18.9–10; Waszink, 25–26.

[21]See pp. 136–40, below, for a full discussion of *An.* 45.3.

sion of dreams: *compos*, here meaning something like "having the mastery, control or power over a thing."[22] Dreams are "empty fantasies" which stir the passions, says Tertullian; we would realize this "if we were in power as we dream" ("si compotes somniaremus"; *An.* 45.4; Waszink, 62). Again, "And in what way, you ask, is the soul able to remember dreams, when it is clear that it is not able to be in power [of itself]?"[23] Here Tertullian deals with a special objection to his argument: how does memory function in the soul? In chapter 24, arguing against Plato, Tertullian maintained that the soul is born, and thus is only "diluted divinity" (*dilutioris divinitatis*), and susceptible to forgetfulness.[24] But Tertullian still argues that the soul is akin to God—it is born from the breath of God and immortal (22.2)—and so he must find a way of explaining the loss of memory that seems to indicate a weakness in the soul.

This partial forgetfulness of dreams, then, "is a property of its [the soul's] *amentia*, which [property] does not exist by the corruption of good health, but by reason of nature: nor does it expel the mind, but diverts it" ("hoc erit proprietas amentiae huius, quia non fit ex corruptela bonae valetudinis, sed ex ratione naturae; nec enim exterminat, sed avocat mentem"; *An.* 45.5; Waszink, 62). A chiasmus follows: the phenomenon is like shaking, not moving; it is not like a destruction, but like a stirring or agitation.

> Therefore, in that (when) memory is present, the mind is sound; when a sound mind, with memory uninjured, is struck senseless (*stupet*), a kind of *amentia* exists. For that reason, we do not call it "madness" (*furere*) but "dreaming"; therefore we are also intelligent (*prudentes*), as at any other time. For although our faculty of knowledge

[22]Lewis and Short, *Oxford Latin Dictionary*, s.v. *compos*.

[23]"Et quomodo, inquis, memor est somniorum anima, scilicet quam compotem esse non licet?" *An.* 45.5; Waszink, 62.

[24]Plato's unborn soul, in contrast, is divine, and shares in immortality, incorruptibility, incorporeality, and other attributes: Tertullian insists that the soul is then equivalent to God, according to Plato. Tertullian argues instead: "we are not ignorant of the fact that it is born and, through this, it is diluted divinity, and feeble happiness, because it is the breath, not the spirit [of God]. And if it is immortal, since it is from divinity, nevertheless it is passible, since it is born, and therefore from the beginning capable of deviation and then taking part in forgetfulness." ("Nos autem, qui nihil deo adpendimus, hoc ipso animam longe infra deum expendimus, quod natam eam agnoscimus ac per hoc dilutioris divinitatis et exilioris felicitatis, ut flatum, non ut spiritum; et si immortalem, ut hoc sit divinitatis, tamen passibilem, ut hoc sit nativitatis, ideoque et a primordio exorbitationis capacem et inde etiam oblivionis affinem"; *An.* 24.2; Waszink, 32; see also his commentary on 303–7).

is overshadowed, it is nevertheless not extinguished, except insofar
as this very power [of knowing] also seems to be lacking at that
time. For this likewise is ecstasy operating according to its own
characteristic(s), so that it thus brings to us images of wisdom, even
as it brings those of error.[25]

Tertullian is trying to explain how one remembers in ecstasy, and what
one learns from ecstasy. Concern with the overshadowing of the faculty
of knowledge is met with reassurance that what is dimmed is the power,
or active force, and not the entire mind. Reference to "images of wisdom"
as well as images "of error" that are gleaned during ecstasy are part of
Tertullian's insistence that ecstasy is epistemically significant.

Although the range of meaning of many terms here—*furo, stupeo, amentia, prudens*—is not clear, we can clearly see that Tertullian is distinguishing
between dreaming and some sort of state of madness, or of being out of
one's mind (*furo*). His argument seems confusing, because he lines up on
the same side terms which might strike us as contradictory. A sound mind
exists when memory is present, even if the sound mind is struck senseless
(*stupeo*)—this is his main contention. He then confirms that dreams and the
knowledge gleaned during *amentia* can indeed be remembered, an important argument since remembering these lessons is necessary to their being
epistemically valuable. Tertullian's description of this *amentia* naturalizes
it, makes it part of our normal dreaming process (which he already argued
is not an accident of sleep, but natural to the always active soul). Just as
earlier, Tertullian had retained the importance of sense perception, so here
the presence of the mental faculties during ecstasy is also emphasized. Ecstasy constitutes neither the full expulsion nor the full presence of the mind,
but some middle state which is epistemically valuable. Tertullian provides
a philosophical and anthropological theory to argue for the usefulness of
what is learned in ecstasy or *amentia*. His argument is complicated. He is
trying to hold onto his idea of the soul's unity, to explain that ecstasy and
dreaming are natural, and at the same time to argue that memory continues
to operate in these moments of *amentia*, and that the mind is present and,

---

[25]"Igitur quod memoria suppetit, sanitas mentis est; quod sanitas mentis salva memoria
stupet, amentiae genus est. Ideoque non dicimur furere, sed somniare; ideo et prudentes, si
quando, sumus. Sapere enim nostrum licet obumbretur, non tamen extinguitur, nisi quod et
ipsum potest videri vacare tunc, ecstasin autem hoc quoque operari de suo proprio, ut sic nobis
sapientiae imagines inferat, quemadmodum et erroris." *An.* 45.6; Waszink, 62.

to some extent, in control. He implicitly argues against a long tradition of ancient scholarship which assumes that dreaming represents the absence and wandering of the mind or the dim images arising from indigestion and the troubles of the day.[26]

In *De anima*, and, as we shall see, in other works, Tertullian makes equivalent the terms ecstasy and *amentia*, grouping prophetic and spiritual powers under the controversial term often translated "madness." How can Tertullian set forth these terms as equivalent? How does *amentia* befall the soul at any point, when we know that Tertullian holds to a Stoic understanding of the soul as rational and unitary (thus excluding the possibility that he thinks the mind is ejected and the soul remains)? In some ways, this very question provides an answer. Tertullian's construction of the soul is so steeped in Stoic ideas of the soul's unity and rationality that, for him, *amentia* does not compromise the essential rationality of the soul. Some philosophers, especially Middle Platonists, put so much emphasis on the mind, or the rational portion of the soul, that the withdrawal of the mind constitutes a true distancing from reason, an instance of the irrational or the mad, the uncontrolled.[27] If the rational portion of the soul leaves, then all one is left with are the passionate and the appetitive aspects of the soul. Tertullian, by contrast, following Stoic insistence on the unity of the soul, can posit the dimming or withdrawal of the mind—which he has demoted to a mere *instrumentum* of the soul, not even its *hegemonikon*—without endangering the soul's fundamental rationality and wholeness.

---

[26]See, e.g., Cicero, *Div.* 2.67; Artemidorus, *Oneir.* 1.1. Tertullian tries to explain further in *An.* 46: using the famous Homeric image of dreams proceeding through gates of horn or of ivory, he explains that some dreams are true, and some are false. Again, he claims to assert the Christian view of all this: while some dreams are true, and prophesy future catastrophe or honor, oracles are generally false, involving spirits that wander freely, even invading our bedrooms. (These "other oracles" wander the tombs of the dead, counterfeit divine power, and grant cures, favors, and even prophecies; see *An.* 46.12.) This stands in contrast to someone like Artemidorus, who admits that some dreams, which he labels *oneiroi*, are true, and others, which he labels *enhypnia*, are merely remaining images and thoughts of the day's events (*Oneir.* 1.1–2). As we saw in ch. 1, above, Tertullian further refines his argument with a taxonomy of dreams (*An.* 47). This taxonomy is Tertullian's way of working out criteria for evaluating the value of the knowledge gained from ecstasy or *amentia*, and for guarding against false knowledge. Dreams can be sent by demons or by God, or they can arise as an ecstasy from the soul itself.

[27]In Philo we saw a variation on this theme: behaviors that appear to be irrational, mad, and uncontrolled are part of the expulsion of the mind, but what is actually going on is a kind of hyperrationality, rather than a distancing from reason.

Leaving aside the question of the philosophical coherence of Tertullian's argument, we can trace the anthropology that undergirds his casual connection of *amentia* and prophecy, and his lack of concern regarding *amentia* and rationality. Tertullian's view is unlike that of some involved in the discussion—for example, Epiphanius's source, who argues that some define ecstasy and prophecy as a horrifying absence of the mind, a step into true madness. Tertullian's view is even unlike that of Philo, for whom ecstasy is a positive absence of the human mind, which sets as the divine mind rises. For Tertullian, *amentia* and ecstasy are generally not "madness" at all, as we might define it. *Amentia* shakes you up, but doesn't destroy you; it provides a glimpse of what is to come, or it is the steady dreaming activity of the ethereal, perpetually working soul. Tertullian expands the sources of knowledge for himself and his community, and at the same time justifies this broadened epistemology. The mind is dethroned in the soul, sense perception and the body offer significant and epistemically useful data, and, most important for this study, the dimming of the mind in *amentia* and ecstasy can be a significant source for knowledge. Indeed, Tertullian argues that ecstasy, or *amentia*, is a charism from God, a charism which signals true Christian identity and the true "spiritual person."

## Tertullian's Debate with the *Psychici*

Tertullian's discussion of the soul and ecstasy is not limited to *De anima*. His ideas about prophecy and *amentia* are rhetorically constructed in different ways in his different writings, as he shifts from issue to issue within intramural Christian struggles over prophecy—struggles which serve to construct Christian identity and claims to true knowledge. Tertullian's interlocutors in *De anima*, as we recall from chapter 3, are difficult to pinpoint, but in some of Tertullian's other writings, his partners in debate are clearer, and the struggle is sharper. *De anima* reveals what is at stake for Tertullian in terms of epistemology: the soul is unified, the mind is not privileged, and thus knowledge gleaned through sense perception or through *amentia* is valuable — as valuable as that gleaned through the mind. Elsewhere in Tertullian's writings, it becomes clear that what is at stake in the debate over prophecy, ecstasy, and *amentia* is not only epistemology, but epistemology as it relates to Christian identity. Tertullian's name-calling and his debate with the so-called *psychici* demonstrate how he attempts to construct and establish his community's identity and his own authority in these struggles over prophecy and the knowledge it brings.

In *Against Marcion* (*Adversus Marcionem*), with which I began this chapter, it is *amentia* that marks Tertullian's Christian identity and that of his community over and against Marcion and his; ecstasy and *amentia* serve to distinguish between Tertullian's view (and that of the New Prophecy, as he says) and Marcion's. Here the term sheds any lingering negative connotations of mental disturbance. In *Marc.* 5.8, charismata, ecstasy, and *amentia* ("in ecstasi, id est in amentia"!) become a litmus test by which the legitimacy of Christian leadership and community is determined:

> Therefore let Marcion exhibit gifts of his god: some prophets, who have spoken yet not from human sense, but from the spirit of God, who have both predicted future events and conveyed hidden things of the heart; let him produce some psalm, some vision, some speech, insofar as it is spiritual, in ecstasy—that is, in *amentia*—if, perhaps, he undertakes an interpretation of tongues. Let him show to me as well a woman who prophesies among them, from these his great holy women, I say. If I can proffer all these things easily, and assuredly these are in agreement with the rules and directions and instructions of the Creator, without doubt Christ and the spirit and the apostle belong to my God.[28]

*Amentia* is used in this passage as a helpful gloss, explaining the word *ecstasis*. There is no whiff of the illicit about it; in fact, it is part of Tertullian's boast about his community's spiritual gifts; spiritual gifts are the weapons with which one may win the fight over true Christian identity. *Spiritalem, in ecstasi*, and *amentia* are used in apposition, as equivalent terms; moreover, they guarantee the truth of the prophecy or charism. Tertullian insists that Marcion should demonstrate that the charismata in his community aren't merely appearances, but are truly propelled by the Spirit, who brings *amentia* and ecstasy. *Amentia* (and ecstasy) has become a sign or marker of true prophecy.

[28]"Exhibeat itaque Marcion dei sui dona, aliquos prophetas, qui tamen non de humano sensu, sed de dei spiritu sint locuti, qui et futura praenuntiarint et cordis occulta traduxerint; edat aliquem psalmum, aliquam uisionem, aliquam orationem, dumtaxat spiritalem, in ecstasi, id est in amentia, si qua linguae interpretatio accessit; probet mihi etiam mulierem apud se prophetasse ex illis suis sanctioribus feminis magnis, dicam: si haec omnia facilius a me proferuntur et utique conspirantia regulis et dispositionibus et disciplinis creatoris, sine dubio dei mei erit et Christus et spiritus et apostolus." *Marc.* 5.8.12; CSSL I.I.688.

Earlier in *Adversus Marcionem*, Tertullian uses the term *amentia* in a similarly positive way in his interpretation of the transfiguration. Reading through Marcion's expurgated Luke in order to discover the weaknesses of Marcion's argument, Tertullian suggests that Marcion, who rejected the "Old Testament" and its God, should have expurgated from his new canon Luke's story of the transfiguration. Its depiction of a friendly encounter between Jesus and those bulwarks of the "Old Testament," Moses and Elijah, hardly fits Marcion's anti-Judaism. Tertullian challenges Marcion:

> Then why does Peter, too, discerning that sharing a tent was worthy for Christ himself, suggest the plan: "It is good that we are here"—good, clearly and obviously, to be where Moses and Elijah were—"and let us make here three tabernacles, one for you, and one for Moses, and one for Elijah"? "But he did not know what he said." How did he not know? Was it by a simple error [that he said this], or was it by a judgment that ecstasy—that is, *amentia*—came together with grace, which we defend in the cause of the New Prophecy. For when a person is in the spirit, especially when he beholds the glory of God, or when God speaks through him, he necessarily is deprived of sense perception, because he is overshadowed by the power of God. Concerning this there is a question between us and the *psychici*; however, it is easy to demonstrate the *amentia* of Peter. For how could he have known Moses and Elijah. . . except in the spirit?[29]

[29]"Igitur et Petrus, meritum contubernium Christi sui agnoscens, <in> indiuiduitatem eius suggerit consilium: bonum est hic nos esse,—bonum plane, ubi Moyses scilicet et Helias—et faciamus hic tria tabernacula, unum tibi et Moysi unum et Heliae unum. 'Sed nesciens, quid diceret.' Quomodo nesciens? Vtrumne simplici errore an ratione, qua defendimus in causa nouae prophetiae gratiae exstasin, id est am<e>ntiam, conuenire? 5. In spiritu enim homo constitutus, praesertim cum gloriam dei conspicit uel cum per ipsum deus loquitur, necesse est excidat sensu, obumbratus scilicet uirtute diuina. De quo cum inter nos et psychicos quaestio est, interim facile est amentiam Petri probare. Quomodo enim Moysen en Heliam cognouisset . . . nisi quia in spiritu uiderat?" *Marc.* 4.22.4–5; CCSL I.I.601–2. *Amentiam* is my emendation; the CCSL text reads *amantiam*. The apparatus indicates no manuscript debate, but *amentiam* is the obvious reading for two reasons: first, *amantiam* does not make much sense, and, second, and more convincing, *Marc.* 5.22 contains almost the same gloss, "dumtaxat spiritalem, in ecstasi, id est in amentia," and our discussion of similar passages in *De anima* demonstrates that Tertullian understands *amentia* and *ecstasis* to be equivalent. Note that *ratione* may be a synonym for δόξα. *Ratio* is defined as the faculty of computing, judgment, understanding, reason, reasoning, reflection. *Doxa*, as we recall from the last chapter, is an important term in some Stoic philosophical speculation on epistemology; if indeed *ratio* is being used in this way, it is a significant piece of evidence that Tertullian considers ecstasy to be the object of a reasoned judgment.

Tertullian goes on to explain that, because of the Jewish prohibition of images, there were no images or statues of Elijah and Moses, thus clinching his argument that Peter saw while in the Spirit: "How, if it were not because he saw in the spirit? And therefore it is clear that he spoke in the spirit, not in his established sense perception: he could not know [what he said]."[30]

From these two passages in *Adversus Marcionem*, we see that when *amentia* refers to prophecy or ecstasy, it carries a positive valuation. The term stands in apposition to *ecstasis* in both cases, and the phrase "id est amentia" may indicate that Tertullian is offering a Latin gloss of the Greek *ekstasis*. But elsewhere in Tertullian's corpus, as we have seen, and certainly more broadly in Latin usage, *amentia* and similar terms refer to madness and folly. Despite the dangers of the term *amentia*, Tertullian uses it to mark his community's spiritual status and to define true Christian identity over and against other Christian communities at the time.

In the passage above, Tertullian distinguishes his community's true spiritual identity not only with the term *amentia*, but also by applying the slur *psychici* or *animales* to another Christian community. Given Tertullian's insistence that no one is naturally spiritual and that all are equal, it is on first glance surprising to see him calling his opponents *animales* or *psychici*—after all, to Tertullian all humans are merely soul-creatures, since the association of divine or demonic spirits with humans is accidental and not natural. But this name-calling is part of early Christian intramural construction of identity and boundaries. To be a "spiritual" person, whether this status was given ontologically or earned by baptism, was the highest state. We have already seen in 1 Corinthians that the status of "spiritual people" is something to be attained, and that this identity is contested in a situation of struggle over spiritual gifts, especially prophecy and glossolalia. Not only *Adversus Marcionem*, but also other of Tertullian's works pick up this terminology of *psychici* and *spiritales*, especially those works explicitly directed against opponents, such as *De resurrectione mortuorum* and *De pudicitia*.[31]

Tertullian's *De resurrectione mortuorum* (*On the Resurrection of the Dead*) is not a neutral treatise on the topic. When he argues for the importance of the

---

[30]"Et ita quod dixit, scilicet in spiritu non in sensu constitutus, scire non poterat." *Marc.* 4.22.5; CCSL I.I.602.

[31]For another struggle with opponents, see *An.* 11, 24–25 and *Val.* 26, regarding Tertullian's view of Valentinus and his followers, and their thoughts about spiritual seed.

flesh, its preciousness and the necessity of its rising again, he argues against
"these *animales*—I will not call them *spiritales*,"[32] implying that he rejects
their self-identification as *spiritales* and uses their own taxonomy against
them, reducing them to merely "living beings," like animals. Tertullian explains that humans will have the *pneuma* or *spiritus* in substance when they
are raised again in the flesh (*Res.* 53); one's anthropology is transformed after
one's resurrection, and the spirit which is now accidental (using the language
of Paul, only a "pledge") will be natural as humans are raised as "spiritual
bodies." Indeed, quoting Joel 2/Acts 2, Tertullian concludes that the Holy
Spirit, poured out in the last days, helps to stop this unbelief regarding the
resurrection of the body (*Res.* 63). Moreover, Tertullian uses christology to
argue about anthropology. Christ is the "last Adam, yet the primary Word,
flesh and blood" who "preserves in himself a deposit of the flesh, a pledge (*ar-
rabonem*) of the entirety" (*Res.* 61). At the same time, humans have received
the pledge of the Spirit (*Res.* 51, 53). But what truly concerns Tertullian is,
first of all, that flesh is real and good, whether Christ's or that of any person,
and, second, that no "diversity" exists among humans: there is no essential
difference or distinction between persons; humans all by nature fall into the
same category (*Res.* 53).[33] Everyone is an *animalis*; it takes something more
to be a *spiritalis*. Tertullian articulates this idea of the human over and against
his rhetorical construction of his opponents' anthropology.

Tertullian criticizes those whom he calls the *psychici* because they
have not received the fullness of the Spirit. In *De monogomia* (*On Monogamy*), he criticizes their ethical lassitude: "The heretics snatch away
marriages; the *psychici* pour them on. The former don't marry even once;

---

[32]"secundum animales istos, ne dixerim spiritales." *Res.* 22.1; CCSL II.II.947.

[33]In *Adversus Marcionem*, *Adversus Valentinianos*, and *De anima*, Tertullian uses Irenaeus's
work (Waszink, "Introduction," 45); it is thus interesting to see Irenaeus's stance in *Haer.* 5.6.1.
Against those who say that when the flesh is removed, the "spiritual man" remains, Irenaeus
redefines the wholeness of the spiritual person, which, he believes, consists of flesh, soul,
and the spirit of God. He argues from Paul, who declares "perfect" those who "have taken
possession of the spirit of God and who speak in all languages, through the Spirit, in such a way
as he himself also spoke, and in the way in which many brethren in the Church have prophetic
gifts, and through the Spirit they speak in all languages, and bring into the open human secrets
for the general benefit, and tell the mysteries of God, who the apostle terms 'spiritual people.'
They are spiritual because they participate in the Spirit, not because of the denial and taking
away of the flesh" (*Haer.* 5.6.1; my translation, from the Greek edition in *Contre les heresies
livre 5* [trans. Adelin Rousseau; SC 153; Paris: Editions du Cerf, 1969] 74).

the latter do not only marry once."[34] We can see that here, far from being strangely rigorist in his ethics, as many modern scholars characterize him,[35] Tertullian presents himself and his community as steering between those whom he characterizes as having no ethics at all—those who marry again and again—and Platonizing Christians—in Tertullian's jargon, heretics—who have twisted ethics and anthropology so that they cannot see the goodness of the body, and thus deny all marriages. Tertullian points to excessive marriage among the *psychici*, those who have not yet truly received the spirit, and the moderation of those who have become spiritual.

In *De pudicitia* (*On Modesty*), Tertullian challenges his "opponents" to demonstrate that they are indeed spiritual; this debate is connected to the question of what demonstrations of the Spirit's power are appropriate to the present time, and who claims and truly has authority. The treatise begins with a criticism of the "pontifex maximus" Victor (and Tertullian uses the title with biting irony), who has issued an edict that Tertullian transcribes: "I dismiss the transgressions of both adultery and fornication to those who have performed (the acts of) repentance." Tertullian follows with his acid wit: "O edict, on which one cannot inscribe 'good deed!' And where should this liberality be displayed? On the very doors of lust, I think!"[36]

Later in *De pudicitia*, Tertullian again raises the question about authority, and about the location of Christian identity. In tones which remind us of his challenge to Marcion, Tertullian demands prophetic evidence so that he might believe that his opponents' Christian identity is real. Prophecy is the guarantor of truth: "Exhibit to me now, apostolic one, proofs of prophecy, that I might perceive your divine nature, and so lay claim for yourself the power

---

[34]"Haeretici nuptias auferunt, psychici ingerunt. Illi nec semel, isti non semel nubunt." *Mon.* 1.1; CCSL II.II. 1229. For interesting epigraphic evidence of some Christians who called themselves πνευματικός/ή, see Tabbernee, *Montanist Inscriptions*, inscription 63 (pp. 401–7), inscription 72 (pp. 452–57), and inscription 93 (pp. 544–47). The provenance and dates of these inscriptions vary, however, so there is no easy way to hypothesize from this epigraphic evidence about a community's self-construction as *pneumatikoi*.

[35]See, e.g., Rankin's discussion ("Was Tertullian a Jurist?," 338), where he mentions Hallonsten's characterization of Tertullian as "severely judicial," and Hanson, who "sees evidence in Tertullian's thought of an Old Testament legalism."

[36]"Pontifex scilicet maximus, quod <est> episcopus episcoporum, edicit: <<Ego et moechiae et fornicationis delicta paenitentia functis dimitto.>> O edictum cui adscribi non poterit: BONVM FACTVM! Et ubi proponetur liberalitas ista? Ibidem, opinor, in ipsis libidinum ianius." *Pud.* 1.6–7; CCSL II.II.1281–82.

of remitting transgressions!"[37] He provides a glimpse of an oracle (which Heine and other scholars declare is one of the few "Montanist" oracles we have)[38] and elaborates a stylized argument about the oracle between himself and an opponent:

> [Opponent:] "But," you say, "the church has the power to forgive sins."
>
> [Tertullian:] This I too acknowledge and dispose of [it] even more [than you], which I have in the Paraclete itself in the new prophets. The Paraclete says, "The church has power to forgive transgression, but I will not do it, lest they should transgress in other things."
>
> [Opponent:] What if a pseudoprophetic spirit said this?[39]

Tertullian in reply emphasizes that a pseudoprophetic spirit is more likely to have been lenient than to have been strict, as this oracle is—no one fakes a prophecy which calls a community to a harder path. Issues of prophetic authority and Christian identity combine as Tertullian moves from this oracle to challenge his opponents in what is clearly a struggle over the identity of the "church": "Now I ask you: whence have you usurped this right of the church?"[40]

Tertullian argues the question further, from Matthew 16, where Jesus declares that the keys and the power to loose and bind are given to Peter. It seems that this text was a point of exegetical debate, and that Tertullian argued that the church was established through Peter, and so those who are spiritual, as Peter was, now possess the power to loose and bind, whereas others asserted that this power is limited to the current representative of Peter in the church. The argument continues:

> What now does this have to do with the church and what indeed with you, *psychice*? For with regard to the person of Peter, this power is conjoined to those who are spiritual (*spiritalibus*), either

---

[37]"Exhibe igitur et nunc mihi, apostolice, prophetica exempla, ut agnoscam diuinitatem, et uindica tibi delictorum eiusmodi remittendorum potestatem." *Pud.* 21.5; CCSL II.II.1326.

[38]Heine, *Montanist Oracles and Testimonia*, 6–7.

[39]"<<Sed habet, inquis, potestatem ecclesia delicta donandi.>> Hoc ego magis et agnosco et dispono, qui ipsum Paracletum in prophetis nouis habeo dicentem: <<Potest ecclesia donare delictum, sed non faciam, ne et alia delinquant.>> Quid, si pseudopropheticus spiritus pronuntiauit?" *Pud.* 21.7–8; CCSL II.II.1326.

[40]"De tua nunc sententia quaero, unde hoc ius ecclesiae usurpes." *Pud.* 21.9; CCSL II.II.1327.

to an apostle or a prophet. Therefore also this very church properly and principally is spirit itself, in which is the trinity of one divinity, Father and Son and Holy Spirit. . . . And, see, indeed, the church will forgive sins, but the church which is spirit, through a spiritual person, not a church which consists of a number of bishops.[41]

In *De pudicitia*'s arguments about oracles and the spirit, at stake are identity, authority, and even epistemology. Tertullian acknowledges the significance of the Paraclete who is in the new prophets, providing access to new knowledge; he attempts to use prophecy and spirit to shore up argumentation, defending and using the oracle; and he seeks to define who and what the church is by means of an appeal to the oracle and by means of an idea of spirit, and of what it means to be a spiritual person. The rhetoric of the "spiritual person" and the "psychic" has the effect of constructing and legitimizing the Christian identity of one group (*spiritales*) over and against others (*psychici*).[42]

In *De anima* itself, Tertullian provides an account of an ecstasy—more specifically, of something that happened *in spiritu*, in the spirit. But here his struggle with other Christian communities over the legitimacy of ecstasy is suppressed. From this passage, we see both that Tertullian values the knowledge gained in ecstasy, and that he understands ecstasy to be a contentious issue. Tertullian knows about the corporeality of the soul not only through reasoning and philosophical argument, but also from evidence gleaned through continued charismata in his congregation.

> Currently, a sister among us receives gifts of revelation, which she experiences (*patitur*) during the rites on the Lord's day. . . . Indeed, truly, the materials for her visions are supplied according to the scripture which is read, or the psalms which are sung, or addresses which are offered, or the petitions which are made. It happened that we were discussing something about the soul—I don't know what[43]—when this sister came to be in the spirit. After the rites, when

[41]"Quid nunc et ad ecclesiam et quidem tuam, psychice? Secundum enim Petri personam spiritalibus potestas ista conueniet, aut apostolo aut prophetae. Nam et ipsa ecclesia proprie et principaliter ipse est spiritus, in quo est trinitas unius diuinitatis, Pater et Filius et Spiritus sanctus. . . . Et ideo ecclesia quidem delicta donabit, sed ecclesia spiritus per spiritalem hominem, non ecclesia numerus episcoporum." *Pud.* 21.16–17; CCSL II.II. 1328.

[42]Of course, this passage is also often cited as an example of Tertullian's antiecclesiastical leanings.

[43]That is, Tertullian was possibly reading from his writing or presenting a talk. See Waszink, 171.

the people have left, we are accustomed to asking her what she saw
(for we diligently set them in order,[44] and examine them).[45]

This is precisely the continuing evidence of true ecstasy and charismata
that Tertullian had accused Marcion's people of not having, precisely the
prophetic evidence that the "psychic" lacks in De pudicitia. Yet Tertullian
must justify and demonstrate the validity of this ecstasy not only for his
argument regarding the soul, but perhaps also against claims that such a
vision might be demonic, or that visions and dreams are not valuable sources
of knowledge, issues he discusses elsewhere in De anima, as we know.
He frames the woman's ecstasy both with an assurance of the frequency
and regularity of her visions, and with a guarantee that her ecstasies have
been tested. He uses the phrase in spiritu and avoids talking about this
moment as an ecstasy or a moment of amentia. In his rhetoric against
Marcion or other "psychics," Tertullian is happy to launch terminology of
ecstasy and amentia multiple times, but in De anima his language is more
circumspect. This vision supports his idea of a corporeal soul: thus he is
careful to acknowledge the importance of the knowledge made available
through the vision, but also to authorize that vision by describing it carefully, and by "guaranteeing" it in various ways.

Tertullian challenges others to prove their Christian identity through
prophecy, ecstasies, and amentia. He too counts visions and dreams as epistemically valuable, but in De anima he is more circumspect than we might
expect. Nonetheless, Tertullian's rhetoric constructs spiritual gifts and a true
and authentic role as spiritual people as necessary elements for powerful,
authoritative, and genuine Christian identity.

## Spiritual Gifts and the Periodization of History

These accusations and self-definitions regarding "spiritual" people cannot be clearly understood without an awareness of the way in which

[44]Quain's translation reads, "all her visions are carefully written down," and is perhaps based
in part on Waszink, 172. But this translation of digeruntur would then assume the correctness
of mainly heresiological accounts of Montanists making collections of their prophecies. See the
discussion on pp. 160–61, below.

[45]"Est hodie soror apud nos revelationum charismata sortita, quas in ecclesia inter dominica
sollemnia per ecstasin in spiritu patitur. . . . Iamvero prout scripturae leguntur aut psalmi
canuntur aut allocutiones proferuntur aut petitiones delegantur, ita inde materiae visionibus

a community's ideas about prophecy, ecstasy, and the status of being "spiritual" are intimately linked to its understanding of time and history. Tertullian and his intended interlocutors employed complex and implicit historiographies: where they stood within history was not agreed upon or given, but a matter of debate. We have already seen that Paul relied upon a periodization of history to challenge the Corinthians' understanding of themselves as knowledgeable and as spiritual people. We shall again see threads of this discourse in Epiphanius's source, where Maximilla's oracle about the end of prophecy and the "consummation" raises questions about whether there is a "limit" or "boundary" to prophetic gifts.

Tertullian has a very precise understanding of the place of spiritual gifts in history. Elucidating his historiography of God's purpose and activity in the world from creation to the end of time helps to make sense of the accusations regarding the *psychici* and their understanding of prophecy and spiritual gifts. Tertullian believes that the spirit is particularly active in the present, since the current period of history is that of the Paraclete or spirit, while his opponents believe that the peak of the spirit's action in history has passed. In *De Virginibus Velandis* (*On the Veiling of Virgins*), Tertullian asserts that the law of faith is permanent, but that "new amendments" are possible because "it is evident that the grace of God operates and advances until the end."[46] Tertullian argues that the devil clearly continues to operate in the earthly sphere; so then does God. Alluding to John 14, he states that "the Lord sent the Paraclete . . . since human mediocrity was not able to grasp all things at once." Through the Paraclete, discipline is regulated and "brought to perfection."[47]

After citing John 16:12–13,[48] Tertullian explains the role of the Spirit: "to direct discipline, to reveal scriptures, to reform the understanding, to make progress toward better things" (*Virg.* 1.5). And then he sets forth the most

---

subministrantur. Forte nescio quid de anima disserueramus, cum ea soror in spiritu esset. Post transacta sollemnia dimissa plebe, quo usu solet nobis renuntiare quae viderit (nam et diligentissime digeruntur, ut etiam proventur)." *An.* 9.4; Waszink, 11.

[46] "operante scilicet et proficiente usque in finem gratia dei." *Virg.* 1.4; CCSL II.II.1209. For easier access to some of the texts discussed in this section, see Heine, *The Montanist Oracles and Testimonia*.

[47] "ad perfectum perduceretur disciplina." *Virg.* 1.4; CCSL II.II.1209.

[48] "I still have many things to say to you, but you cannot bear them now. When the Spirit of truth comes, he will guide you into all the truth; for he will not speak on his own, but will speak whatever he hears, and he will declare to you the things that are to come."

interesting part of his argument, weaving Eccl 3:1—"There is a time for everything"—with an appeal to all of creation, which "is advanced to fruit gradually." The created world progresses through many stages to become the ripe fruit; "so also righteousness . . . was at first in an originary state, when it revered God by nature; then it progressed in its infancy through the law and prophets, then it advanced in its youth by the gospel. Now through the Paraclete it is brought to maturity."[49] Tertullian's description conforms roughly to the historiographical paradigm, well established in antiquity, of the world passing through ages of life just as a human does.[50] In the present, the spirit's role in history and God's activity in the world are fully mature.

Elsewhere, Tertullian's discourse of the periodization of history intertwines with issues of canon and revelation. In *On the Resurrection of the Dead* (*De resurrectione mortuorum*), Tertullian states that God "has purged the pristine instruments from the obscurity of all ambiguity, by making clear their words and illuminating their sense."[51] The "heresies" resorted to the scriptures (*scripturarum*), and while these "pristine instruments" (*pristina instrumenta*) may have seemed to support heretical arguments, Tertullian can refute heresy by means of the very same instruments, reading them through the interpretive lens of the spirit and the New Prophecy: ". . . now [the Holy Spirit] has dispersed all former ambiguities by the open and clear foretelling of the entire mystery [of the resurrection of the flesh] through the new prophecy which is overflowing from the Paraclete."[52]

*On Monogamy* (*De monogamia*) offers a similar argument: the Paraclete does not introduce novel practices, but defines more clearly what has already been set forth (*Mon.* 3.10–12). It is clear that some claim that Tertullian and others ascribe "whatever is new and burdensome" to the Paraclete; the

[49]"Sic et iustitia . . . primo fuit in rudimentis, natura Deum metuens; dehinc per legem et prophetas promouit in infantiam, dehinc per euangelium efferbuit in iuuentutem, nunc per Paracletum componitur in maturitatem." *Virg.* 1.7; CCSL II.II.1210.

[50]Arnoldo Momigliano, "The Origins of Universal History," in *On Pagans, Jews, and Christians* (Middletown, Conn.: Wesleyan University Press; Scranton, Pa.: Harper & Row, 1987) 35–36.

[51]"et pristina instrumenta manifestis uerborum et sensuum luminibus ab omni ambiguitatis obscuritate purgauit." *Res.* 63.7; CCSL II.II.1012. See also the preface to the *Martyrdom of Perpetua and Felicitas*.

[52]"idcirco iam omnes retro ambiguitates et quantas uolunt parabolas aperta atque perspicua totius sacramenti praedicatione discussit per nouam prophetiam de paraclito inundantem." *Res.* 63.9; CSSL II.II.1012.

*psychici* even hint that such insights may come from a "rival spirit" (*Mon.* 2.1–4).[53] Moving focus off the hot topic of the Paraclete, Tertullian appeals to what they have in common: "Let us withdraw from mention of the Paraclete as having some authority for us. Let us unroll the common instruments of the original scriptures."[54] Then, he says, all will see that the Paraclete is not an innovator but a restorer: monogamy (that is, Tertullian argues against second marriages) is represented by figures from Noah to Peter (*Mon.* 4–9).

In this work on monogamy, Tertullian again sets history into periods, as he did in *On the Veiling of Virgins*. He states that "hardness of heart reigned up until Christ, and weakness of the flesh had reigned up to the Paraclete. The new law removed divorce . . . ; the new prophecy removed second marriage."[55] History is divided into increasingly ethically developed periods which match the increase of spirit over time. In *De jejunio* (*On Fasting*), which is explicitly addressed to so-called *psychici*, Tertullian exposes more of the problem. From Phil 3:15 (" 'And if you are ignorant of anything,' he says, 'the Lord will reveal it to you' "), Tertullian supports the idea of the ongoing revelation through the "Paraclete, the leader of all truth" (compare John 16:13). He explains that the *psychici* are in cahoots with heresy and pseudoprophecy; they accuse the Paraclete of being Satan by stating that the Paraclete's prophets offer messages from the devil (*Jejun.* 11).[56] In the midst of this debate, the fixing of boundaries, temporal and otherwise, is disputed:

> But again you set boundaries for God, as concerning grace, so concerning discipline, as concerning charismata, so concerning rites, so that just as official observances have ceased, in the same way also God's benefits have ceased. And so you deny that duties are still imposed by God, because of this: "the law and the prophets were until John" (Luke 16:16).[57]

[53]"ab aduersario spiritu." *Mon.* 2.3; CCSL II.II.1230.

[54]"Secedat nunc mentio Paracleti, ut nostri alicuius auctoris. Euoluamus communia instrumenta scripturarum pristinarum." *Mon.* 4.1; CCSL II.II.1233.

[55]"Regnauit duritia cordis usque ad Christum, regnauerit et infirmitas carnis usque ad Paracletum. Noua lex abstulit repudium . . . , noua prophetia secundum matrimonium." *Mon.* 14.4; CCSL II.II.1249.

[56]In *Jejun.* 12, Tertullian complains that his interlocutors will not accept the Paraclete in Montanus.

[57]"Sed rursus palos terminales figitis deo, sicut de gratia, ita de discipline, sicut de charismatibus, ita et de sollemnibus, ut perinde officia cessauerint, quemadmodum et beneficia eius, atque ita negetis usque adhuc eum munia imponere, quia et hic lex et prophetae usque ad Iohannem." *Jejun.* 11.6; CCSL II.II.1270. I found Heine (*Montanist Oracles and Testimonia*, 85) helpful in translating this passage.

Those whom Tertullian calls *psychici* must have used Luke 16:16 as an argument that prophecy and "gifts" had ceased, as well as certain "duties."[58] Tertullian instead holds to a different tripartite division of history, which corresponds to infancy (the time of the law and the prophets), adolescence (the time of Christ), and maturity (the present period of the Paraclete).

It is difficult to know exactly what spiritual manifestations and practices were appropriate to this new age, in Tertullian's view, especially given that discussions of spiritual people and spiritual gifts are always already embedded in a rhetorical context of polemic or persuasion. We have seen hints of what Tertullian might want in his *Against Marcion* (5.8), where he demands true ecstasy and prophecy "in the spirit." I would argue that the imprecision and the lack of description regarding what constitutes a community or person who is spiritual is deliberate. How can one define the actions of a spirit that is accidental to one's essence? Even dreams, which are natural occurrences, cannot be controlled by the dreamer; how much more indefinable are the *accidentia* which befall the human in ecstasy or *amentia* of the Holy Spirit?

The difficulty of defining this ecstasy and *amentia* is not only due to its accidental character, but also to the fact that its very mention is part of a rhetorical construction of ecstasy as part of true Christian identity over and against the "false" Christian claims of Marcion and his followers. Tertullian's appeal to charismata and *amentia* is embedded within a rhetorical context of struggle. Authority and Christian identity are interwoven with mentions of spiritual gifts and of ecstasy, and thus references to charismata and *ecstasis* are conveniently vague. This fortifies Tertullian's rhetorical stance: his community has what the *psychici* do not, but the exact content of this spiritual activity is conveniently impossible to define.

Tertullian's understanding of the present as the age of the Paraclete, and his mocking use of the term *psychici*, which denies the spiritual status of his opponents, shore up his claims to the truth and appropriateness of ecstasy

---

[58]See also Heine, "Role of the Gospel of John in the Montanist Controversy," 1–19. The issue of time, boundaries, and prophecy arises again in Epiphanius *Pan.* 48; see ch. 5, below. In his *Homilies on Luke*, Origen uses Luke 16:16 to insist that prophecy has come to an end (Hällstrom, *Charismatic Succession*, 32). For uses of Luke 16:16 in conjunction with Montanism and discussions of the Phrygians, see Pseudo-Athanasius, *Sermon Against All Heresies* 10 (Heine, *Montanist Oracles and Testimonia,* 113); and Pseudo-Athanasius, *Synopsis scripturae sacrae liber XVI, Canticum canticorum* 24 (Heine, *Montanist Oracles and Testimonia,* 159).

and visions in his own community. Tertullian thus asserts the epistemic value of ecstasy and dreams in order to establish his own claims and the practices of his community (such as the restrictions on second marriages) as truth and true Christianity, over and against his opponents.

## Conclusions

Tertullian is often read as a "Montanist" writer, who advocates prophecy and charismata at the expense of reason, or as a "rigorist," who demands strict new Christian practices and supports them willy-nilly through appeals to the Paraclete, visions, oracles, and prophecy. But such readings distort his work. This chapter and the previous one make better sense of Tertullian and his arguments by reading him within a model of struggle, as a participant in a broader debate over prophecy, ecstasy, and *amentia*.

In *De anima,* we see that *amentia* or ecstasy, clear evidence of divine gifts active in one's community, is also a significant source for true knowledge. Although the term *amentia* is generally — almost always — used negatively in early Christian debates over prophecy, Tertullian, like Philo, uses it almost casually with no hint of the pejorative, explaining that certain dreams and ecstasy are a kind of madness. Epiphanius's source, we shall see, does just the opposite: it uses a variety of accusations of madness, folly, and unstable intellect to chip away at the authority of the Phrygians. Tertullian uses the term *amentia* casually because his rhetorical strategy is focused elsewhere in *De anima*. In a move analogous to his argument about Jerusalem (instead of Athens) as a center of knowledge, Tertullian shifts the weight of authority away from the mind and toward the soul, which he argues is unitary and undivided — not tripartite, as Plato states. This undivided and wholly rational soul is God's breath (*afflatus*) and partakes in divine qualities. This is the weightiest argument in the treatise, drawing all others toward it. In arguing that the soul is simple and uniform, and that the mind is merely the soul's instrument, Tertullian allows for the possibility of behavior that looks like madness, but that is not characterized by true loss of the mind. Tertullian collapses the tripartite Platonic schema of the soul, with its noetic, its appetitive, and its desirous portions of the soul, into one rational, uniform, and uncompounded soul, which knows what it knows not only through the mind, but also through sense perception, dreams, and ecstasy. Sense perception then becomes a significant and reliable source for knowledge, since the senses gather information and educate the mind (*An.* 18.7–8). Tertullian can thus also use *amentia* to describe certain kinds of ecstasy and dreaming. Since the soul is wholly rational, and the mind is an instrument of the soul, the *appearance* of madness or the dimming of the mind in prophecy does not concern Tertullian.

Indeed, in *Against Marcion*, Tertullian dares Marcion and his followers to provide evidence of ecstasy and *amentia*, challenging them to a good intramural match over spiritual gifts. Thus *amentia*, evidence of spiritual gifts, becomes a characteristic of a true Christian identity, according to Tertullian. But it is an identity that is not innate or ontologically given. No one is born spiritual. No ontological divide exists between humans such that some are spiritual, some are material, and some are psychic; and no one should claim a special, natural status over and against another. Although Genesis indeed says that an ecstasy fell upon Adam, and that he prophesied, this does not indicate that Adam was naturally and ontologically spiritual, but rather that a spirit is an *accidens*, something accidental and secondary to one's nature. According to Tertullian's interpretation, Genesis cannot be used to claim universal spiritual status, using the example of Adam, or even special spiritual status, using the example of Seth.[59] Just as Paul demoted the Corinthians, informing them that their self-identification as πνευματικοί was unjustified, and that they were still merely σαρκικοί, so also Tertullian calls his opponents *psychici*, knowing that they too claim the status of spiritual people (*spiritales*).

Tertullian's understanding of Christian history defies a Weberian model of the decline of charismata and of institutionalization opposed to the spirit and its manifestations. Tertullian does not understand Christian community to be in decline from its spiritual origins, nor does he present the church as an institution which hinders prophetic charism even in its examination of a sister's vision. Indeed, participating in a discourse of the periodization of history, Tertullian offers a different twist: spiritual activity and the presence of the Spirit are only becoming stronger in the current generation of Christians. He asserts this as part of his larger argument over and against other forms of Christianity. In arguing that the mind is merely an instrument, and that sense perception is epistemically valuable, in arguing that ecstasy and *amentia* prove the legitimacy of one's Christian identity, in understanding Adam's ecstasy in Gen 2:21–24 to be an accident of the spirit, and in insisting that spiritual gifts are available through the Paraclete in the present, Tertullian offers a picture of Christian identity and legitimizes a realm of knowledge that are quite different from the identity and epistemology of Epiphanius's source.

[59]See Tertullian, *Val.* 29.1–3, pp. 121–22, above.

# "An Ecstasy of Folly": The Sound and Unsound Mind in Epiphanius's Anti-Phrygian Source

Tertullian provided an encyclopedic — both exhaustive and exhausting — explanation of the human soul and its activity during ecstasy. The contemporaneous source found in Epiphanius's *Panarion* 48 provides only glimpses of and fragments from the larger debate over prophecy and ecstasy, brief allusions that are puzzling and tantalizing. Since *Pan.* 48.1.4–13.8's methods and topics of argumentation are similar to Tertullian's, this chapter reads Epiphanius's source as participating in a common discourse with Tertullian — in a kind of conversation, even if the two works do not respond to each other directly.[1]

Tertullian and Epiphanius's source are generally understood to sit on opposite sides of the fence, one Montanist and heretical, one orthodox and anti-Montanist. They lie closer to each other than one might think, however, and any labelling that occurs — any challenge to true Christian identity — is part of these opponents' rhetorical constructions of each other. They engage in a shared discussion about prophecy and ecstasy, and they share certain philosophical foundations, methods of argument, and even conclusions. Any struggle between their ideas — and there is strong disagreement! — is the result of an intimate conflict over the same sources and concerns. Although these texts have often been relegated to the opposing scholarly (and sometimes ancient) categories of "Montanist" and "orthodox," the intimacy of the conflict between them, and the frequent similarity of their conclusions, helps to challenge these very categories.

---

[1]Pierre de Labriolle (*Les sources de l'histoire du Montanism,* liii), too, does not see a direct relation between the texts.

I begin this chapter by summarizing scholarly definitions of Montanism and by examining Epiphanius's own late-fourth-century C.E. context, in order to isolate the early-third-century Anti-Phrygian source's concerns from later treatments of it, whether fourth-century or modern. A careful analysis of the source itself follows. I trace the way in which the source uses a discourse of madness and rationality and a discourse of the periodization of history by looking at several sections in *Pan*. 48.1.4–13.8: its introductory argument, which challenges one of Maximilla's oracles; its account and refutation of several of Maximilla's and Montanus's oracles; and its assertion of a catalog of great past prophets — prophets who, according to the source, were rational and sober-minded, unlike Montanus, Maximilla, and their followers. Epiphanius's source makes these arguments even as it asserts that its community possesses true Christian identity, over and against the "Phrygians," and that the Phrygians' ecstasies lead to questionable and foolish realms not of knowledge, as they claim, but of falsehood.

## Inventing Montanism

Much of our information about the diversity of early Christianity comes through the voices of ancient heresiologists — authors who taxonomize "deviant" forms of Christianity or, rather, what is not Christianity. Especially before the discovery of the Nag Hammadi manuscripts in the middle of the twentieth century, scholars often adopted for themselves ancient heresiologists' categorizations and labels. Thus, nomenclature forged in the crucible of intramural Christian polemic, such as "Valentinian," "Marcionite," or "Phrygian," has been reified.

Recent scholarship has noted this problem, attempting to understand these texts within their rhetorical contexts and to reconstruct early Christian ideas and practices without reduplicating the categories of "orthodox" and "heretical."[2] In the case of *Pan*. 48.1.4–13.8, however, a source which does not even use the term "Montanist" has been often labeled as such and has been read in the context of a later set of information, dealing with different events and figures, which Epiphanius includes at the end of *Panarion* 48 and 49. Scholars have also elided *Pan*. 48.1.4–13.8 with Eusebius's *Hist. eccl.* 5.16–18 and

---

[2]See especially King, *What is Gnosticism?*, introduction and ch. 7. Walter Bauer (*Orthodoxy and Heresy in Earliest Christianity* [ed. Robert A. Kraft and Gerhard Krodel; Philadelphia: Fortress, 1971]) was revolutionary in his reversal of Tertullian's argument that truth precedes heresy, even if Bauer does not attempt to deconstruct the categories of orthodoxy and heresy as such.

various other sources in order to construct "Montanism" in antiquity. Little attention has been paid to geographical or temporal variation among those who called themselves adherents of the "New Prophecy," or, even more significant, to the fact that "Montanism" is a category manufactured by ancient heresiologists and then utilized by modern scholars.[3]

Montanism is accused of various things: moral rigorism, excessive asceticism, prohibition of second marriages, pricking children with needles and consuming their blood, paying their priests, having women officiants, trying to introduce new texts as scripture, millennialist notions, and promoting voluntary martyrdom that amounts to suicide. Early heresiologists conflated sources and rumors about Montanism; scholarship often follows suit, and tries (fairly unsuccessfully) to make sense of a long list of supposed aberrations in practice and thought.[4] W. H. C. Frend, for example, characterized Montanism in this way: "Christians must embrace an entirely spiritual life. Marriages were to be dissolved, continence to be observed, rigorous fasts ('dry fasts' or xerophagies) to be undertaken, and the name of Christ confessed openly to the

---

[3]For an example of an article that resists the category of "Montanism," see Alistair Stewart-Sykes, "Papyrus Oxyrhynchus 5: A Prophetic Protest from Second Century Rome," *Stud. Pat.* 31 (1997), esp. 202–5. See also the work of William Tabbernee, which eschews the term "Montanist" even while reluctantly using it merely for the purposes of shorthand (e.g., "Recognising the Spirit: Second-Generation Montanist Oracles," paper presented at the Oxford Patristics Conference, Oxford, England, 18–23 August 2003).

[4]Montanism, with its emphasis on prophecy, has been cast in many roles in the history of early Christianity. August Neander saw Montanism "as a reaction against Gnosticism's perversion of Christianity" (Trevett, *Montanism*, 6). Albert Schwegler understood it to be a form of legalistic Jewish Christianity; F. C. Baur, like Harnack, "took note of the parallel rise of monarchical episcopacy and he saw in Montanism a more ancient and Jewish form of Christianity which was now in opposition to a hierarchical, Hellenised form" (ibid., 7). Albrecht Ritschl thought Montanism was a sect strongly influenced by Gentile Christian and pagan practices. Ritschl and Harnack thought that Montanism warned the Church as the latter moved toward alliance with the Roman state, but that Montanism became arrogant and legalistic in its own turn. Christine Trevett (ibid., 10) states: "Montanism's rise as critic, irritant, or even heresy is sometimes regarded as a watershed for the young Church. It rose alongside the growth of episcopal authority and certain forms of Gnosticism. Hence the history of ecclesiology and of doctrine has tended to be understood with reference to these two (Montanist and Gnostic) aberrant and abhorrent forces." Roman Catholic historiography later sees Gnosticism, paganism, and Montanism as separate dangers to the second-century church, while others try to demonstrate that there are affinities between Gnosticism and Montanism. Later twentieth-century studies of Montanism have tended to focus on its possible pagan roots (ibid., 8; see also Susanna Elm, "Montanist Oracles," in *Searching the Scriptures: A Feminist Ecumenical Commentary and Translation* [ed. Elisabeth Schüssler Fiorenza; 2 vols; New

point that martyrdom should be courted."[5] Klawiter argued that Montanism is often characterized as apocalyptic because of its supposed obsession with martyrdom, and the rumor that they called Pepuza,[6] a small town in Phrygia, a "New Jerusalem." Other scholars focus on Montanus, who is said to be the founder. For example, some scholars reconstruct an early Montanism in which Montanus was a *gallus* of Kybele, and participants in Montanist ritual were familiar with roles as sacred slaves of Apollo.[7]

Despite the various strange practices, aberrant behaviors, and problematic origins of which Montanism has been accused, and despite various shifts and turns in early Christian history with which Montanism has been credited, there may be no "there" there: upon closer examination, the very category of "Montanism" unravels. The term itself is suspect, since it does not appear until the late fourth century,[8] and because there is no clear evidence with which to reconstruct with precision the temporal and geographical variations of those whom heresiologists tended to lump under the category "Phrygians" or "Kataphrygians" or "Montanists." It is impossible to pinpoint the origins of a separate movement called "Montanism," or, for that matter, even the earliest prophecies of the man named Montanus.[9] These discrepancies make

York: Crossroad/Continuum, 1994] 2:131–38). But as Trevett (*Montanism*, 7) says, "The same questions are still in the air. Frederick Klawiter's thesis has asked whether Montanism was a prophetic reform movement of protest against secularisation and spiritual decline in catholic circles (so Baur and Campenhausen), or whether it was perhaps the revolution of martyrs in political revolt against Rome."

[5]W. H. C. Frend, "Montanism: Research and Problems," in *Archaeology and History in the Study of Early Christianity* (London: Variorum Reprints, 1988) 523.

[6]The exact location of Pepuza is unknown, although William Tabbernee has recently proposed a site near Susuzören in the province of Uşak, Turkey ("Portals of the Montanist New Jerusalem: The Discovery of Pepouza and Tymion," paper presented at the North American Patristic Society Annual Meeting, Loyola University, Chicago, Ill., 23–25 May 2002). See also idem, *Montanist Inscriptions*, 27. For the possible connection of *Panarion* 49's mention of Pepuza with Sirach 24 and wisdom traditions, see John C. Poirier, "Montanist Pepuza-Jerusalem and the Dwelling Place of Wisdom," *JECS* 7 (1999) 491–507.

[7]Elm, "Montanist Oracles," 135. See also Trevett, *Montanism*, 8. But such scholarly reconstructions depend on ancient critiques of Montanus as founder; such critiques of Montanus are part of a larger pattern within ancient heresiology that challenges the origins and leader of a community in order to undermine the authority of a whole group.

[8]It is first used by Cyril of Jerusalem, cited in Trevett, *Montanism*, 2.

[9]Eusebius gives information that helps to date Montanus's activity to 171 C.E.; Epiphanius dates it too early, at 156 C.E. The customary focus on Montanus alone is even problematic, as Anne Jensen (*God's Self-Confident Daughters: Early Christianity and the Liberation of*

it difficult to establish with confidence the beginnings of the prophetic activity of Montanus, Priscilla, and Maximilla,[10] much less the content of the prophecies or the rituals or geographical diffusion of those who followed these prophets. Montanism, like Gnosticism, serves a variety of purposes in scholars' reconstructions of early Christianity.[11] Often considered a watershed in early Christian history, Montanism has been used to explain several phenomena: canon formation, the rise of church office and institutionalization, and the "orthodox" emphasis on community benefit rather than individual and elite spiritual practice. Montanism is constructed within and used to support a Weberian model of decline of charism. Canon squelches Montanism's spirit; priesthood and office usurp its charism; orthodoxy, seeing Montanism's attempt to renew the spirit of Christianity, shores up its institutions and routinizes spiritual gifts, casting aside prophecy and other more effervescent charismata.

Montanism therefore functions as an explanatory device—or even a driving engine—for various historiographies of early Christianity. Adolf von Harnack, for example, maintained that while spiritual phenomena were important for early Christian mission and propaganda, they brought with them an implicit danger of fraud, exaggeration, and misuse. As the New Testament canon solidified, prophecy naturally declined, since the time of revelation was thought to have passed. The climax of ecclesiastical development occurred only after the Montanist controversy; it was in its struggle over Montanism that the church learned again how to "[bind] the individual closely to itself."[12] Thus, in the second century, according to Harnack, there

---

*Women* [1992; trans. O. C. Dean, Jr.; Louisville, Ky.: Westminster John Knox, 1996] 139) has pointed out, since it marginalizes the roles of Priscilla and Maximilla.

[10]See Timothy Barnes's careful analysis in "The Chronology of Montanism," *JTS* n.s. 21 (1970) 403–8. Frederick Klawiter hypothesizes that Montanism may have arisen in approximately 175 C.E. in Asia Minor because of sudden new persecutions there at the time of Marcus Aurelius, which inspired an apocalyptic viewpoint that easily accepted martyrdom: see "The Role of Martyrdom and Persecution in Developing the Priestly Authority of Women in Early Christianity: A Case Study of Montanism," *Church History* 49 (1980) 251–61.

[11]See King, *What is Gnosticism?*, for an exemplary method for challenging heresiological categories.

[12]Von Harnack (*The Mission and Expansion of Christianity*, ch. 4) asserted that unlike the individualism of Montanism, the church binds the person into its οἰκοδομή; scholars construct a Montanism which is analogous to Paul's depiction of the Corinthians: both are accused of focusing on the individual's benefit, rather than the church. See also Cecil Robeck's discussion of Harnack (*Prophecy in Carthage*, 7).

is a diminishing of charismata, and although Montanism brings a renewed burst of gifts, this phenomenon waned in the third century.

Others, too, understand Montanism to be a final burst of charisma in the face of increasing institutionalization of church office and the strictures of canon. Von Campenhausen drew a direct connection between Montanism and canon formation, and in his assessment, Montanism, with its emphasis on revival, eschatology, and prophecy, was a "reactionary" movement that recalled "the spirit of primitive Christianity." Its emphasis on prophecy necessarily clashed with the "canonical norm."[13] E. R. Dodds went a step further to theorize that Montanists developed a "Third Testament" from their prophecies.[14] Yet the very idea that a canonical norm existed at the time of Montanus and his immediate successors, in the late second and early third centuries, is

[13]Von Campenhausen, *The Formation of the Christian Bible,* 221. See also McDonald's excellent summary of von Campenhausen's views (*The Formation of the Christian Biblical Canon,* 174–75). As I discussed in the introduction, von Campenhausen (*Ecclesiastical Authority and Spiritual Power,* 2) resisted the Weberian model prevalent in his day. He offered a measured argument that office and charismatic types of authority cannot be set in opposition, because "in the real life of history each has his allotted place in relation to the other, and each must affirm the other; indeed, to a certain extent each assimilates the other." He also attempted to break the impasse between a liberal-Protestant emphasis on Spirit and a Roman Catholic emphasis on tradition by demonstrating that neither Spirit nor tradition can be traced back in a pure uncomplicated line to Christian origins (294). He locates the culmination of spiritual power and "official" authority in the person of Jesus, however, falling into the trap of seeking a pure origin in Jesus, if not in early Christian communities (see ch. 1). According to von Campenhausen, early Christianity then divides into two branches, one represented by the anti-office stance of Paul and his emphasis on spirit, the other represented by the presbyterial system evolving, as von Campenhausen has it, out of Jewish Christianity. A third phase occurs as Luke-Acts tries to weave both traditions together in his story of early Christianity. Finally, von Campenhausen states, in the face of the "Gnostic crisis," the church again turns to "an increasing emphasis on office and its authority" (298) in the second century. By the third century, "exclusive authority of office attains its full stature" (299) and the spirit is increasingly "an individual and private matter" (300). But he also stated that the decrease of prophecy is connected to the increasingly formalized transmission of the apostolic tradition. Any struggle between the ecclesiastical and the charismatic dissipates as "officers" come to possess the Spirit.

[14]E. R. Dodds, *Pagan and Christian in an Age of Anxiety* (Cambridge: Cambridge University Press, 1965) 64–68. This concept of a "Third Testament" is the elaboration of von Campenhausen's theory that Montanists "wrote down many of their prophecies and visions in books that they claimed were inspired and that these books were then read in their assemblies." See von Campenhausen, *The Formation of the Christian Bible,* 229; MacDonald, *The Formation of the Christian Biblical Canon,* 174.

problematic, since different regions and different communities considered a variety of texts to be important until the fourth century and beyond.[15]

Scholars' reconstructions of Montanism thus frequently utilize a model of charismatic origins and subsequent decline of charismata into institution. Dodds's theory about Montanism, canon, and the Spirit, for example, is undergirded by a model of decline:

> The eventual defeat of Montanism was inevitable. It is already foreshadowed in the sage advice whispered by the Holy Spirit to Ignatius: "Do nothing without the Bishop." In vain did Tertullian protest that the Church is not a collection of Bishops; in vain did Irenaeus plead against the expulsion of prophecy. From the point of view of the hierarchy the Third Person of the Trinity had outlived his primitive function.[16]

Some more recent studies exhibit similar assumptions and models of Spirit's "primitive" vibrancy and subsequent decline. David Aune's *Prophecy in Early Christianity and the Ancient Mediterranean World*, the most complete study of early Christian prophecy yet, characterizes Montanism as a "charismatic renewal movement" in the midst of the decline of spiritual gifts. Prophets had an integral role in community until the beginning of the second century C.E., but then "inevitable forces of institutionalization banished prophets from their roles as leaders and marginalized the revelatory significance of their proclamations."[17] David Hill theorizes that the Montanist renewal movement gave prophecy a bad name within Christianity, resulting in a decrease in prophetic activity among mainstream Christians.[18]

[15]On debates over dating of canon, see MacDonald, *The Formation of the Christian Biblical Canon*. Our earliest canon lists appear only in the fourth century with Eusebius's *Ecclesiastical History* and Athanasius's *Thirty-Ninth Festal Letter*, and since communities struggled long thereafter over what texts were recognized for public and private use (see Wilhelm Schneemelcher, "General Introduction," in *New Testament Apocrypha*, vol. 1: *Gospels and Related Writings* [ed. Edgar Hennecke, Wilhelm Schneemelcher, and R. McL. Wilson; 5th ed.; Westminster: John Knox, 1991] 9–75).

[16]Dodds, *Pagan and Christian in an Age of Anxiety*, 67. He goes on to say, "He [*sic*; the Spirit] was too deeply entrenched in the New Testament to be demoted [?!], but he ceased in practice to play any audible part in the counsels of the Church."

[17]Aune, *Prophecy in Early Christianity*, 189.

[18]Hill, *New Testament Prophecy*, 190; see Robeck's discussion of Hill in *Prophecy in Carthage*, 7.

Scholarly reconstructions of Montanism and its place within early Christianity are rooted in assumptions about the nature of early Christian history, about early Christianity as a monolithic phenomenon, and about Montanism's role in early Christian history. Does Montanism provide spiritual renewal at a time when routinization is setting in? Does it represent a synthesis of Christianity with Dionysian or "barbarian" traditions? Scholarship is now engaged in a serious reconsideration of assumptions about Montanism and about "heresy" more broadly. Like other so-called heresies, Montanism is a category manufactured in order to define Christian normativity and thus to construct the boundaries of orthodox Christian identity.

In working with Epiphanius's source, I set aside scholarly constructions of and debates over Montanism and focus instead on the source's own rhetoric against the "Phrygians" and its engagement in a debate over prophecy and ecstasy. In doing so, I follow scholars like Ronald Heine, who carefully refrain from harmonizing early sources which mention Montanus and the New Prophecy, but instead note differences among texts, plotting trends according to time and geographical location.[19] This chapter and the previous chapters on Tertullian take a similar approach, reading Tertullian (usually accused of being a Montanist) and Epiphanius's source (usually read as opposing Montanism) not as evidence of a Montanist controversy, but as texts which partake in a broader context of debates over prophecy and ecstasy in antiquity. To accomplish this reading, it is necessary to distinguish Epiphanius's source's interests and rhetorical strategies from Epiphanius's use of the source for heresiological purposes.

## Reading With Epiphanius

*Pan.* 48.1.4–13.8 is one of the many sources that Epiphanius absorbs in order to construct his massive heresiology. From approximately 375 to 378

---

[19]Heine, "Role of the Gospel of John in the Montanist Controversy," 1–19. He concludes that the debate in Asia Minor is characterized by conflicts over interpretation of scripture (but lacks a focus on passages about the Paraclete), while the debate spreading out of Rome and into North Africa centers on the question of whether there are prophets after the apostles, and uses the Gospel of John (including its mention of the Paraclete) extensively. In this latter context, the issue was not whether a given prophecy was true or false, as it was in Asia Minor; rather, some stated that there was no more prophecy after the apostles, while others argued that while the Holy Spirit was in the apostles, the Paraclete is now present, working even greater things.

C.E., this bishop of Salamis in Cyprus produced his *Panarion* ("Medicine Chest") against eighty "heretical sects."[20] Like other heresiological materials, the *Panarion* attempts to establish Christian identity in the midst of the other—an intimate other, which also claims to be Christian. Its very genre as a catalog of the deviant and its rhetorical conceits make clear that, on some level, this is an exercise in invention.[21] "I am writing you a preface to give the gist of my <treatise> against sects," Epiphanius begins.

> Since I shall be telling you the names of the sects and exposing their unlawful deeds like poisons and toxic substances, matching the antidotes with them at the same time—cures for those who are already bitten, and preventatives for those who will have this experience—I am drafting this preface here for the scholarly, to explain the "Panarion," or chest of remedies for the victims of wild beasts' bites. It is a work in three volumes and contains eighty sections, which stand symbolically for wild animals or snakes.
>
> But "one after the eighty" is at once the foundation of the truth, the teaching and the saving treatment of it, and Christ's "holy bride," the Church. (Proem 1.1.1–3; ET Williams, 1:3)

Thus, two metaphors govern the *Panarion*. The number of sects described— and note that Epiphanius makes up names[22] and may divide and relabel

---

[20]Frank Williams, "Introduction," in idem, trans., *The Panarion of Epiphanius of Salamis* (2 vols.; Leiden: Brill, 1987–1994) 1:xiii. There are eleven manuscripts of the *Panarion*; none is complete, and "all descend from one carelessly copied archetype, and the text has been further contaminated by Atticizing scribes" (x). For another interpretation of Epiphanius's list of heresies, see Aline Pourkier, *L'hérésiologie chez Épiphane de Salamine* (Paris: Beauchesne, 1992) ch. 3. In this chapter, unless otherwise noted, I use the Greek edition of Epiphanius cited in chapter 1, p. 74 n. 11, above, and abbreviated as "Dummer." Unless otherwise noted, all translations are my own. I found Frank Williams's excellent translations helpful as I prepared my own.

Epiphanius claims that he uses "observation, documentation, and oral testimony": "Some of the things which I shall tell the reader <about> sects and schisms, I owe to my fondness for study. Certain things I learned from hearsay, though I experienced some with my own ears and eyes. I am confident that I can give an account of some sects' origins and teachings for accurate report . . . of these things. I know one from the works of ancient authors, another from the report of men who confirmed my notion precisely" (*Pan.* 1.2.4; ET Williams, 1:12). Williams admits that we also find "historical conjecture on Epiphanius' part." Williams, "Introduction," 1:xix.

[21]See Michael Williams, *Rethinking "Gnosticism": An Argument for Dismantling a Dubious Category* (Princeton, N.J.: Princeton University Press, 1996) 39–40, 44–50.

[22]Epiphanius is well known for inventing names for various sects (see pp. 165–66, below); he himself admits it with regard to the "Alogi" of *Panarion* 51.

communities in order to make his quota—corresponds to the image of the eighty concubines of the Song of Solomon. Echoing the virgin-whore dichotomy of antiquity, Epiphanius genders these "sects" as female but they are illegitimate compared to the bride: the eighty concubines "are not lawful wives and have no dowry from the king and no guarantee that their children can inherit."[23] The bride (the church) too, is feminine, but she is equated with truth, and is given a position of primacy.

In Epiphanius's *Panarion*, the metaphor of concubines and of the feminine is analogically linked to that of wild beasts and poisonous snakes. Epiphanius draws on late antique associations of the feminine with the poisonous, the wild, the uncontrolled, the animal, the irrational;[24] heresies are females who do not stay within their proper bounds. He not only employs the well-established trope of feminizing and sexualizing (in antiquity, the two often work together) one's opponent, but also makes less abstract claims about aberrant (as he claims) leadership roles of real women in arguing against various heresies.[25] Epiphanius's second governing metaphor bestializes other

---

[23]See especially the elaboration of the metaphor in *Pan.* 80.10.1ff. Epiphanius states (*Pan.* 80.10.4) that there are only seventy-five concubines, and five mothers, four of which he names as Hellenism, Judaism, the Samaritan sect, and Christianity ("from which the separated sects have been broken off like branches" [*Pan.* 80.10.5; ET Williams, 2:637]). The fifth may be the Scythians, mentioned in *Pan.* 80.10.3 but omitted here. Note also that the philosophies are allegorically associated with the "young girls without number." See especially *De fide*, at the end of the *Panarion*, for a discussion of the bride-virgin and the characteristics of the Church.

[24]Consider, in the plays of Euripides, e.g., Medea's use of poisons (*Medea*) and women's behavior as wild beasts (*Bacchae*). See Page DuBois, *Centaurs and Amazons: Women and the Pre-history of the Great Chain of Being* (Ann Arbor, Mich.: University of Michigan, 1982) 151.

[25]Epiphanius directly protests women's authority among the "Quintillianists" or "Priscillianists"—here he uses the names of female prophets usually associated with Montanism, and constructs entirely new heresies based upon their leadership. (*Panarion* 49 hints at fascinating interpretive debates about Eve and women's roles in Christian community. See J. A. Cerrato, "Hippolytus' *On the Song of Songs* and the New Prophecy," *Stud. Pat.* 31 [1997] 268–73). In *Panarion* 79, opposing what he sees as the worship of Mary, Epiphanius states: "women are unstable, prone to error, and mean-spirited. As in our earlier chapter on Quintilla, Maximilla, and Priscilla, so here the devil has seen fit to disgorge ridiculous teachings from the mouths of women" (*Pan.* 79.1.6; ET Williams, 2:621). See also the continuation of the argument: "let us adopt a manly frame of mind and dispel the madness of these women" (79.2.1) and "never at any time has a woman been a priest" (79.2.3, followed by arguments from scripture).

Regarding the feminization of heresy, see, for example, Virginia Burrus, "The Heretical Woman as Symbol in Alexander, Athanasius, Epiphanius, and Jerome," *HTR* 84 (1991) 229–48. More broadly in early Christian literature, we see that Montanus, for example, is described as effeminate

Christians, characterizing "heresies" as the poison of snakes, reptiles, and insects, and as the bites of wild beasts. The title itself—*Panarion*, "Medicine Chest"— conjures fear of this illness and infection.[26] *Panarion* 48, for example, characterizes the Phrygian sect as a blood-sucking snake: "I have crushed its poison, and the venom on its hooked fangs, with the cudgel of the truth of the cross. For it is like the viper of hemorrhage."[27] At times, Epiphanius expresses the concern that by describing these heresies he may unwittingly attract his audience to that which he describes as repulsive. He thus emphasizes heresies' impurity, their ability to invade and corrupt; he offers promises of inoculation and apotropaic tools.[28] Epiphanius, like the best kind of health maintenance organization, provides preventative health care, spiritual vaccines for the as-yet uninfected.

Heresiological texts name, construct, and taxonomize the other. Because of Epiphanius's organization of his sources, *Panarion* 48 and 49 are usually read together as materials for reconstructions of the Montanist controversy. As in Epiphanius's other entries, the "heresy's" identity as other is immediately established. These groups are not given the privilege of the name "Christian"; sometimes Epiphanius creates names for them, or refers to other, prior heresiological literature for already appended labels. In *Panarion* 48, the group is defined geographically as the "sect of the Phrygians" (1.1; αἵρεσις ... τῶν Φρυγῶν).[29] According to Epiphanius, its origin and its lineage neither point

---

and as wearing make-up (Apollonius in Eusebius, *Hist. eccl.* 5.18.11); Priscilla's virginity is questioned (ibid., 5.18.3); the role of female prophets and leaders in Montanism is mocked ("Dialogue between an Orthodox and a Montanist"; see Heine, *Montanist Oracles*, 113–27). It is interesting that *Pan.* 48.1.4–13.8 does not launch any critique of female Phrygian prophets *as females*, further lending support to the idea that Epiphanius is borrowing from a source.

[26]Elsewhere in Greco-Roman literature, we find the idea that a *superstitio* or even a religion might infect others. See, e.g., Pliny and Trajan's correspondence, in which Christians are seen as a contagion (Pliny, *Letters* 10.96–97), or John Chrysostom's first *Discourses against the Jews*, in which Judaism is depicted as a disease.

[27]ET Williams, 2:21.

[28]*Panarion* 48 offers a remedy for the bloodthirsty snake, the Phrygians: "And I prepare a sort of medicine made of refutation from the words of sacred scripture and right reasonings, and compound <it> in the Lord for two purposes: for the recovery of the sufferers from their illness and great pain, but for a prophylactic, as it were, for those who have never contracted the disease" (*Pan.* 48.15.3–5; ET Williams, 2:20–21).

[29]Dummer, 219. Note that Williams' translation of "Montanists" in *Pan.* 48.1.2 is a misleading elaboration: the Greek merely reads οὗτοι, referring back to τῶν Φρυγῶν. See also Jensen, *God's Self-Confident Daughters*, 135, who argues that this geographical designation serves to localize the New Prophets and thus undercut their "catholicity."

backward to true Christian origins nor forward to the true stream of orthodoxy which runs into the future; this sect arose at the same time as the Encratites and "is their successor." It belongs within the succession of heresies, not to genealogy of true Christian identity.

A proliferation of labels arises in *Panarion* 48, and is echoed in *Panarion* 49. Epiphanius starts out by using an early-third-century source's epithet: the "Phrygians." But *Pan.* 48.14.3–5 turns chaotic:

> But to omit nothing that bears on the name of every sect I have discussed, I shall also speak, in its turn, of the Tascodrugians. For this name is used either in this sect itself, or the one after it, which is called the sect of the Quintillianists—for this name too originates with these people themselves . . . They say that a shocking, wicked thing is done in this sect—or in its sister sect, the one called the sect of the Quintillianists or Priscillianists, and Pepuzians.[30]

*Pan.* 49.2.6 adds yet a new name to the confusing mix: the Artotyrites, or "Bread and Cheese" people, so called for their alleged use of these materials in ritual. Epiphanius himself cannot settle on a name or on a single group; heresies intermingle, reproduce, and proliferate like wanton concubines.

Despite this profusion of names, even Epiphanius finds it hard to say how the Phrygian sect is different from the "true church." Epiphanius first admits how the Phrygians are the same as his version of Christianity: they "accept every scripture of the Old and the New Testaments and affirm the resurrection of the dead as well" (*Pan.* 48.1.3). They are different, however, in that "they boast of having Montanus for a prophet, and Priscilla and Maximilla for prophetesses." At the end of *Panarion* 48 Epiphanius cites what scholars agree is yet another source. This source talks about Pepuza as an important site to the Kataphrygians: they celebrate mysteries there, and say that Jerusalem will descend there (*Pan.* 48.14).[31] *Pan.* 49.1 goes on to mention that one of the prophetesses ("either Quintilla or Priscilla") had a vision of Christ as a woman at Pepuza. Often, scholars read Epiphanius's source in *Pan.* 48.1.4–13.8 against this later material, which they often characterize as "Montanist," apocalyptic, and bizarre, thus distorting the reading of the prior source.

[30]ET Williams, 2:20.

[31]On the importance of this site in terms of relics and shrines, see William Tabbernee, "'Our Trophies are Better than Your Trophies': The Appeal of Tombs and Reliquaries in Montanist-Orthodox Relations,'" *Stud. Pat.* 31 (1997) 206–17.

Epiphanius's taxonomy of heresies often serves a different rhetorical purpose than the sources which he uses within the *Panarion*. *Pan*. 48.1.4–13.8 is essential to fill the quota of the eighty concubines, but there is little evidence that Epiphanius is deeply engaged with the issues raised by his source. The *Panarion* as a whole is not consistently concerned either with discussing rationality or the unsound mind or with the debate over prophecy and ecstasy, as the source is. In turn, the Anti-Phrygian source does not evidence the *Panarion*'s broader interest in gendered metaphors or in bestializing the other. It is the *Panarion* 48's early-third-century source, with its deep involvement in the debate over ecstasy and rationality, rather than Epiphanius and his late-fourth-century context, that is central to my argument.

## Reading Without Epiphanius: The Anti-Phrygian Source (*Pan.* 48.1.4–13.8)

Although many historians of early Christian and of Montanism call Epiphanius's source in *Panarion* 48 the "Anti-Montanist," this term does not arise from the text. Thus, I call Epiphanius's source the Anti-Phrygian, adopting the terminology of *Pan*. 48.1.4–13.8. While a heresiologist like Eusebius clearly establishes that he is incorporating an external source in the *Ecclesiastical History* by markers such as "he speaks in this manner in his preface" (*Hist. eccl.* 5.16.2), Epiphanius (frustratingly) weaves sources into his own narrative without any such markers.

At least three arguments support the idea that Epiphanius uses a late-second- or early-third-century source in *Pan*. 48.1.4–13.8 although the question of how much Epiphanius added to or altered this source is still open.[32] First, Richard Adelbert Lipsius, Heinrich Voigt, and Karl Holl (the editor of the first critical edition of Epiphanius's *Panarion*) agree that the source is limited roughly to 48.1.4–13.8, arguing in part on the basis of strong similarities to various texts which predate Epiphanius, including Hippolytus's *Syntagma* and Pseudo-Tertullian's *Adversus omnes haereses*.[33] Pierre de Labriolle, too,

---

[32]Because of Epiphanius's technique of weaving sources into his own writing, elements within this section may be later impositions from Epiphanius himself. References to the "Old Testament and New Testament," for example, suggest a later, fourth-century influence, as do trinitarian references in *Pan*. 48.12.12–13. Similarly, the name of the church with which the source identified itself seems to shift from ἁγία ἐκκλησία to ἁγία καθολική ἐκκλησία.

[33]For discussions of dating, see Dennis E. Groh, "Utterance and Exegesis: Biblical Interpretation in the Montanist Movement," in *The Living Text: Essays in Honor of Ernest*

agrees that *Panarion* 48.2–13 is from an earlier source, noting the similarity of the first paragraph (*Pan.* 48.1) to Epiphanius's introductory style in other sections, while *Pan.* 48.2–13 present a "correction of Montanist sentiment" which Epiphanius has reproduced from another source. Labriolle also points to the specificity of the oracles cited, which he surmises must then have been taken from a written source, and the fact that the content of the source matches debates of the early third century, not debates over Montanism in Epiphanius's own late-fourth-century context.[34]

Second, scholars have noted that elements of *Panarion* 48 are similar to Tertullian's early-third-century writings; these similarities are so strong that they point to an early-third-century debate rather than Epiphanius's late-fourth-century context. As we saw in chapter 1, the Anti-Phrygian source's debate over Gen 2:21 and the long discussion of sleep are closely matched by Tertullian's *An.* 11.4, 21.2, 43.12, and 45.3–6. Dennis Groh, Labriolle, and others agree that the evidence does not warrant a hypothesis of direct literary conversation between the two,[35] but some scholars have suggested that the two shared a common sourcebook of scriptural prooftexts and inter-pretive arguments, and then tweaked the interpretation of these scriptures in slightly different ways.[36] This similar concern about defining ecstasy and interpreting Gen 2:21 indicates a close time frame, however, since later de-bates over Montanists or Phrygians are more concerned with other issues, such as women's leadership or ideas about canon.[37]

---

*W. Saunders* (ed. Dennis E. Groh and Robert Jewett; New York: University Press of America, 1985) 80. Groh discusses the work of Richard Adelbert Lipsius (*Zur Quellenkritik des Epiphanios* [Vienna: Braumüller, 1865]) and Heinrich Gisbert Voigt (*Eine Verschollene Urkunde des Anti-montanistischen Kampfes: die Berichte des Epiphanius über die Kataphryger und Quintillianer* [Leipzig: Fr. Richter, 1891]). According to Lipsius (*Epiphanios*, 221–31), the Anti-Phrygian source extends from 48.2 to 48.13; according to Voigt (*Antimontanistischen Kampfes*, 27–112), the source begins in the middle of the first paragraph; according to Holl, the source extends from 48.1.4 (line 5) to 13.8 (Groh, "Utterance and Exegesis"). See also Trevett, *Montanism: Gender, Authority and the New Prophecy,* 27–37. Frank Williams, however, without discussing the debate at all, states that "the Epiphanian style, and the absence of the marks of the adaptation of sources, make it certain that Epiphanius's refutation is his own" (*The Panarion of Epiphanius of Salamis*, 2:6 n. 1).

[34]Labriolle, "Introduction," *Les sources*, l; see also xlviii–liv.

[35]Groh, "Utterance and Exegesis," 82; Labriolle, "Introduction," *Les sources*, liii (against Voigt).

[36]See Groh, "Utterance and Exegesis"; Williams, 2:6 n. 1.

[37]See, for example, the fourth-century sources collected in Heine's *Montanist Oracles and Testimonia.*

Third, the semantic field of *Pan.* 48.1.4–13.8 supports the argument that Epiphanius uses a source. Various forms (and various parts of speech) of εὐσταθεία (steadiness, calm, tranquility) and διάνοια (understanding or mind), παρακολουθῶ (follow closely, follow with the mind, be aware, conscious) and ἐρρωμένη (powerful, healthy, vigorous) pepper the text. Other relevant terms are λόγος and its cognates, as well as κατάστασις (stability) and φρόνησις (purpose, intention). An investigation of some of the key terminology of *Pan.* 48.1.4–13.8 reveals that this particular vocabulary of reason and sound-mindedness is not widely replicated in other contemporary texts or elsewhere in the *Panarion*.[38] A test case of ερρωμεν- and διανοι- (uninflected and partial for the purpose of search parameters, and searching for occurrences of both terms within five words) in the *Thesaurus Linguae Graecae*, for example, indicates that the Anti-Phrygian source contains a preponderance of these references. Of the twenty-five references to ερρω- μεν- and διανοι- (again searching for occurrences of both terms within five words) found in the fourth century,[39] a full eleven come from Epiphanius; of

[38]TLG results:

| Search Field | 2d c. C.E. | 3d c. C.E. | 4th c. C.E. |
|---|---|---|---|
| ευσταθ- and λογ- | 8 | 0 | 31 (2 from Epiphanius, *Panarion* 48) |
| ευσταθ- and διανοι- | 0 | 0 | 3 (2 from Epiphanius) |
| ερρωμεν- and διανοι- | 5 | 0 | 25 (11 from Epiphanius) |
| παρακολουθ- and διανοι- | 4 | 1 | 7 (2 from Eusebius; 2 from Basil, 3 from Epiphanius, *Panarion* 48) |

All searches allowed for an interval of five words between terms. The TLG search is of course somewhat inconclusive for date, since it does not account for the fact that texts may contain earlier sources.

[39]The range of uses of the five second-century references (references that are roughly contemporaneous to the Anti-Phrygian, rather than to Epiphanius) helps to expand our understanding of the conceptual field evoked by this term. Two references associate health and διάνοια ἐρρωμένη (Galenus, *In Hippocratis aphorismos commentarii vii* 17b.529–32; and Claudius Aelianus Soph., *De Archia et Myscello* 346). Clement of Alexandria's two uses of the term, both of which appear in *Paidagogos* (2.4.44; 2.10.107) have an ethical force; διάνοια ἐρρωμένη stands in contrast to some sort of excessive, and even erotic, behavior (*Paid.* 2.4 discusses banquets; the passage at hand has to do with the singing of songs to God at banquet [2.4.44.5]. The second reference deals with women's diaphanous and provocative clothing [2.10.107.5]). The last reference in the second century, from Philostratus (*Major Soph.* 2.24.3), deals with the straightforward mind of Herakles.

these, eight appear in *Pan.* 48.1.4–13.8.[40] This particular phrase is idiomatically favored in *Panarion* 48, and does not represent vocabulary significant in the *Panarion* as a whole. The *Thesaurus Linguae Graecae* search reveals two things: first, it provides further evidence to support the theory held by Voigt, Labriolle, Groh, and others that Epiphanius here uses a source; second, it exposes that, within the whole of the *Panarion*, *Pan.* 48.1.4–48.13.8 is particularly concerned with terminology of rationality and a sound mind.

This Anti-Phrygian source does not reveal much about his or her own community, except to align it with true and rational prophecy in scripture and with the "holy church." Montanus and Maximilla, in contrast, are portrayed as irrational and deceptive, as self-confuting, arrogant toward the divine, contradicting scripture; their followers are ignorant and deluded. This characterization allows the Anti-Phrygian source to establish its grounds for authority and to question the epistemological value of certain forms of ecstasy, and even the reality of those realms of knowledge. The source also works hard to define ecstasy as a rational, noncompulsory phenomenon.

The Anti-Phrygian's argument progresses through three main parts: a discussion of charismata based on a refutation of an oracle proclaimed by Maximilla; a catalog of "great men," that is, examples of prophets from Scripture; and a series of oracles from Montanus and Maximilla, along with the Anti-Phrygian's refutation of these oracles. Accusations of sexual impropriety, of economic exploitation and greed, of strange ritual practice, so

---

[40]The first use of the phrase is found in *Pan.* 26.18. This long discussion of "gnostics" includes a recurring debate (see also *Pan.* 26.11.5) over the exegesis of Jude 8: "Yet in the same way these dreamers also defile the flesh, reject authority, and slander the glorious ones" (Ὁμοίως μέντοι καὶ οὗτοι ἐνυπνιαζόμενοι σάρκα μὲν μιαίνουσιν κυριότητα δὲ ἀθετοῦσιν δόξας δὲ βλασφημοῦσιν). Epiphanius emphasizes that Jude is not talking here about actual dreaming ("dreaming in body"; *Pan.* 26.13.7, οὐκ εἶπεν . . . περὶ ἐνυπνιαζομένων ἐν σώμασιν), but about those who "say their words as though they were dreaming, and not in the recovery of the wakefulness of their reasoning powers" (τῶν λαλούντων ὡς δι᾽ ὀνειράτων τὰ αὐτῶν ῥήματα καὶ οὐκ ἐν ἀνάνηψει γρηγορήσεως λογισμῶν). Jude 10 refers to those who "[speak] of what they do not know." The text concludes, feeling that it has proved its point: "And he showed that he was not speaking about a dream experienced while sleeping, but concerning their pompous sayings and foolish speech which was said during sleep and *not from a sound understanding*" (καὶ ἔδειξεν ὅτι οὐ περὶ τῆς ἐνυπνιάσεως τοῦ ὕπνου λέγει, ἀλλὰ περὶ τῆς μυθώδους αὐτῶν τραγῳδίας καὶ ληρολογίας, ὡς διὰ ὕπνου λεγομένης καὶ οὐκ ἀπὸ ἐρρωμένης διανοίας). (Emphasis mine; the edition is Holl's, taken from the *TLG*). Elsewhere, the phrase is used to denote sanity in contrast to the ideas of heretics (again, regarding the "Gnostics," *Pan.* 33.2.1; regarding Bardesanes, *Pan.* 56.1.2).

popular in Eusebius's account of "the Phrygian heresy" (*Hist. eccl.* 5.16–19) or later in Epiphanius's own comments, are absent in *Pan.* 48.1.4–13.8. The Anti-Phrygian is concerned instead with rationality and the unsound mind, with true prophecy and false understandings of ecstasy.

In the pages that follow, I shall investigate several interlocking rhetorical strategies that the Anti-Phrygian employs. The source employs the discourse of rationality and madness, accusing the Phrygians of having unsound minds, and holding up in its own community a genealogy of right-thinking prophets. It also employs a discourse of periodizing history, subtly constructing an argument that relegates prophecy and ecstasy to a God-infused distant past. I shall demonstrate this below in two sections. First, I explain the Anti-Phrygian's complicated introductory argument, in which the author constructs identity and difference (and, concomitantly, truth and falsehood), critiquing the Phrygians for having separated and created intentional differences with the true church. Second, I show how the Anti-Phrygian constructs certain ideas of madness and rationality through appeals to great prophets of old and through critiques of oracles from Montanus and Maximilla. These rhetorical strategies go to the heart of this study's concerns with the construction of identity and otherness, and with the ways in which accusations of madness and claims of reason function in polemic.

### What's the Difference? Identity and Otherness, Truth and Falsehood

The Anti-Phrygian's introductory argument centers on which community truly possesses the "gifts of grace." Indeed, "their" slogan ("we [the "Phrygians"] too must receive the charismata")[41] becomes ammunition against the Phrygian sect, as the source asserts that the "holy church" has received the "real" gifts of grace (τὰ ὄντως χαρίσματα, *Pan.* 48.1.5). The debate is not between those who believe that charismata are important and alive and those who think that they are insignificant; rather, the source questions whose charismata are true. In fact, the Anti-Phrygian later reveals the real bone of contention: the Phrygians claim to have left "the church" over the issue of charismata.[42]

The Anti-Phrygian's intricate introductory argument challenges one of Maximilla's oracles, accusing her of having an unsound mind, and question-

---

[41]δεῖ ἡμᾶς . . . καὶ τὰ χαρίσματα δέχεσθαι. *Pan.* 48.1.4–5; Dummer, 220.

[42]Πῶς τοίνυν, ὦ Φρύγες, . . . πῶς πεισθῶμεν ὑμῖν λέγουσι διὰ χαρίσματα ἀφεστάναι τῆς ἐκκλησίας; *Pan.* 48.12.1; Dummer, 235.

ing her place and the place of her disciples within the history of Christian prophecy (which for the source, of course, includes Israelite prophets). The Anti-Phrygian insists that "God's holy church" (that is, *not* the Phrygians) has received the "real" gifts. In the "holy church of God" (ἡ ἁγία δὲ τοῦ θεοῦ ἐκκλησία), charismata are real and have been tested by prophets, apostles, and the Lord (*Pan.* 48.1.5–7). This boast that the true church tests (δεδοκιμασμένα) the spirits is bolstered by appeals to "the apostle John" (1 John 4:1; 2:18–19). Just as John writes of those who "were not of us," so too these Phrygian prophets are "not of the saints." They have departed in contentiousness (τῇ φιλονεικίᾳ), devoting themselves to "spirits that are erring and fictions" (πνεύμασι πλάνης καὶ μυθολογίαις).[43] Not only does the source construct the Phrygians as "other" than the church; it also undermines the Phrygians' claims to truth and knowledge through spiritual gifts. The Anti-Phrygian, asking why "they no longer have prophets after Montanus, Priscilla, and Maximilla," mocks the Phrygians: "they cannot fulfill what they have contentiously undertaken"—that is, the Phrygians, after insisting that "we too must receive the gifts," no longer have prophets.

This accusation is puzzling, given what we know of the continuing prophetic activities of the "New Prophecy," which seems to be what this group called itself. The Anti-Phrygian source grounds this accusation in an oracle it attributes to Maximilla: "After me, there will no longer be a prophet, but the end," or "consummation."[44] The Phrygians take Maximilla's oracles seriously, the source insists. They also take seriously their own slogan, that "we too must receive the charismata." The source was at first defensive in the face of this Phrygian slogan, as it made the source's own community look less interested in gifts. The Anti-Phrygian then lashed back, insisting that the "true church," as the source identifies its community, indeed has real gifts of grace. But now the source challenges the Phrygians, saying that by their own leader's oracle, there should be no more prophets. And so the source delivers another blow:

> For either they will show that there are prophets after Maximilla,
> in order that the grace which they speak not be inoperative, or

---

[43]This may be another reference to 1 Timothy. The Pastoral Epistles have often been considered to be written in opposition to Marcion or the Encratites; it is interesting to see how they are also used against the "Phrygians." See the quotation of 1 Tim 4:1 in *Pan.* 48.1.4. Later the Anti-Phrygian argues in a similar fashion, labeling Maximilla's prophecy as counterfeiting truth, and as coming from spirits of error (*Pan.* 48.12.7).

[44]μετ᾽ ἐμὲ προφήτης οὐκέτι ἔσται, ἀλλὰ συντέλεια. *Pan.* 48.2.4; Dummer, 222.

Maximilla's disciples will be found to be pseudoprophets, daring to be inspired and to delude those who listen to them after the limit of prophetic gifts,[45] [speaking] not from the Holy Spirit, but from spirits (*daimones*) of error.[46]

Here the source uses the puzzling phrase "after the limit of prophetic gifts." This is the only time in the entire introductory argument that the Anti-Phrygian source attaches the adjective προφητικά, "prophetic," to charismata. It does so precisely to set a temporal limit on prophetic gifts, to push them into the past. The text also seems to insist that Maximilla and Priscilla could not have prophesied after a certain temporal boundary (that of the "holy apostles"[47]) and, thus, their prophecies are false:[48] "Grace is not ended in the holy church! Not at all! But if those who prophesied prophesied up to a certain time, and [then] they prophesied no longer, then neither Maximilla nor Priscilla prophesied after the prophecies which have been tested through the holy apostles in the holy church."[49] These two

---

[45]μετὰ τὸν ὅρον τῶν προφητικῶν χαρισμάτων. *Pan.* 48.2.3; Dummer, 221. Ὅρος can denote a conceptual, spatial, or a temporal boundary; for example, it is used as the name of an aeon among Valentinians, according to Irenaeus (see Lampe, s.v. ὅρος, definition A.3); it can refer more generally to a period of time (Lampe, definition A.2; cf. also LSJ, definition I); it refers to a boundary or landmark (LSJ, definition I); or it can refer to a limit or definition of the passions (Lampe, definition B).

[46]ἢ γὰρ δείξωσιν εἶναι προφήτας μετὰ Μαξίμιλλαν, ἵνα μὴ ἀργήσῃ ἡ παρ᾽ αὐτοῖς λεγομένη χάρις, ἢ οἱ περὶ Μαξίμιλλα ψευδοπροφῆται εὑρεθήσονται, μετὰ τὸν ὅρον τῶν προφητικῶν χαρισμάτων τολμήσαντες οὐκ ἀπὸ ἁγίου πνεύματος, ἀλλ᾽ ἀπὸ πλάνης δαιμονίων ἐνθουσιασθῆναι καὶ φαντασιάσαι τοὺς ἀκούοντας αὐτῶν. *Pan.* 48.2.3; Dummer, 221.

[47]The question of who was defined as "apostle" in early Christian communities has no easy answer, but in the Anti-Phrygian source, the title does not seem to apply to any present church leaders. See *Pan.* 48.1.6, 48.2.2.

[48]Note that Eusebius's anonymous source (*Hist. eccl.* 5.16–17) offers a close parallel: "And again after a little he goes on, 'For if the Montanist women succeeded to Quadratus and Ammia in Philadelphia in the prophetic gift, let them show who among them succeeded the followers of Montanus and the women, for the apostle grants that the prophetic gifts shall be in all the church until the final coming, but this they could not show, seeing that this is already the fourteenth year from the death of Maximilla" (*Hist. eccl.* 5.17; ET Lake, 1:484–85). Eusebius's anonymous source presents a fascinating parallel, both in content and time period, to the issues raised in Tertullian and Epiphanius's source. It uses many of the same rhetorical strategies as the Anti-Phrygian, but Eusebius inserts his own comments, thus fragmenting his anonymous source.

[49]οὐκ ἀργεῖ δὲ ἡ χάρις ἐν ἁγίᾳ ἐκκλησίᾳ· μὴ γένοιτο. εἰ δὲ ἕως τινὸς προεφήτευσαν οἱ προφητεύσαντες καὶ * οὐκέτι προφητεύουσιν, ἄρα οὔτε Πρίσκιλλα οὔτε Μαξίμιλλα

dense arguments, put together, expose the Anti-Phrygian's own conclusion that *prophetic* charismata are limited to the past, even if God's grace and other gifts exist currently in the church.[50] The Anti-Phrygian reclaims charismata as part of the "holy church's" identity. The source's argument implies that the Phrygians had claimed that their communities were more truly Christian because of their concern with charismata. But the Anti-Phrygian emphasizes that charismata are part of his or her community, and that the gifts that Maximilla and her disciples displayed were defunct and contradictory, anyway. At the same time, the Anti-Phrygian pushes the term charismata in a different direction, emphasizing its etymological connection with grace (χάρις, see 48.2.1), rather than its connection with prophetic gifts.[51]

Although the Anti-Phrygian source argues strenuously that the "true" church has received charismata, it never appeals to the correct behavior of prophets in its community nor argues that its community engages in ongoing prophetic charismata. The Anti-Phrygian's community may have gifts, but it has no prophetic ones. It cannot compete with the Phrygians on this playing field, and it presents a periodization of history that justifies its understanding of spiritual gifts. The source states that "although they will again wish to say that the first gifts are not like the last, whence are they able to prove this? For the holy prophets and the holy apostles prophesied in a manner similar to one another."[52] For the Anti-Phrygian, the first spiritual gifts are represented by

---

προεφήτευσαν, * μετὰ τὰς προφητείας τὰς διὰ τῶν ἁγίων ἀποστόλων ἐν τῇ ἁγίᾳ ἐκκλησίᾳ δοκιμασθείσας. *Pan.* 48.2.1–2; Dummer, 221. Jürgen Dummer suggests that αἱ προφητεύσασαι be added before μετά; certainly this or more plainly προφητεύσασαι can give a clear meaning of "since they prophesied after the prophecies which were tested by the holy apostles in the holy church." Annewies van den Hoek pointed out in a helpful conversation that this is not necessary; rather, the text reads: "neither Priscilla nor Maximilla prophesied after the prophecies which were tested through the holy apostles in the holy church."

[50]The Anti-Phrygian's references are carefully sustained in the imperfect tense: "for when there was a need for prophets," the source argues, "the same saints were prophesying everything by a true spirit and a sound understanding and a conscious mind." ὅτε γὰρ ἦν χρεία προφητῶν, ἐν ἀληθινῷ πνεύματι καὶ ἐρρωμένῃ διανοίᾳ καὶ παρακολουθοῦντι νῷ οἱ αὐτοὶ ἅγιοι τὰ πάντα επροφήτευον. *Pan.* 48.3.1; Dummer, 223.

[51]Note the etymological connection between χάρις and χάρισμα. The two are also connected in Rom 12:6–8, the themes of which are similar to 1 Corinthians 12. *TDNT*, s.v. χαίρω κτλ., 372–406; see also ch. 2, above.

[52]>>οὐχ ὅμοια τὰ πρῶτα χαρίσματα τοῖς ἐσχάτοις<< . . . ὁμοίως γὰρ ἀλλήλοις οἱ ἅγιοι προφῆται καὶ οἱ ἅγιοι ἀπόστολοι προεφήτευσαν. *Pan.* 48.8.1; Dummer, 229. The equivalence of apostle and prophet in this passage is interesting and is reminiscent of *Didache* 12.

the "holy prophets" and the last spiritual gifts are represented by the "holy apostles," thus shutting out the possibility of present prophetic gifts. Scripture and the apostles are a continuous part of the authority of this "holy church," while the Phrygians are "severed" from this tradition.

In this introductory argument, the source also critiques Maximilla's rationality; she is not like true prophets who speak "in full possession of their understanding, and their words have been accomplished and are still being fulfilled,"[53] since she wrongly predicted the "end."[54] The source catches her on a historical technicality (albeit a large one): the end has not come; Maximilla's understanding of prophecy and of her place within history are both wrong; her disciples are thus wrong and irrational, just as she was. The Anti-Phrygian uses both a discourse of periodizing history, and a discourse of rationality and madness, comparing Maximilla unfavorably to the ancient, true, accurate prophets who spoke "in full possession of their understanding."

This question of the different ages or periods in which charismata are operative also arises in Tertullian's writings. In the last chapter, we saw that Tertullian argues that a new and greater age had come, the age of the Paraclete, where great gifts are to be expected. Similarly, the editorial introduction to the *Martyrdom of Perpetua and Felicitas*, which is contemporaneous with Tertullian, and which he may have written,[55] chides those who think that great spiritual events do not happen in the present, asserting instead:

[53]ὅσα γὰρ οἱ προφῆται εἰρήκασι καὶ μετὰ συνέσεως παρακολουθοῦντες ἐφθέγγοντο, καὶ ἐτελέσθη τὰ παρ' αὐτῶν εἰρημένα καὶ ἔτι πληροῦται. *Pan.* 48.2.5; Dummer, 222. The Anti-Phrygian argues that her oracle is wrong: two hundred and six years (Epiphanius has most likely modified his source's date) have passed, and the συντέλεια has not yet come.

[54]In the Anti-Phrygian source, we find a discrete oracle which uses the term συντέλεια. This term often refers to the end times; in its uses in Matthew (13:39, 40, 49; 24:3; 28:20) and in Hebrews (9:26), it is linked to the word αἰών and refers to the end of an age (or the end of the ages). Eusebius's anonymous source refers to this meaning, although not this precise oracle; it must have had access to a different version of the saying: "In the same book, again, after other refutations of the false prophecies of Maximilla, in a single passage he both indicates the time at which he wrote this, and quotes her predictions, in which she foretold future wars and revolutions, and he corrects the falsehood of them as follows: 'Has it not been made obvious already that this is another lie? For it is more than thirteen years today since the woman died, and there has been in the world neither local nor universal war, but rather by the mercy of God continuing peace even for Christians'" (*Hist. eccl.* 5.16.18–19; ET Lake, 1:480–81). See also *Pan.* 48.2.6–7.

[55]Cecil Robeck (*Prophecy in Carthage*, 17), among others, argues that the arguments that Tertullian is the editor of the *Martyrdom* are questionable. Robeck states two significant problems: the redactor did not name him- or herself, and so to insist upon Tertullian as editor is to argue from silence, and Tertullian's *An.* 55.4 wrongly ascribes Saturus's vision to Perpetua.

Let those then who would restrict the power of the one Spirit to times and seasons look to this: the more recent events should be considered the greater, being later than those of old, and this is a consequence of the extraordinary graces promised for the last stage of time. For *in the last days, God declares, I will pour out my Spirit upon all flesh and their sons and daughters shall prophesy and on my manservants and my maidservants I will pour my Spirit, and the young men shall see visions and the old men shall dream dreams.* So too we hold in honour and acknowledge not only new prophecies but new visions as well, according to the promise.[56]

This evidence, paired with the Anti-Phrygian's complete avoidance of any discussion of present-day prophecies, indicates that the Anti-Phrygian source understands the progress of history in a fundamentally different way than some other Christian communities do.

For the Anti-Phrygian, the timing and the nature of "true charismata" is at the heart of articulations of identity and difference. Using a discourse of the periodization of history, the Anti-Phrygian states that the difference between "us" and "them" is a result of different understandings of charismata, and also indicates that the Phrygians may have understood charismata to have varied depending upon the age: thus the gifts in the end times are not necessarily the same as those first spiritual gifts. The source argues that the prophets and apostles prophesied in a similar manner (*Pan.* 48.8.1), implying that despite their different periods, they nevertheless are practically the same, and are the standard against which all subsequent prophecy must be judged. A pristine past is the standard against which to judge the present times.

In this section of the Anti-Phrygian source, the Phrygians are also impugned as duped, deluded, false: whatever knowledge they may claim to have through their prophetic charism is part of a delusion. This argument fits well with the Anti-Phrygian's overall rhetorical strategy: to convince the reader/hearer that Maximilla, Montanus, and the Phrygians in general lack "stability of reason" (οὐκ ἐν εὐσταθείᾳ τινὶ λόγου).

This introductory argument is not the only time the Anti-Phrygian challenges the Phrygians' claim to the name "Christian." Elsewhere, the source also accuses the Phrygians of separating from the church over the issue of

---

Tabbernee rightly states that Tertullian and the editor of the *Martyrdom* share a common ethos in the New Prophecy. See Tabbernee, *Montanist Inscriptions*, 56.

[56]*Martyrdom of Saints Perpetua and Felicitas* 1, in Herbert Musurillo, *Acts of the Christian Martyrs* (Oxford: Clarendon, 1994) 107.

charismata, a claim that functions rhetorically to present the Phrygians as voluntary schismatics:

> How then, Phrygians, who have again risen up against us as enemies, and who have changed your title to "Christian," who have risen up in barbarians' battle and have imitated the hostility of the Trojan and Phrygians—how can we be persuaded by you, when you say you have separated from the Church because of charismata? For they are no longer charismata which are other than real charismata and are contrary to the character professed by the Lord, like the ones your prophets speak. You in turn introduce to us again Maximilla: For even your names are different and most frightful, and are not gentle or at all pleasant, but something wild and barbaric. For immediately Maximilla, who belongs among those thus called *kata Phrygas*—listen, children of Christ, to what she says.[57]

Here the Anti-Phrygian mocks the provenance of the movement, and reminds the audience of the traditions of barbarism that surround Phrygia. Phrygia was considered to be a backwater of empire, associated with the cults of Dionysos and Kybele, which were frequently characterized as primitive and frenzied. In Greek myth and culture, this region was not associated with the "pure" Greeks invented by the pan-Hellenic myth of the *Iliad* and echoed in the Roman *Aeneid*. More broadly, in the Greco-Roman world, the division between Greek and barbarian was a method of constructing the educated and verbally coherent self over and against the wild and unintelligible other. We have already seen that Tertullian plays with this trope in two (opposite!) ways: Tertullian uses Marcion's "barbarian" origins to slander him, and Tertullian reclaims a sort of barbarian identity by embracing knowledge from Jerusalem and fishermen rather than Athens and its philosophers.

This convenient trope, this association of the geographical label "Phrygian" with war-like barbarians, constructs the Phrygians as geographically

---

[57]Πῶς τοίνυν, ὦ Φρύγες ἡμῖν πάλιν ἐπαναστάντες πολέμιοι καὶ μεμορφωμένοι εἰς Χριστιανικὴν ἐπίκλησιν, βαρβάρων δὲ ἐπανηρημένοι μάχην καὶ τῶν Τρώων καὶ Φρυγῶν μιμούμενοι τὸ πολέμιον, πῶς πεισθῶμεν ὑμῖν λέγουσι διὰ χαρίσματα ἀφεστάναι τῆς ἐκκλησίας; οὐκέτι γὰρ χαρίσματα εἴη τὰ ἀλλότρια χαρισμάτων ὄντα καὶ παρὰ τὸν χαρακτῆρα τὸν ὑπὸ κυρίου ὑπισχνούμενον, ὡς οἱ καθ᾽ ὑμᾶς προφῆται λέγουσιν. εἰσάγετε δὲ ἡμῖν πάλιν καὶ Μαξίμιλλαν· καὶ γὰρ καὶ τὰ ὀνόματα ὑμῶν διηλλαγμένα καὶ φοβερώτατα καὶ οὔτε προσηνές τι καὶ γλυκύτατον ἔχοντα, ἀλλὰ ἄγριόν τι καὶ βαρβαρικόν. εὐθὺς γὰρ αὕτη ἡ Μαξίμιλλα ἡ παρὰ τοῖς τοιούτοις κατὰ Φρύγας οὕτω καλουμένοις—ἀκούσατε, ὦ παῖδες Χριστοῦ, τί λέγει. *Pan.* 48.12.1–4; Dummer, 235.

and culturally other, as well as returning to the argument that the Phrygian prophets do not sound like the apostles (the passage continues with vague appeals to phrases from Peter, "the Lord," and Paul). Criticism based on the interwoven strands of geography, culture, and language is shuttled into the larger argument about charismata and soundness of mind. Reference to "barbarian" and to the strangeness of Maximilla's name provides a concrete example of difference, and supports the idea of the Phrygians' harsh and nonsensical speech, *logos* literally unravelling. This argument is particularly effective in the midst of a larger attempt to discredit their ecstasies and prophecies as unreasonable and strange. Their very adoption of the name "Christian" is secondary and part of their vice, and even the name of one of their prophets is strange and alienating. And without citing the argument of the other side, the Anti-Phrygian states that these barbarian Phrygians even admit that the nature of their charismata is different from the kind that "the Lord promises."[58] The second person plural derisively addressed to the Phrygians shifts quickly to the second person plural of the audience, who are constructed and appealed to as the "children of Christ."

The theme of alienation or otherness continues in the terminology that the Anti-Phrygian uses to describe "their" charismata: they are τὰ ἀλλότρια, "other than," or "alien to," the true charismata. This accusation resonates with the source's constant statements that when the Phrygians prophesy, they lack sound understanding (ἐρρωμένη διάνοια) and awareness (παρακολουθοῦντες); they are "neither stable nor do they have awareness of reason" (οὐδὲ εὐσταθοῦντες φανοῦνται οὔτε παρακολουθίαν λόγου ἔχοντες, *Pan.* 48.3.10–11; Dummer, 224). Their ecstasy is one of folly (ἐν ἐκστάσει γέγονεν ἀφροσύνης, *Pan.* 48.5.8; Dummer, 227). The accusation that the Phrygians have risen up in a "barbarian's battle" is part of the larger discourse of rationality and madness, and a fragment of a larger attempt to discredit the Phrygians' ecstasies and prophecies as unreasonable and strange.

## Reason and Mental Instability in the Anti-Phrygian

Two major sections of *Pan.* 48.1.4–13.8 work to establish the reasonableness of true prophecy and the unsound mental functions of the Phrygians.

---

[58]*Pan.* 48.12.2. If the New Prophecy did make such a claim, it might have been based in a historiography (like Tertullian's) that divides time into various periods and thinks that the Paraclete would bring charismata that are different from those at the time of Jesus.

A catalog of great prophetic men[59] and of their encounters with the divine forms the foundation of the Anti-Phrygian's argument about how reasonable true prophecy is. Each figure is applauded as proof of rationality in prophecy: "And you see how it is evident that everything was said in truth by the prophets, and by a sound mind and with sober reasoning, and not in madness."[60] The catalog of great men is mirrored by a catalog of several of Montanus's and Maximilla's oracles, along with refutations of their soundness. As the Anti-Phrygian source contrasts the prophets of old and the Phrygians, it makes the Phrygians foils to the true, sound, and sober prophets. The source reinforces by sheer repetition the importance of the true prophets' sound and sober thought, while never specifically defining either the criteria by which it selects them, or the concepts of rationality or an unsound mind.

Even more interesting, while Montanus and Maximilla are cast as less than sane, the Anti-Phrygian never accuses them of madness in the way in which we might expect. Their behavior is not described as frenzied. The author tells no stories of ascents to heaven and painful, fatal falls to earth, as Eusebius's anonymous source does of Theodotus, a "trustee" (ἐπίτροπος) of Montanus (*Hist. eccl.* 5.16.14). The Phrygians' lack of sound mind seems to consist in their being bad interpreters of Scripture (especially in debates over LXX Gen 2:21 and LXX Ps 115:2), in the failure of their prophecies to come true (Maximilla's first cited oracle), or in their advancement of claims that compete with the role and power of God or of Christ.

What then is at stake for the Anti-Phrygian source, if these frontal attacks against Montanus and Maximilla, representatives of the Phrygians, are full of terms denoting madness and instability of thought, and yet the examples given are so bland, relatively speaking? The Anti-Phrygian source has several concerns, some of which remain more or less suppressed. First and foremost, it is concerned to argue that each legitimate prophet's actions and speech are not compulsory. These prophets talk back to God, and refuse to follow

---

[59]Exclusion of women may be deliberate, given the number of women that seem to be associated with New Prophecy and later accusations that so-called Montanists appeal to past female prophets and allow women to have roles in liturgy and church office. See, e.g., Eusebius's anonymous source, recorded in *Hist. eccl.* 5.17.1–2; Origen, *Comm. Matt.* 28; idem, *Catenae on Paul's Epistles to the Corinthians* 14.36; *Debate of a Montanist and an Orthodox Christian*; Ambrosiaster, *Ad Timotheum prima* 3.11; and especially Epiphanius, *Pan.* 49.1–3.

[60]καὶ ὁρᾷς ὡς ἔστιν ἰδεῖν τὰ πάντα ἐν ἀληθείᾳ παρὰ τοῖς προφήταις εἰρημένα καὶ ἐν ἐρρωμένῃ διανοίᾳ καὶ σώφρονι λογισμῷ, καὶ οὐκ ἐν παραπληξίᾳ. *Pan.* 48.7.10; Dummer, 229.

God's commands if the commands seem puzzling or nonsensical. The prophet speaks in his or her own voice, not in the voice of God; that is, the prophet is not a puppet of a divine ventriloquist, or compelled or out of control in any way. Second, the Anti-Phrygian wants to define ecstasy in such a way as to preclude *mania* and folly from the purview of Christian prophecy (by "Christian," Israelite prophets are also meant). The Anti-Phrygian proceeds by establishing a canon of great men as exemplars of "true" prophecy, and by citing oracles from Montanus and Maximilla that can be undermined in various ways.

Concerned throughout to emphasize that nothing happens through compulsion to prophets or to those in ecstasy, the Anti-Phrygian argues against the idea that a prophet would speak as God—in God's own voice. A prophet speaking with God's voice might be understood to be merely an instrument of the divine, a vessel for God's communication that is hollowed out, volitionless, unable to speak freely. The image of the divine speaking through the prophet appears frequently in antiquity, across cults.[61] We have seen this image of a prophet in Philo, and even Paul hints at it.

We see this anxiety about who is speaking as the divine and who is speaking for the divine in an interpretive "correction" that the Anti-Phrygian makes. The Anti-Phrygian hints that some understand the accusation that everyone is a liar (in LXX Ps 115:2: "I said in my ecstasy, 'Everyone is a liar.'") to be God's words, not David's. "In saying, 'I said,'" the Anti-Phrygian insists, "he was speaking for himself, and, concerning all people, he said, that they lie" (καὶ Δαυὶδ δὲ ὁ ἅγιος εἶπεν ὅτι >> <εἶπον ἐγώ·> πᾶς ἄνθρωπος ψεύστης<<. ὁ δὲ λέγων >>εἶπον ἐγώ<< ἰδίᾳ ἔλεγεν, καὶ περὶ τῶν ἀνθρώπων ὅτι, ἔλεγε, ψεύδονται, *Pan.* 48.7.6; Dummer, 228–29).[62] The sheer repetition of forms of λέγω in this one sentence—three times,

---

[61]On the body as the instrument of the soul, and the soul as the instrument of God, see, for example, Plutarch, *The Oracles at Delphi No Longer Given in Verse* 404B–C; on the soul not acting of its own volition, see 404F. But also see Plutarch, *The Obsolescence of Oracles* 414E: "it is foolish and childish in the extreme to imagine that the god himself after the manner of ventriloquists . . . enters into the bodies of his prophets and prompts their utterances, employing their mouths and voices as instruments" (*Plutarch: Moralia* [trans. Frank C. Babbitt; LCL; Cambridge, Mass.: Harvard University Press, 1936] 5:377). While of course each text has its own rhetorical context and reasons for depicting (or not depicting) a prophet in this way, many hold a rather neutral attitude to the idea that God would speak through a person, and that God's voice would be heard directly in the prophet's ecstatic utterance—that God would speak as Godself through a human.

[62]εἶπον ἐγω is omitted in the manuscript the first time, although it obviously belongs.

not counting the quotation of εἶπον ἐγώ—indicates that the Anti-Phrygian is concerned about who did the talking. David spoke for himself about the vast difference between humans and God: "he granted truth-telling to the Lord alone" (μόνῳ κυρίῳ τὸ ἀληθεύειν ἐπέδωκε, *Pan.* 48.7.7; Dummer, 229). This knowledge that David attained in an ecstasy "evidences the true spirit, which spoke in the prophets and revealed to them the depths of the precise knowledge of God" (ἵνα δείξῃ τὸ ἀληθινὸν πνεῦμα, τὸ ἐν προφ-ήταις λαλῆσαν καὶ τὰ βάθη αὐτοῖς ἀποκαλύψαν τῆς τοῦ θεοῦ γνώσεως ἀκριβείας, *Pan.* 48.7.7; Dummer, 229). Emphasis on the true spirit and God's truth-telling serve not only to construct the Anti-Phrygian's identity and that of his or her community over and against the Phrygians, but also to limit a "precise knowledge of God" to the few prophets in whom the true spirit moved. Human inability to tell truth is linked to a human inability to perceive correctly, the Anti-Phrygian would argue—it has to do with the fact that humans don't truly *know*. The Anti-Phrygian's interpretation of Ps 115:2 emphasizes the difference between humans—liars all—and the divine. As the source writes, "[David], astounded and amazed by God's *philanthropia*, was amazed by the things which the Lord had proclaimed to him" (ἐκπληττόμενος δὲ καὶ θαυμάζων τὴν τοῦ θεοῦ φιλανθρωπίαν καὶ τὰ αὐτῷ παρὰ τοῦ κυρίου κεκηρυγμένα ἐθαύμαζε, *Pan.* 48.7.6; Dum-mer, 229). God's *philanthropia* consists not in giving ecstasies which lead to new knowledge, but in God's mercy toward humans, whose knowledge falls so short of truth. The Anti-Phrygian implies that the Phrygian prophets just don't get it; they hubristically claim to speak as God, instead of rely-ing upon (ancient evidences of) God's *philanthropia*. Moreover, the source undercuts the Phrygians' claims to knowledge through the spirit: they are not like those to whom the Spirit has revealed the "depths of the precise knowledge of God."

The Anti-Phrygian source, in its interpretation of David's speech, assures the reader that God does not use David as an instrument; it is not God but David who insists that everyone is a liar. The Anti-Phrygian does not often directly assault the idea of humans being compelled by God, but instead ac-complishes this critique by deliberately misreading oracles from Montanus and Maximilla. That is, although the idea that the divine speaks through a prophet in the first person is common in antiquity, the Anti-Phrygian deliber-ately reads Montanus's and Maximilla's oracles as evidence of their unstable minds and as examples of their insane willingness to compete with God or with Christ. The Anti-Phrygian distinguishes between the true prophets, who ascribe all of their prophecy to God by the introductory phrase, "Thus says the Lord" (see *Pan.* 48.10.1–2; 48.13.5),[63] and the false prophets Montanus and Maximilla, who falsely and hubristically take on the voice of the divine as their own.

The Anti-Phrygian source argues against speaking in God's voice and refutes the idea that humans have access to certain kinds of knowledge from the divine. It does so in part by critiquing three oracles of Maximilla and Montanus. The source opposes these oracles because, as it claims, their content seems to compete with God or with Christ. David Aune, in his survey of prophecy in the ancient Mediterranean, discusses what he calls the "oracle of self-commendation," in which "the speaker claims to be an authentic vehicle of divine revelation. Functionally, self-commendation oracles serve to legitimate the medium through whom the divinity is thought to reveal his will."[64] Of the seven oracles of Montanus and Maximilla cited by the Anti-Phrygian, three fall under this oracular type. The self-commendation form is generally only an introduction to an oracle or part of a larger context of prophecies. The Anti-Phrygian, however, cites these as the entire oracles: it is as if the readers are given only an introductory line, and no more, and then the oracles are refuted on this basis,[65] as though self-commendation were the sum of the Phrygians' prophecy. The Anti-Phrygian interprets these introductions to oracles as the oracles themselves, and as examples of the Phrygian prophets' hubristic understanding of themselves as God.

Montanus is said to have proclaimed, "I am the Lord God, the Pantokrator, dwelling in a man" (*Pan.* 48.11.1). The Anti-Phrygian states that Scripture demonstrates the "course (ἀκολουθία) of the Holy Spirit's teaching"; the Phrygian prophets are beside, or outside of, this true course. Scripture also gives warnings about "the counterfeits of the strange spirit and the opposites of the truth."[66] The accusation is that Montanus comes in his own name — and Jesus had warned that "one will come in his own name, and you will receive

---

[63] Aune (*Prophecy in Early Christianity*, 89–90) labels this "the messenger formula."

[64] Ibid., 70–71.

[65] For a very different interpretation, which understands many of these oracles in terms of second-century theological debates, see Sheila McGinn, "The 'Montanist' Oracles and Prophetic Theology," *Stud. Pat.* 31 (1997) 128–35. McGinn tries to revive Gillespie's idea (see p. 92 n. 91, above) of early Christian prophets as theologians. This interpretation squeezes too much out of the oracles and does not sufficiently take into account their formal structure.

[66] τὰ μιμηλὰ τοῦ ἀλλοτρίου πνεύματος καὶ τὰ ἀντίθετα πρὸς τὴν ἀλήθειαν. *Pan.* 48.11.1; Dummer, 233–34.

him" (John 5:43)—and that Montanus is "in total disagreement with the sacred scriptures."[67] Montanus has claimed to be the Father, and has not announced Christ as "all the ancient [prophets]" did. The Anti-Phrygian chooses to read this beginning of an oracle in the worst possible sense of Aune's "oracle of self-commendation": Montanus points to himself, and in doing so glorifies himself, not Christ, thereby demonstrating how far from Christ he is. The Anti-Phrygian delivers a final, particularly painful blow, because it discounts the charismata the Phrygians held so dear: instead of having received the charismata, Montanus parts ways with them.[68]

The Anti-Phrygian treats another of Montanus's oracles in a similar way, citing it as, "Neither angel nor elder, but I the Lord, God the Father, have come" (*Pan.* 48.11.9). Again, the source misreads the oracle, arguing that Christ only said he was the Son, while Montanus goes so far as to claim he is the Father. While the Anti-Phrygian's refutation of the previous oracle (*Pan.* 48.11.1) accused Montanus of a strange spirit, of counterfeiting, and of standing opposite to truth, the refutation of this oracle separates Montanus from both Christ and the church and gifts by stating that "Christ has given in *truth* every ecclesiastical gift (χάρισμα) in the holy church."[69] The Anti-Phrygian claims to speak for the church (note the use of ἐκκλησία and its cognate) and claims that this church has been given charismata "in truth," in contrast to Montanus' falsehood.

Finally, the Anti-Phrygian derides Maximilla's oracle, "Do not listen to me, but listen to Christ" (*Pan.* 48.12.3). Although this oracle may appear to be precisely the sort that the Anti-Phrygian would encourage—it points not to the prophet, but to God—instead the source argues that although this seems to glorify Christ, it does not. Again reality and truth are rhetorically constructed on the side of the Anti-Phrygian:

> While she lies, she speaks the truth, even if she does not want to. For she says rightly not to listen to her, but to Christ. For many times the unclean spirits are compelled to condemn themselves as

[67]*Pan.* 48.11.4. One of the accusations is that Montanus asserted that he was greater than Christ, since a greater era had dawned with the coming of the Paraclete.

[68]The Anti-Phrygian then reminds the reader that even if Jesus does say that he will send the Paraclete (John 16), this Paraclete will glorify Jesus (*Pan.* 48.11.5). Even from our spotty sources, it is clear that the Paraclete is especially significant for the Phrygians.

[69]My emphasis. Χριστὸν μὴ δοξάζεν, ὃν πᾶν χάρισμα ἐκκλησιαστικὸν ἐν ἐκκλησίᾳ τῇ ἁγίᾳ δοθὲν ἐν ἀληθείᾳ ἐδόξασεν. *Pan.* 48.11.9; Dummer, 235.

being not of the truth, and, willing or unwilling, to show who their
Lord is, on account of necessity.[70]

The vocabulary here is not insignificant—the Anti-Phrygian source picks
up the terms of the oracle that it discusses next (*Pan.* 48.13.1). In that
oracle, according to the source, Maximilla both uses the phrase "willing
or unwilling" (θέλοντα καὶ μὴ θέλοντα) and refers to being compelled
(ἠναγκασμένον). To discredit Maximilla, the Anti-Phrygian argues that she
was not in a rational state (παρηκολούθει), since someone rational does
not condemn him- or herself. Moreover, she could not have been speaking
in the Spirit because the Spirit is "one," not divided against itself.

The oracle above, and the Anti-Phrygian's reaction to it, expose most
clearly the Anti-Phrygian's concerns. Issues of rationality, compulsion, will,
God's *philanthropia*, and truth and falsehood converge in this oracle and its
refutation. As the Anti-Phrygian cites it, Maximilla's oracle is syntactically
confusing:

> The Lord has sent me to be a founder and revealer and interpreter
> of this labor and covenant and promise; I am compelled, willing
> and unwilling, to know the knowledge of God.
>
> ἀπέστειλέ με κύριος τούτου τοῦ πόνου καὶ τῆς συνθήκης καὶ
> τῆς ἐπαγγελίας αἱρετιστὴν μηνυτὴν ἑρμηνευτήν, ἠναγκασμένον,
> θέλοντα καὶ μὴ θέλοντα, γνωθεῖν γνῶσιν θεοῦ. (*Pan.* 48.13.1;
> Dummer, 237)

Although Maximilla proffers this oracle, the participles which describe her
(ἠναγκασμένον, θέλοντα καὶ μὴ θέλοντα) are masculine. Karl Holl believes
this to be a "careless oversight" on the part of Epiphanius's source.[71] The
Anti-Phrygian may indeed have carelessly elided the gender of the participles
with the masculine of the preceding nouns (αἱρετιστὴν μηνυτὴν ἑρμηνευ-
τήν). But masculine participles may be an intentional manipulation that
makes possible the source's later accusation that "she claimed to compel
the willing and the unwilling" (with the masculine singular as a generic)

---

[70]αὕτη δὲ ἀληθεύει ψευδομένη, καὶ μὴ βουλομένη. καλῶς γὰρ λέγει φάσκουσα μὴ
αὐτῆς ἀκούειν, ἀλλὰ Χπιστοῦ. πολλάκις γὰρ τὰ ἀκάθαρτα πνεύματα ἀναγκάζεται ἑαυτὰ
καθαιρεῖν, <ὡς> οὐκ ὄντα τῆς ἀληθείας, καὶ ὑποφαίνειν τὸν κύριον αὐτῶν, θέλοντα καὶ
μὴ θέλοντα, δι' ἀνάγκην. *Pan.* 48.12.6; Dummer, 235–36.

[71]"wohl Flüchtigkeitsversehen"; Holl, *Pan. Haer.*, 237.

and its biting critique of her claims to knowledge: "For she did not teach to those who were willing the knowledge of God—a knowledge which she did not know—nor did she compel the unwilling."[72]

In the Anti-Phrygian text, Maximilla's oracle is immediately followed, as expected, by a statement regarding the incorrectness of its message and its source in a strange spirit. This is not surprising since, as we have seen, the Anti-Phrygian has already used the oracle's terminology to refer to unclean spirits who are compelled to denounce themselves (*Pan.* 48.12.6). Again turning the oracle against Maximilla, the Anti-Phrygian adopts her language of compulsion or necessity and reverses it, stating that she "denounced herself out of necessity, not acting freely of her own opinion" (ἠναγκασμένον ἑαυτὸν ἀποφήναντα, οὐχ ἑκουσίᾳ γνώμῃ, *Pan.* 48.13.3; Dummer, 237).

The importance of this issue of compulsion is evident in the fact that the argument turns suddenly to the Anti-Phrygian's insistence that

> Our Lord was not sent against his will to the world, nor was he sent with compulsion by the Father, but together with the Father and the Holy Spirit he willed to give himself up. And just as he, together with the Father, wanted to give—without compulsion, but through the excess of God's love for humanity—grace to each, so also those whom he called, he called by [their own] choosing, not laying necessity nor placing a prisoner's collar [on them]. (*Pan.* 48.13.3–4)

This passage's abrupt shift to a discussion of the death of Jesus makes sense if, as I have argued above, the central concern of the Anti-Phrygian is to work against the idea that God compels or forces anyone. God is not a God of compulsion, and God's *philanthropia* does not consist in God-given ecstasies.

The Anti-Phrygian avoids mentioning genuine Pauline materials, despite this oracle's use of ἑρμηνεῖα, a term Paul uses twice to discuss spiritual gifts, and despite the importance of Paul's epistles to the conversation about charis-

---

[72]καὶ γὰρ καὶ Μαξίμιλλα τοὺς θέλοντας καὶ μὴ θέλοντας ἔλεγεν ἀναγκάζειν. . . . οὔτε γὰρ θέλοντας ἐδίδαξε γνῶσιν θεοῦ ἣν οὐκ ᾔδει οὐδὲ τοὺς μὴ θέλοντας ἠνάγκασεν. *Pan.* 48.13.7; Dummer, 238. See Williams's note to Epiphanius, *Pan.* 48.13.7 (2:19 n. 69). It is also possible, given the polemic immediately following, that Epiphanius's source knew that Maximilla's oracle was spoken in the voice of Christ—that is, that Christ through Maximilla proclaimed this oracle, necessitating masculine adjectives and thus provoking the Anti-Phrygian's argument regarding Christ's volition.

mata and prophecy.[73] This is in part because of the danger that Maximilla's
oracle will be understood in terms of Paul's "fool's speech" in 2 Cor 12:11, which
Paul claims to have been compelled (ὑμεῖς με ἠναγκάσατε), and because
of the ambiguity of Paul's stance on tongues, prophecy, and interpretation
in 1 Cor 12:10 and 14:26, where Paul talks about the role of the "interpreter
of tongues."[74]

The Anti-Phrygian presents the Phrygians as compelled by unclean spirits and thus undercuts whatever knowledge they claim to reveal. We have
already seen the Anti-Phrygian source argue that God's *philanthropia* consists not in God's bringing frenzied ecstasies (and strange knowledge) upon
humans—and thus, perhaps, compelling them into ecstasies—but in God's
granting of an ecstasy of sleep and rest, in the case of Adam (LXX Gen 2:
21), or an ecstasy of amazement at God's grace, in the case of David (LXX
Ps 115:2). The Anti-Phrygian concludes its critique of Maximilla's oracle
with what I believe is an intentional misreading of ἠναγκασμένον, θέλοντα
καὶ μὴ θέλοντα, γνωθεῖν γνῶσιν θεοῦ as meaning that Maximilla claimed

---

[73]The only place where the Anti-Phrygian quotes a genuine Pauline passage (and, notably,
one from 1 Corinthians, which one would expect to be of broader interest to the source) is 1
Cor 11:1 ("Be imitators of me . . ."; see *Pan.* 48.12.5).

[74] Ἑρμηνεία is used twice, in 1 Cor 12:10 and 14:26, during discussions of the charismata
given by the Spirit. According to 1 Corinthians, "interpreter of tongues" is one of the roles
given by the Spirit (see 1 Cor 2). The most interesting reference containing the verb ἀναγκάζω
comes in 2 Cor 12:11, where Paul cries, "I have been a fool! You forced me to it, for I ought to
have been commended by you" (Γέγονα ἄφρων, ὑμεῖς με ἠναγκάσατε. ἐγὼ γὰρ ὤφειλον ὑφ᾽
ὑμῶν συνίστασθαι· οὐδὲν γὰρ ὑστέρησα τῶν ὑπερλίαν ἀποστόλων εἰ καὶ οὐδέν εἰμι). This
passage is fascinating in light of the Anti-Phrygian's argument. First, the idea of compulsion is
associated with the idea of foolishness, with the idea that one is at less than one's full mental
capacity, something that the Anti-Phrygian opposes. Second, the passage is part of Paul's
reluctant narrative of his trance or vision (see ch. 2, above). Paul is cagey about whether
he experienced *ekstasis*—"I know a person in Christ who fourteen years ago was caught
up to the third heaven—whether in the body or out of the body I do not know; God knows.
And I know that such a person—whether in the body or out of the body I do not know; God
knows—was caught up into Paradise and heard things that are not to be told, that no mortal
is permitted to repeat" (2 Cor 12:2–4 NRSV). Third, this vision is followed by an experience
of bodily harm, and Paul implies that God keeps him weak and in suffering, whether Paul
desires the experience or not: "Therefore, to keep me from being too elated, a thorn was given
me in the flesh, a messenger of Satan to torment me, to keep me from being too elated. Three
times I appealed to the Lord about this, that it would leave me, but he said to me, 'My grace is
sufficient for you, for power is made perfect in weakness'" (2 Cor 12:7b–9a NRSV). Embedded
in this last passage, we see not only revelatory speech from the divinity, but also some sort of

to compel people, willing or unwilling, to know God. "All those in the world do not know what Maximilla's name is," the author counters, as evidence that she compelled no one.[75] The Anti-Phrygian opposes the idea that God compelled prophets, or spoke through them in an unmediated way.[76]

## The Discourse of Periodizing History: The Catalog of Past Prophets

The Anti-Phrygian source's resistance to the idea that God compels prophets is further demonstrated by the way in which it constructs a tradition of great prophets, and aligns itself and its community with these great and rational prophets. The genre of this section seems to be a florilegium, a catalog of biblical *exempla* trotted out on occasions like this, when prophecy and ecstasy were on trial.[77] This method of presenting *exempla*, as we

---

bodily harm which may be sent from Satan, but which is certainly condoned by God. Thus we find at least three of the Anti-Phrygian's least favorite ideas here—that Paul is compelled, that he admits a kind of folly, that God has inflicted something on Paul against Paul's will.

[75]*Pan.* 48.13.8.

[76]The Anti-Phrygian seems to claim that the Phrygians' ecstatically revealed knowledge attacks the holy church's way of life, especially with regard to marriage and virginity. *Pan.* 48.8.6–9.8 is the only point in the extant fragment of the source where concrete concerns about Christian practice (outside of prophecy) emerge. This section reads as a kind of excursus on the themes of virginity and marriage, with "Paul's" injunction in 1 Tim 4:3 (regarding some who "forbid marriage and enjoin abstinence from foods which God created to be received with thanksgiving by those who believe and know the truth") wielded against "you," that is, the Phrygians. This passage is part of a larger debate of the second and third centuries, which centered around Paul and his views on marriage. 1 Timothy attempts, for example, to curb the genuine Paul's advocacy of singleness in 1 Corinthians 7, while the *Acts of Thecla* attempts to place Paul in the opposite light, as someone who believes that virginity is salvific, and attracts the beautiful Thecla to such a life. The Anti-Phrygian may be attacking the content of the Phrygians' oracles without providing the reader with that content: the Phrygians may have claimed to know, through ecstasies, that second marriages and even marriage in the first place are dubious in God's eyes.

[77]Another such catalog can be found in Eusebius's anonymous source (*Hist. eccl.* 5.17.3–4); the source indicates that the New Prophets themselves compiled such lists: "But they cannot show that any prophet, either of those in the Old Testament or of those in the New, was inspired in this way; they can boast neither of Agabus, nor of Judas, nor of Silas, nor of the daughters of Philip, nor of Ammia in Philadelphia, nor of Quadratus, nor of any others who do not belong to them" (ET Lake, 1:485). This concluding phrase indicates that the New Prophecy claimed prophets as their own spiritual lineage. It is interesting to note that this list and the Anti-Phrygian's catalog share only the figure of Agabus, and that Eusebius's source names female prophets.

have seen in Tertullian before, is a well-known rhetorical technique for proving one's point.[78] The catalog echoes with forms of the word *eksta-sis*. In fact, the list may have been first compiled by those who wanted to demonstrate the legitimacy of ecstasy by referring to authoritative or popular early Christian texts. But the Anti-Phrygian answers this catalog point by point, admitting that the term "ecstasy" may arise, but honing the meaning of "ecstasy" so as to exclude certain associations. The driving concern in this catalog of great figures, like the driving motivation of the refutation of oracles, is to prove that no true prophet spoke in an ecstasy that occurred under compulsion.

The Anti-Phrygian's argument about ecstasy and compulsion is rooted in a discourse of the periodization of history which fits so well with our present-day understandings of linear, chronological time that it is easy to universalize this idea of history. It is easy to employ again the model of charismatic origins and decline of spirit into institution, and to be unaware of the discursive nature of the Anti-Phrygian's presentation. But the source's assumption that in the ancient times of the prophets and apostles, there was prophecy, but no longer, is launched in a particular rhetorical setting of debates over prophecy and history. The Anti-Phrygian emphasizes figures from the Hebrew scriptures, who bring rhetorical heft because of the antiquity of Judaism. Examples are distinctly from the past; the author avoids any present or recent prophets. Indeed, because of the authority associated with antiquity, the source here rhetorically constructs a catalog that gains authority through a list of prophets historically located in some more God-infused distant time.

Within what I am calling this "great men" catalog, ten men and one group are named: Moses, Isaiah, Ezekiel, Daniel, Adam, Peter, David, Abraham, those who saw the angels as Christ ascended ("men of Galilee"), Agabus, and Paul himself, who is included on the basis of quotations from the non-Pauline 1 and 2 Timothy. A glance at this catalog is in itself surprising: some of the figures mentioned do not immediately come to mind as great prophets in scripture. While the reasons for selecting these particular figures are opaque, we can hypothesize that they represented important prooftexts in the ongoing discussion of ecstasy and prophecy; the Anti-Phrygian turns

---

Other such lists of great figures occur in Sirach and in Hebrews. Thanks to AnneMarie Luijendijk and Melanie Johnson-DeBaufre for pointing this out to me in conversation. Here too the catalogs function to construct a community's self-understanding, both in terms of lineage/genealogy and in terms of certain qualities toward which the community is encouraged.

[78]See Kennedy, *Quintilian*, 66–71.

to these authoritative figures to control them rhetorically, demonstrating that their prophecies were in no way compulsory or tainted with madness.

The catalog starts with four figures—Moses, Isaiah, Ezekiel, and Daniel—who are used as evidence that "a prophet always spoke with fixedness of reasoning powers and with awareness, and spoke forth (φθέγγομαι) by the Holy Spirit" (*Pan.* 48.3.4). The emphasis is on speech and sight: the text continues, "saying all things formidably like Moses, 'the servant of God and faithful in (his) house, who saw'—he is called 'the prophet' in the Old Testament." The brief citation in the Anti-Phrygian source (Μωυσῆς ὁ θεράπων τοῦ θεοῦ καὶ πιστὸς ἐν οἴκῳ ὁ βλέπων) serves as a prompt for the passage in LXX Num 12:8, as Dummer's edition rightly points out. In context, it reads:

> And the Lord came down in a pillar of cloud, and stood at the door of the tent, and called Aaron and Miriam; and they both came forward. And he said, "Hear my words: If there is a prophet among you, I the Lord make myself known to him in a vision, I speak with him in a dream. Not so with my servant Moses; he is entrusted with all my house. With him I speak mouth to mouth, clearly, and not in dark speech; and he beholds the form of the Lord."[79]

Moses was the quintessential prophet in Jewish apologetics and discussion at this time, and his face-to-face (literally "mouth-to-mouth") encounter with the divine is the subject of Paul's discussion in 2 Cor 3:12–18—an interpretation that the Anti-Phrygian ignores.[80] By this brief allusion to Numbers, the Anti-Phrygian intends to conjure up Moses' unmediated and unusual contact with God, which happens in clarity and not in enigmatic riddles, and which happens in the act of seeing, just as Philo's significant moments of contemplation were joined with intense visual clarity.[81]

---

[79]Num 12:6–8b; the LXX reads: Ἀκούσατε τῶν λόγων μου· ἐὰν γένηται προφήτης ὑμῶν κυρίῳ ἐν ὁράματι αὐτῷ γνωσθήσομαι καὶ ἐν ὕπνῳ λαλήσω αὐτῷ. οὐχ οὕτως ὁ θεράπων μου Μωυσῆς· ἐν ὅλῳ τῷ οἴκῳ μου πιστός ἐστιν· στόμα κατὰ στόμα λαλήσω αὐτῷ, ἐν εἴδει καὶ οὐ δι᾽ αἰνιγμάτων, καὶ τὴν δόξαν κυρίου εἶδεν.

[80]According to Daniel Boyarin, midrashic sources stress Moses' intimate level of contract with God by stating that all the prophets saw through seven mirrors, but Moses saw through only one. Personal communication, spring 2000. Paul's discussion of Moses in 2 Corinthians 3 is surprising because it offers an unusual interpretation of the veil over Moses' face: instead of understanding the veil to protect the Israelites from the glory of God shining in Moses' face, Paul understands the veil to conceal the fading of that glory.

[81]See p. 43, above.

The Anti-Phrygian's interest in sight is confirmed by what immediately follows; the text next discusses the vision (ὄρασις) of Isaiah, who saw the Lord. Forms of the verb ὁράω are used three times, and the words of the Lord have to do with sense perception: "Hear indeed and you will not understand; and see indeed, and you will not perceive" (*Pan.* 48.3.5; see Isa 6:9–10). The Anti-Phrygian emphasizes that the blunted sense perception of the people stands in contrast to the clear speech of Isaiah as he conveys these words. The source reads: "And after hearing by the Lord, he [Isaiah] came to the people and said, 'The Lord says these things.' " The Anti-Phrygian follows this introductory marker of oracular speech (a variant of the "Thus says the Lord" discussed above) with the question, "Do you not see that the speech is that of an aware person, and not of one in ecstasy, nor is the oracle given like that of ecstatic understanding?"[82] Thus the text implicitly hedges against a "wrong" interpretation of Isaiah's vision and description of it, an interpretation that might emphasize that Isaiah himself was hearing and not understanding, seeing and not perceiving. The Anti-Phrygian argues that Isaiah was not in some sort of ecstatic frenzy marked by jumbled sense perception when he saw the Lord on a throne, and the seraphim and cherubim, and that afterwards, recounting these events, Isaiah's speech was also comprehensible.

The Anti-Phrygian continues to argue for the clarity of the true prophet's mind. Ezekiel, for example, is proven to have a mind which is sound and rational (ἐρρωμένην ἔχων τὴν διάνοιαν καὶ παρακολουθοῦσαν) because he resists the command of the Lord to "bake bread on human dung." Ezekiel is clearly praised for having resisted God's "threat" (ἀπειλή).[83] Acts 10:14 is later cited because similarly Peter resists God's command to eat unclean animals: "he did not obey like a person of unsound mind, but told the Lord, 'Not so, Lord.' "[84] The Anti-Phrygian thus rejects the idea that God would

---

[82]οὐχ ὁρᾷς ὅτι παρακολουθοῦντος ὁ λόγος καὶ οὐκ ἐξισταμένου, οὔτε ὡς ἐξισταμένης διανοίας ἡ φθογγὴ ἀπεδίδοτο; *Pan.* 48.3.6–7; Dummer, 224.

[83]The story of Ezekiel is full of such commands, which do sound like threats against his very life. For example, Ezekiel 3:14 reads, "The spirit lifted me up and bore me away; I went in bitterness in the heat of my spirit, the hand of the Lord being strong upon me"; the effect of this is that Ezekiel sat "stunned, for seven days" (3:15) until the Lord came to him and commanded him to warn the house of Israel. If Ezekiel obeys, God assures him, he will save his own life (3:19).

[84]*Pan.* 48.7.5; see also 48.8.3. Regarding later interpretations of Acts 10, see François Bovon, *De Vocatione Gentium: Histoire de l'interprétation d'Act. 10,1–11, 18 dans les six premiers siècles* (Tübingen: Mohr/Siebeck, 1967) esp. 92–165. Bovon points to the importance of Acts 10:17 in texts associated with the "Montanist" controversy.

compel a human to do something that s/he did not want to do or thought was wrong—the very sort of compulsion that Maximilla embraces in her oracle, in the Anti-Phrygian's opinion.[85]

By calling up a catalog of great past prophets, the Anti-Phrygian source seeks to control the definition of ecstasy. It did something similar in its interpretation of LXX Gen 2:21 as Adam's "ecstasy of rest" and sleep, as we recall from chapter 1, above. The Anti-Phrygian returns to a refrain about the difference between "them"—who are unsound in mind—and "the prophets" who are reasonable. The means by which one discerns the unsoundness of one's ecstasy and the stability of another's prophecy, however, are difficult to define. The Anti-Phrygian attempts to define ecstasy in a way that suits his or her purposes and that distances the "true" or "real" church and its charismata from those which the Phrygians claim to have.

The Anti-Phrygian interrupts the catalog of great men with a reminder of the contrast between these *exempla* of rational understanding and "them," the Phrygians: "But when they profess to prophesy, it is plain that they are not sound of mind and rational. Their words are ambiguous and odd, with nothing right about them."[86] This argument appeals to common sense, but is strikingly devoid of content. By what criteria does one discern that words are "ambiguous and odd"? The Anti-Phrygian attempts to bolster this accusation by citing another oracle: "Montanus, for instance, says, 'Behold, the human is

---

[85]Clarity of mind is again emphasized by the story of Daniel, who solved the riddles of both the content of Nebuchadnezzar's dreams and their interpretation. Discussion of Daniel is peppered with significant terms. He is celebrated for his "healthy/powerful and stable condition and the superiority of his gift" (ἐρρωμένη καταστάσει καὶ ὑπερβολῇ χαρίσματος, *Pan.* 48.3.10; Dummer, 224). The term gift (χάρισμα) recalls to the listener's mind the discussion about gifts in Paul, and the importance of charismata to the author and the author's opponents. Reference is also made to Daniel's great wisdom, and the spirit who gives this wisdom "in reality" (ὄντως) instructs "the prophet and those who, through the prophet, are deemed worthy of the teaching of the truth." The ante is upped here as the reference to Daniel shifts from evidence of Daniel's gift to references to "truth." This deployment of terms denoting the "real" from the false is a strategy similar to that used in the discussion of Maximilla's oracle. The author next moves to contrast the exemplum of Daniel with something less than true—an oracle of Montanus. The source contrasts the truth of the ancient prophet, who has a true gift of the Holy Spirit, and who "has an understanding that was most extraordinary, beyond any human," to the meaningless and strange phrases of Montanus, in whom, the Anti-Phrygian insists, the Holy Spirit "never spoke" (*Pan.* 48.4.3).

[86]ἃ δὲ οὗτοι ἐπαγγέλλονται προφητεύειν, οὐδὲ εὐσταθοῦντες φανοῦνται οὔτε παρακολουθίαν λόγου ἔχοντες. λοξὰ γὰρ τὰ παρ' αὐτῶν ῥήματα καὶ σκαληνὰ καὶ οὐδεμιᾶς ὀρθότητος ἐχόμενα. *Pan.* 48.3.11; Dummer, 224.

like a lyre and I, I fly over as a plectron. The human sleeps, and I, I am fully awake. Behold, the Lord is the one who makes human hearts ecstatic, and gives a heart to humans.'"[87] The trope of a human as an instrument played by the divine or by divine spirits is no innovation in antiquity. As we have seen, it is even found in Philo (*Her.* 266); it is also found in Christian texts such as Hippolytus's *De antichristo* 2.[88] But the Anti-Phrygian argues that this oracle is defective in multiple ways. Montanus's words are not similar to those of true prophets. Aspersions are cast upon the vocabulary itself:

> For he said this, "I fly" and "I strike" and "I am awake" and "The Lord has made hearts ecstatic"; these are the words of an ecstatic and not at all of one who is aware, but of one who shows forth another character beside the character of the Holy Spirit who has spoken by the prophets.[89]

The Anti-Phrygian models his or her own audience—that is, attempts to convince the reader to have a certain disposition—and flatters them by placing them on the side of the rational and true prophets by stating that "those who are aware and who have received the word of benefit and care for their own life"[90] condemn Montanus's speech and boastful attempt to enroll himself among the prophets. Moreover, the Anti-Phrygian has tried to appeal to, but even more to construct, a certain kind of audience by calling upon those who are concerned about their lives and about the "word of benefit." Reference to this "word of benefit" calls to mind Paul's

---

[87]Εὐθὺς γὰρ ὁ Μοντανός φησιν >>ἰδού, ὁ ἄνθρωπος ὡσεὶ λύρα κἀγὼ ἐφίπταμαι ὡσεὶ πλῆκτρον· ὁ ἄνθρωπος κοιμᾶται κἀγὼ γρηγορῶ. ἰδού, κύριός ἐστιν ὁ ἐξιστάνων καρδίας ἀνθρώπων καὶ διδοὺς καρδίαν ἀνθρώποις<<. *Pan.* 48.4.1; Dummer, 224–25.

[88]The latter citation is taken from H. J. Lawlor, "The Heresy of the Phrygians," reprinted in *Orthodoxy, Heresy and Schism in Early Christianity* (ed. Everett Ferguson; New York: Garland, 1993) 336. Note also John Chrysostom's use of the image in terms of creation and animation: "you see, this body created in the Lord's design was like an instrument needing someone to activate it, rather like a lyre that needs someone who can by his own skill and artistry raise a fitting hymn to the Lord through his own limbs, as though by the strings of the lyre" (Homily 13; ET *Homilies on Genesis 1–17*, 173).

[89]μὴ δυναμένου τὰ ὅμοια λέγειν προφήταις; οὔτε γὰρ πνεῦμα ἅγιον ἐλάλησεν ἐν αὐτῷ. τὸ γὰρ εἰπεῖν >>ἐφίπταμαι καὶ πλήσσω καὶ γρηγορῶ καὶ ἐξιστᾷ κύριος καρδίας<<, ἐκστατικοῦ ῥήματα ὑπάρξει ταῦτα καὶ οὐχὶ παρακολουθοῦντος, ἀλλὰ ἄλλον χαρακτῆρα ὑποδεικνύντος παρὰ τὸν χαρακτῆρα τοῦ ἁγίου πνεύματος τοῦ ἐν προφήταις λελαληκότος. *Pan.* 48.4.2–3; Dummer, 225.

[90]τίς τοίνυν τῶν παρακολουθούντων καὶ μετὰ συνέσεως δεχομένων τὸν τῆς ὠφελείας λόγον καὶ τῆς ἑαυτῶν ζωῆς ἐπιμελομένων. *Pan.* 48.4.2; Dummer, 225.

arguments from benefit in 1 Corinthians and his emphasis upon benefit for the one body. This reference to benefit recalls to the model reader that one *should* be concerned with benefit, which has to do with unity among members of a community, not individualism.[91] The appeal to the audience as those who are rational and concerned with "benefit" masks the shakiness of an argument that begins somewhat strongly—accusing Montanus of engaging in ecstatic speech, based on the formal dissimilarity of this oracle to others—but evolves into an attack based upon vocabulary.

What troubles the Anti-Phrygian is that this oracle champions the passivity of the prophet. Again, issues of compulsion and control are at the forefront. The human sleeps (κοιμᾶται) while the "I" of the oracle is awake; the passive (deponent) tense of the verb "to sleep" is highlighted by the active verb "I awake," which stands in immediate contrast to it (γρηγορῷ). Montanus's oracle implies that in the moment of his own prophecy, he is essentially asleep, as God moves over him, playing him like an instrument. In a world where gender and status divide less along the lines of biological sex (male-female) and more along the lines of active-passive (a binary that subsumes into itself master-slave and male-female, for example),[92] this image of passivity both feminizes the prophet and puts him in the position of a slave before a master.[93] Accusations of passivity function rhetorically to discredit an opponent: the slave and the woman, for example, are of low status, and, given their situations, are not the sort of people who appreciate or even have the rights to free will and self-control in the first place. These accusations of passivity are also applied to Montanus, Maximilla, and their followers, who expound the idea that God compels God's followers to speak as prophets.

[91]See Margaret Mitchell's discussion of the language of concord and factionalism, cited in ch. 2, above.

[92]See Bernadette Brooten, *Love Between Women: Early Christian Responses to Female Homoeroticism* (Chicago: University of Chicago Press, 1996) 1–2.

[93]For an interpretation of Montanus's passivity that reaches different conclusions, based upon the idea that Montanus's and Maximilla's religious experience was formed by their earlier participation in Phrygian slave-religion and worship of Kybele, see Elm, "Montanist Oracles," 135.

# Conclusions

The Anti-Phrygian, more than any other source investigated in this book, insists that true prophets are characterized by rationality, a sound mind, and sober judgment. Even though the source carefully discusses the multiple meanings of *ekstasis*, as we saw in chapter 1, it is clear throughout that ecstasy is essentially a negative term. For the Anti-Phrygian, ecstasy generally indicates a mind that is unclear and unable to follow the sequence of events in a reasonable way. But since the term appears in various authoritative scriptures, and is picked up by the Phrygians to support their own ecstatic practices and utterances, the Anti-Phrygian responds by trying to take back the scriptural proofs and to shift and control the meaning of *ekstasis*.

The Anti-Phrygian source does not, however, turn to the rhetoric of Bacchic frenzy when challenging the Phrygians' ecstasy, accusing them of certain behaviors, such as odd bodily movements in ecstasy or speaking in tongues. Its use of a discourse of madness and rationality does not accuse the Phrygians of the expulsion of the human mind or the appearance of drunkenness—qualities that Philo associates with ecstasy, especially with the best sort of ecstasy. Yet it still accuses the Phrygians of an "ecstasy of folly," of unsound thinking and irrationality. The Anti-Phrygian source argues by insisting that its own community represents the "true" or "holy" church, and so tries to rob the "Phrygians" of Christian identity; it argues implicitly that true prophecy and correct ecstasy are things of the past; and it turns Maximilla's and Montanus's oracles against them and against their followers, challenging the idea that their prophecies provide knowledge from the divine. What is at stake for the Anti-Phrygian is the identity of true Christianity, along with its proper practices, and the ability to anchor one's claim to be part of the true church in a secure realm of knowledge, not some flimsy and insupportable claim to ongoing prophetic charismata. The source rhetorically achieves this end using several techniques.

The Anti-Phrygian tries rhetorically to control the terms of the debate over prophecy in order to shore up his or her viewpoint as that of the true, holy church. The source tries to corner the market on Christian identity. Much of this battle occurs simply through adjectives: are a community's charismata true and real? Are they like the first, or do they claim to be the last? Similarly, the source tries to redefine ecstasy by trotting out a catalog of great men, and by modifying the Phrygians' claims to ecstasy by insisting that these are ecstasies of folly, that they are unreal and false. The Anti-Phrygian is in a struggle over identity with the proximate other. Thus the debate consists of modifiers and attempts to control the meaning of key words like *ekstasis* and *ekklesia* and even charismata, which the author implies are no longer prophetic charismata.

The Anti-Phrygian also argues that prophecy does not occur under compulsion. While someone like Philo might argue that God's love is expressed through ecstasies that bring about mad behavior and stunning clarity of thought, the Anti-Phrygian insists that God's *philanthropia* consists in bringing rest to humans. The Anti-Phrygian is trying to control the term "ecstasy" over and against Phrygian claims to it and the (to the Anti-Phrygian's mind demonic, false, and innovative) knowledge which they insisted resulted from these ecstasies. The Anti-Phrygian takes a set of oracles in which Montanus and Maximilla claim to have access to the divine through ecstasy and twists them into hubristic claims to *be* the divine in order to discredit the realms of knowledge to which they (may have) claimed access. Indeed, the source entirely edits out the new knowledge which the oracles provided or claimed to provide. The Anti-Phrygian source is also concerned to emphasize the distance between the human and the divine both by its use of a periodization of history, and by its critique of the Phrygians' elision of themselves with the divine in the moment of ecstasy. Prophetic charism, the source implies, is something of the past, and the Phrygians do not stack up to the catalog of prophets and apostles of a former time. The fact that the source does not argue from any evidence of its own community's charismata may indicate that the debate is largely exegetical and theoretical. By theoretical, I do not mean that it has no bearing on life. I mean rather that what *appears* to be under discussion—the definition of ecstasy, proper examples of prophecy, a description or definition of rationality in the face of all this—slides rather quickly out of the way, and other more key concerns arise from these purported discussions.

The source also protests several oracles on the grounds that Montanus or Maximilla has claimed to be God, or to speak as God, or to be able to do more than God, and also emphasizes that God never compels people to do things. Indeed, humans can stand at a distance and refuse God's strange demands to violate dietary laws, while Maximilla's claims that she was compelled by God expose her falsehood. Rather than discussing prophecy as an *accidens*, an ecstasy where the divine spirit comes upon a person secondarily, as Tertullian does, the Anti-Phrygian discounts recent claims to the inbreaking of knowledge from the divine. Tertullian and the Anti-Phrygian source, although contemporaries, live in different periods of history, and embrace radically different claims about ecstasy, madness, and rationality.

# Conclusions

The Anti-Phrygian source contemptuously accused its opponents of engaging in an "ecstasy of folly." Tertullian defiantly used the term *amentia*, "madness," to talk about the ecstasies that, he asserted, open up divine realms of knowledge and even define true Christian identity. Paul challenged the Corinthians to embrace a divine folly that is greater than human wisdom, but at the same time attempted to rank and limit the spiritual gifts that the community enjoys. How are we to make sense of these competitions and fights, of the contentious accusations of madness and the puzzling embraces of folly? Moreover, we recall that the Anti-Phrygian argued that the time of prophetic gifts was in the distant past; Tertullian argued that the present is an especially vibrant time for the Spirit's activity, for prophecy and ecstasies. Paul argued that true gifts and knowledge are deferred to the future. How do we make sense of the many different understandings of the periodization of history that emerge in ancient debates over prophecy?

The debates over prophecy and ecstasy that we have explored in the preceding pages employ sophisticated rhetoric to persuade, to convince, and to construct a community's self-definition in terms of that community's place within a God-driven history and its access to God-given realms of knowledge. Present-day historiographers of early Christianity must be aware of these rhetorical constructions lest we pick up the argumentative strategies of ancient texts and deploy them as historical fact. Ancient discussions of prophecy or ecstasy do not provide data to be picked up like tesserae, turned over carefully, and inserted into the clearly patterned mosaic of early Christianity. No one mosaic plot exists to be filled in, and these fragments of rhetoric are not passive like tesserae or silent like shards of glass. They are alive and compelling, and to me fascinating precisely because their arguments are fragmentary and bright. The texts we have read do not provide static evidence, but argue for a certain view of Christian history; they do not reflect glimmers of understandings of prophecy and ecstasy, but seek to mold the readers' understanding, to persuade the reader, then and now, to a certain vision of spiritual gifts, knowledge, and one's place within history.

## Authority, Identity, and Epistemology

This book has argued that texts like Paul's, Tertullian's, and the Anti-Phrygian's are best read in terms of a model of struggle. Analyzing a range of texts in antiquity, we found that despite all their accusations of madness and rationality and their uses of *mania*, *amentia*, and terminology of a sound mind, they are not interested in defining reason or madness or in setting forth a theory of history's periodization. Rather, by using these discourses, the texts seek to shore up their own authority and that of their community, to establish a community's identity and borders over and against others, and to delimit realms of knowledge—to fix the boundaries of what can be known and how it can be known.

Even the taxonomies of madness, ecstasy, and dreams set forth in chapter 1 indicate that not all forms of a phenomenon are equal, and that taxonomies are not necessarily neutral lists, but can function to express hierarchy of organization. Plato championed the lover's madness, which makes the soul gaze upwards to new realms of heavenly sight and knowledge. Philo, allegorically interpreting the story of Abraham, understood Abraham's true heir to be one who abandons the flesh, sense perception, and even the *logos*, reason itself. He celebrated a prophetic ecstasy in which the human mind sets and the divine mind rises, resulting in a behavior that looks drunken, frenzied, or corybantic, but that somehow offers an epistemic revolution and dispenses clear knowledge. Tertullian puzzled over dreams, and was most interested in the type of dream in which the soul is in ecstasy or *amentia*. The Anti-Phrygian source tried desperately to wrest the term "ecstasy" away from the likes of Philo or Tertullian, arguing that ecstasy is really just God's means of giving rest, as God granted quiet to Adam in Gen 2:21.

In 1 Corinthians, Paul presented his own kind of taxonomy of spiritual gifts, ranking and ordering the *pneumatika* of the Corinthian community. This ranking is driven by Paul's attempts to persuade the Corinthians about what sort of knowledge a human can reach in the present and by his attempts to shift their understanding of their own community identity—they are not truly wise or spiritual yet. Paul insisted that present knowledge is incomplete and dim. The resurrection has not already occurred; complete transformation and the "spiritual body" will occur at a distant future time, when the "last trumpet" sounds (1 Corinthians 15). In 1 Corinthians 13, Paul argued in a similar vein: in the present, one can only know as in a warped mirror; face-to-face knowledge of the divine is deferred to a later time.

According to Paul, the Corinthians desired to be (and understood themselves to be) wise, knowledgeable, perfect, and, especially, spiritual in the present. Paul's argument about the inaccessibility of certain realms of knowledge is interwoven with his attempt to re-form the Corinthians' self-understanding and identity: despite their self-understanding as *pneumatikoi*, they are not spiritual, perfected people, but are only fleshly people. Paul made this argument within a larger project of reordering the charismata of the Corinthian community, admitting the importance of prophecy, but splitting this spiritual gift off from glossolalia and the interpretation of tongues. Paul offered his interpretation: tongues, prophecy, wisdom, and knowledge are incomplete and imperfect in the present; only in the future can the Corinthians truly enjoy full knowledge and full status as *pneumatikoi*. In the present, he argued that he could barely call them *psychikoi*, and that *sarkikoi* is really the term that best describes them. To bolster this argument, Paul constructed his own identity as a founder, father, and apostle to that community, and at the same time critiqued the Corinthians for not being who they think they are—spiritual people truly concerned with wisdom and knowledge.

Tertullian too was engaged in a debate about what it means to be a spiritual person, but his rhetorical approach differed from that of Paul. In *De anima*, Tertullian was concerned to argue that the soul is undivided. Speculating about the soul, he insisted that anything spiritual about it is a secondary phenomenon, an *accidens spiritu* rather than a natural part of the human. Thus he opposes anyone who argues that certain humans are (almost) naturally *spiritales*, an elitist idea he attributed to the Valentinians. In his broader corpus, Tertullian launched this rhetoric of anthropology by calling his opponents *animales* or *psychici*. Tertullian argued that his community's ethics and access to divine revelation is superior to that of his opponents. In calling the opponents *psychici*, he challenged what was most likely their own self-appellation as *spiritales*, and he constructed his Christian identity and that of his community over and against their false claims to spiritual superiority.

Tertullian's *De anima* was the third portion of a larger argument against the philosopher Hermogenes and others. Tertullian's self-construction as antiphilosophical (and especially anti-Platonic) allowed him to justify a variety of sources as epistemically valuable in his attempt to explain the human soul.

Tertullian's main philosophical argument in *De anima* was that the soul is unified, an assertion that might look uninteresting on the face of it, but that challenges not only Platonic anthropology, with its tripartite soul, but also Platonic epistemology, with its emphasis on the intellect as the best means of gaining knowledge, especially knowledge of the divine. While Paul sought to limit the realms of knowledge to which the Corinthians thought they had access, in a very different rhetorical context Tertullian constantly called for a broader epistemology. He did so on several fronts. He argued that Greek philosophy, especially Platonic, did not have a monopoly on truth, and indeed that simpler, truer knowledge can be found in Judea, in common fishermen, and especially in straightforward divine revelation. Using a modified Stoic epistemology, Tertullian also argued that sense perception is a valuable epistemic source and broadened his authoritative *exempla* to include legends, medical data, and scripture as significant sources of knowledge about the soul. Tertullian also understood the present to be a unique time of the Spirit's activity in human history; the Spirit's gifts are especially vibrant and mature in the present, and are manifest through spiritual gifts such as ecstasy, or *amentia*, and the knowledge this brings.

Epiphanius's Anti-Phrygian source did not deploy the rhetoric of "spiritual people" or *pneumatikoi*, but engaged in the construction of community identity at a different level. The source used the language of the "true church" and "real charismata" to shore up its own authority and in order to construct group boundaries over and against the Phrygians. Two main (and interwoven) rhetorical strategies against the Phrygians are employed: the source tainted the Phrygians with the brush of barbarism and mental instability, and it insisted that they did not stand within an ancient tradition of prophets and apostles, but are "other than" that true and authoritative tradition.

The Anti-Phrygian argued vigorously against the new knowledge that Montanus, Maximilla, and other "Phrygians" claimed to present through their ecstasies. Instead, it located valuable knowledge and true prophecy in Scripture, in past figures such as Moses, Daniel, and Peter. Such figures had sound minds, the source claimed, and even had the wherewithal and knowledge to defy God's strange commands when necessary. Any present claims to ecstasies granted by God and the special knowledge they bring are delusional. The Anti-Phrygian source never referred to ongoing prophetic charismata in its own community, even as it insisted that its church had the "real" charismata. Twisting the words of Maximilla's and Montanus's oracles, the Anti-Phrygian made their claims to spiritual gifts of ecstasy and prophecy seem like vehicles for a hubristic attempt to assert equality with God. God's love is *not* manifest in the world through ecstasies such as these, argued the Anti-Phrygian; ecstasy merely brings rest, not new knowledge. Moreover, the Anti-Phrygian source used identity boundaries to reinforce this limiting of epistemology, marking off its community as the "true church" over and against what it claimed were the Phrygians' false claims to divine revelation.

Knowledge and the means to knowledge is a central theme in the debate over prophecy and ecstasy in antiquity. 1 Corinthians, Tertullian's works, and the Anti-Phrygian source are interested not only in constructing their own authority and in setting up boundaries for what constitutes community identity, but also and especially in negotiating the bounds of epistemology. What you can know, how you can know, and when you can know it are matters of contention in these texts. The Foucauldian dictum that knowledge is power is now found everywhere, from the blackboards of the academy to the print copy of advertising. In the ancient world as well, in debates over prophecy and ecstasy, epistemology and power are intertwined. At first glance, these texts may seem to provide information about an "orthodox" rejection of ecstasy or prophecy, or snippets of data about Montanists. On closer investigation, however, they expose a complexly structured, rhetorically sophisticated debate over claims to certain kinds of knowledge. The stakes are high: the question of who has true, real (divine) knowledge is linked to issues of authority and identity in communities. For the early-third-century texts we investigated, debates over prophecy and ecstasy are tied to the issue of who is truly Christian, who is part of the "true church" and who stands outside it.

This study has brought together a diverse set of texts under the topic of prophecy and ecstasy. These texts are frequently characterized as Jewish or Christian, Platonist or Stoic, orthodox or heretical. This study, however, has demonstrated two things about assertions of group identity in antiquity. First, such categories do not so much mark ethnicity, religion, or positionality, but are deployed as part of the larger project of the rhetorical construction of identity over and against others engaged in the debate over prophecy. Second, in antiquity, the interest in prophecy and ecstasy and the discursive construction of rationality and madness overran identity boundaries — almost everyone was talking about it.

## Ancient and Modern Discourses

The ancient discourses of madness and rationality and of the periodization of history that have been discussed here not only occupied a variety of ancient communities; they have been inscribed onto a variety of modern discourses as well. The terms and stratagems of the ancient discourse have been adopted in many fields, including modern anthropology, for example, as Mary Douglas, Victor Turner, or I. M. Lewis pick up ancient Christian materials and read them as evidence of a certain kind of ecstasy, without taking into account the rhetorical context of the texts or the contexts of modern authors' own rhetoric and reconstruction. These anthropologists also tend to associate liminal behaviors such as ecstasy with those who are disenfranchised (such as the poor, women, immigrants). In doing so they reduplicate both an idea of Enlightenment progress, in which those who are at the center of society rely upon reason rather than religious effervescence, and at the same time veer toward Romantic valorizations of the primitive, the mad, and the wild in their fascination with such "liminal" behaviors. We see glimmers here of the ancient discursive struggle over madness and rationality and over history and its progress, but set in a modern context. The claim that truth is manifest in divine communication through ecstasy and spiritual gifts and the counterclaim that truth is manifest in an ancient, reasoned tradition of interrogation and clear, rational behavior have been reified, rather than read within a rhetorical context of struggles over knowledge.

Thus, the structures of antiquity's discourses on madness and rationality and on history's periodization are reduplicated faintly in modern scholarship and issues, for modern rhetorical purposes. The discipline of church history, for example, has picked up one strand of the debate, the idea of the decline of charismata, and has often read this as historical datum rather than rhetorical argument. My book contributes to historiographies of early Christianity that counter a Weberian view of effervescent charismatic origins and the subsequent decline of a moment into institution and routinization. The model of struggle which I employ instead focuses on moments of rupture and negotiation, rather than attempting to construct a historiography based in principles of linear progress (or devolution). In this, I am influenced by postcolonial theorists such as Ashis Nandy and Dipesh Chakrabarty who critique the Western Enlightenment category of "history," with all its assumptions about the self in modernity, the primitive nature of religious experience and the communities' evolution toward secularism, and the world's linear development towards progress and rationality. In rejecting the term "Montanism" and in questioning its use as an explanatory category in early Christian historiographies, I have read Tertullian's *De anima* and the Anti-Phrygian source not as the last moment of active charismata in Christianity and their contestation before the boom of routinization and church office fell. The rhetoric of Tertullian and that of the Anti-Phrygian, situated in a broader context, become part of a large, active debate over prophecy and ecstasy in antiquity, rather than a fight about the last gasps of prophecy in early Christianity.

By attempting to challenge implicit and explicit scholarly reliance on a model of charismatic origins and subsequent decline, I have tried to elucidate that all attempts at a historiography of early Christianity, ancient and modern, are rhetorically constructed to convince and persuade. A model of struggle lays bare that all historiography of "Christian origins" is forged in the crucible of negotiation and argument over Christian identity, whether that historiography be ancient or modern. Like the ancient texts we have studied here, more recent historiographies are also gripped by the authority of origins. This time, however, the origins cited are not creation stories per se, but instead are narratives about the beginnings of Christianity. Were early Christians interested in charismata? Were they Spirit-filled? Authentically in touch with divine revelation? Were they all that way? Did unity indeed precede diversity? Does a spirit-filled early Christianity render Christian origins more authentic?

This study presents another historiography, one no less interested in persuasion, but willing to acknowledge that it takes part in an ongoing struggle over early Christian historiography and the definition of early Christian origins. Since Albert Schweitzer, if not before, scholars have been aware of the deep investments that drive studies of the historical Jesus. Historiographies of early Christianity are also invested and fraught with meaning. They are often part of an attempt to argue for (an ideal and pristine) Christian identity that might serve as a model for Christianity or community in the author's own time, and for a story of Christianity that makes sense of the author's own present commitments and concerns. My work contributes to the ongoing deconstruction of the idea and privilege of origins, however, by arguing that early Christian debates over prophecy do not really provide a glimpse at one pure origin. Rather, these debates show struggle and conflicting opinions in the first century and beyond. Moreover, early Christian debates over prophecy were rooted in an older and broader discourse that included Plato and Philo and others — more sources and conversations than merely those produced by early Christians.

This book has investigated a set of texts using the topic of prophecy and ecstasy as a principle of selection, rather than seeking out texts that are only Jewish, orthodox, or of one particular philosophical bent. In antiquity, prophecy, ecstasy, dreams, and visions were part of a vital ongoing philosophical debate; arguments about prophecy's decline or ecstasy's inappropriateness are not particular to early Christian historiography, but are part of a larger rhetorical context of struggle over community identity and claims to various realms of knowledge. Although in our own time prophecy and ecstasy no longer hold sway as a center of philosophical and theological debate, we have seen the ripple effects of this ancient discourse in modern times. In the present, we find similar ongoing battles not only in anthropology and current early Christian historiography, but also in recent debates about experience as a source of theological reflection, or current insistence by feminists and others that privileged epistemologies be rethought and reconfigured to value a greater range of sources and voices. Speculation continues, in Christian theology and elsewhere, over whether the divine compels humans to act in certain ways, and over human vulnerability in the face of the divine. And communities, both scholarly and those more broadly constituted, make assumptions about the nature of religion and the givenness of history's progress as they discuss the role of religion in society, questioning in violent times whether religion and its effervescence can or must be tamed, rationalized, or institutionalized. These fascinating present-day discussions trace patterns similar to those that underlie the ancient debates over prophecy and ecstasy and the discourse of madness and rationality.

Debates over prophecy and ecstasy, especially as they use the rhetoric of madness and rationality, are threads in a dense fabric. Communities are weaving their identities, authors are attempting to establish the authority of their understanding of things, realms of knowledge are delimited and restricted as groups debate the connection between the human and the divine in prophecy and ecstasy. By tracing the threads of the discourse of madness and rationality and the discourse of history's periodization, this book has, I hope, provided some insight into the finely woven strands of this debate.

# Selected Bibliography

## A. Ancient Sources

*The Apostolic Fathers.* Translated by Kirsopp Lake. 2 vols. Cambridge: Cambridge University Press, 1985.

Artemidorus. *Interpretation of Dreams.* Translated by Robert J. White. Park Ridge, N.J.: Noyes, 1975.

*Ascension of Isaiah.* In *Writings Relating to the Apostles, Apocalypses, and Related Subjects.* Vol. 2 of *New Testament Apocrypha.* Edited by Edgar Hennecke, Wilhelm Schneemelcher, and R. McL. Wilson. 5th edition. Louisville, Ky.: Westminster/John Knox, 1991.

Athanasius. *On the Incarnation of the Word: Christology of the Later Fathers.* Edited by Edward Hardy and Cyril Richardson. Library of Christian Classics 3. Philadelphia: Westminster, 1954.

*Biblia patristica: index des citations et allusions bibliques dans la littérature patristique.* 5 vols. Paris: Éditions du Centre national de la recherche scientifique, 1975– .

John Chrysostom. *Homilies on Genesis 1–17.* Translated by Robert Hill. FoC 74. Washington, D.C.: Catholic University of America Press, 1986.

*Cicero: De senectute, De amicitia, De divinatione.* Translated by William A. Falconer. LCL. 1923. Repr., Cambridge: Harvard University Press, 1996.

Epiphanius. *Panarion.* Translated by Frank Williams. 2 vols. Leiden: Brill, 1994.

Epiphanius. *Panarion haer. 34–64.* Edited by Karl Holl. 2d rev. ed. Edited by Jürgen Dummer. GCS. Berlin: Akademie-Verlag, 1980.

Eusebius. *Historia ecclesiastica.* Translated by Kirsopp Lake. 2 vols. LCL. 1926. Repr., Cambridge: Harvard University Press, 1953.

Heine, Ronald E. *The Montanist Oracles and Testimonia.* NAPS Monograph Series 14. Macon, Ga.: Mercer University Press, 1989.

Irenaeus of Lyon. *Contre les heresies livre 5*. Translated by Adelin Rousseau. SC 153. Paris: Editions du Cerf, 1969.

Jerome. *On Illustrious Men*. Translated by Thomas P. Halton. FoC 100. Washington, D.C.: Catholic University of America, 1999.

Labriolle, Pierre de. *Les sources de l'histoire du montanisme. Textes grecs, latins, syriaques*. Freiburg: O. Gschwend and Paris: Ernest Leroux, 1913.

*Martyrdom of Perpetua and Felicitas*. In Herbert Musurillo, *Acts of the Christian Martyrs*, 106–39. Oxford: Clarendon, 1994.

Origen. *Contre Celse*. Translated by Marcel Borret, S.J. SC 150. Paris: Cerf, 1969.

———. *Contra Celsum*. Translated by Henry Chadwick. Cambridge: Cambridge University Press, 1953.

———. *Homelies sur la Génèse*. Translated and edited by Louis Doutreleau. SC 7. 1976. Repr., Paris: Editions du Cerf, 1996.

———. *Homilies on Genesis and Exodus*. Translated by Ronald E. Heine. FoC 71. Washington, D.C.: Catholic University of America, 1981.

*Patrologia Latina database*. 4th ed. Alexandria, Va.: Chadwick-Healey, 1995.

Philo. *De Somniis*. Translated by F. H. Colson and G. H. Whitaker. Vol. 5. LCL. 1934. Repr., Cambridge: Harvard University Press, 1988.

———. *Quis Rerum Divinarum Heres*. Translated by F. H. Colson and G. H. Whitaker. Vol. 4. LCL. New York: Putnam's, 1932.

*Philo of Alexandria: the Contemplative Life, the Giants, and Selections*. Translated by David Winston. Classics of Western Spirituality. New York: Paulist Press, 1981.

*Philonis Alexandrini Opera Quae Supersunt*. Edited by Leopold Cohn and Paul Wendland. 7 vols. Berolini: Georg Reimer, 1896–1930.

Plato. *Phaedrus*. Translated by Robin Waterfield. Oxford: Oxford University Press, 2002.

———. *Platonis Opera*. Edited by John Burnet. 5 vols. Oxford: Clarendon, 1937.

Plutarch. *The Oracles at Delphi* and *The Obsolescence of Oracles*. In *Moralia*. Translated by Frank C. Babbitt. Vol. 5. LCL. 1936. Repr., Cambridge: Harvard University Press, 1993.

*Soranus' Gynecology*. Translated by Oswei Temkin. 1956. Repr., Baltimore, Md.: Johns Hopkins University Press, 1991.

Tatian. Oratio ad Graecos *and Other Fragments*. Edited and translated by Molly Whittaker. Oxford: Clarendon, 1982.

Tertullian. *De anima*. In *Tertullian: Apologetical Works and Minucius Felix Octavius*. Translated by Edwin A. Quain, S.J. FoC 10. 1950. Repr., Washington, D.C.: Catholic University of America Press, 1962.

———. *De Anima*. Edited by Jan H. Waszink. Amsterdam: J. M. Meulenhoff, 1947.

———. *On the Soul* and *On the Veiling of Virgins*. Translated by Peter Holms. ANF 3. Grand Rapids, Mich.: Eerdmans, 1989.

———. *Opera*. 2 vols. CCSL 1–2. Turnholt: Brepols, 1954.

*Thesaurus Linguae Graecae*, CD-ROM. Irvine, Calif.: University of California, 1992.

## B. Modern Sources

Aland, Kurt. "Bemerkungen zum Montanismus und zur frühchristlichen Eschatologie." In idem, *Kirchengeschichtliche Entwürfe: alte Kirche, Reformation und Luthertum, Pietismus und Erweckungsbewegung*, 105–48. Gütersloh: Gütersloher Verlagshaus, 1960.

Amat, Jacqueline. *Songes et visions: L'au-delà dans la literature latine tardive*. Paris: Études Augustiniennes, 1985.

Anatolios, Khaled. *Athanasius: The Coherence of his Thought*. New York: Routledge, 1998.

Asad, Talal. *Genealogies of Religion: Discipline and Reasons of Power in Christianity and Islam*. Baltimore, Md.: Johns Hopkins University Press, 1993.

Ash, James L., Jr. "The Decline of Ecstatic Prophecy in the Early Church." *JTS* 37 (1976) 227–37.

Aune, David. *Prophecy in Early Christianity and the Ancient Mediterranean World*. Grand Rapids, Mich.: Eerdmans, 1983.

Ayers, Robert H. *Language, Logic, and Reason in the Church Fathers: A Study of Tertullian, Augustine, and Aquinas*. Altertumswissenschaftliche Texte und Studien 6. Hildesheim: Georg Olms, 1979.

Barnes, Timothy D. "The Chronology of Montanism." *JTS* n.s. 21 (1970) 403–8.

———. *Tertullian: A Historical and Literary Study*. Oxford: Clarendon, 1971.

Barrett, Michèle. *The Politics of Truth: From Marx to Foucault*. Cambridge, England: Polity Press, 1991.

Bauer, Walter. *Orthodoxy and Heresy in Earliest Christianity*. Edited by Robert A. Kraft and Gerhard Krodel. Philadelphia: Fortress, 1971.

Betz, Hans Dieter. "The Problem of Rhetoric and Theology according to the Apostle Paul." In *L'apôtre Paul, personalité, style et ministère*, 16–48. Edited by A. Vanhoye. Leuven: Leuven University Press, 1986.

———. *2 Corinthians 8 and 9*. Hermeneia. Philadelphia: Fortress, 1985.

Blenkinsopp, Joseph. *A History of Prophecy in Israel*. Revised edition. Louisville, Ky.: Westminster John Knox, 1996.

Borgen, Peder. "Philo of Alexandria." In *Jewish Writings of the Second Temple Period: Apocrypha, Pseudepigrapha, Qumran Sectarian Writings, Philo, Josephus*, 233–82. Edited by Michael E. Stone. Philadelphia: Fortress, 1984.

Boring, M. Eugene. *The Continuing Voice of Jesus: Christian Prophecy and the Gospel Tradition*. Louisville, Ky.: Westminster/John Knox, 1991.

Bornkamm, Günther. "History of the Origin of the So-Called Second Letter to the Corinthians." *NTS* 8 (1962) 258–64.

Bostock, Gerald. "The Sources of Origen's Doctrine of Pre-Existence." In *Origeniana quarta: die Referate des 4. Internationalen Origens-kongresses (Innsbruck, 2–6 September 1985)*, 259–64. Edited by Lothar Lies. Innsbrucker theologische Studien 19. Innsbruck, Austria: Tyrolia-Verlag, 1987.

Botha, Jan. "On the 'Reinvention' of Rhetoric." *Scriptura* 31 (1989) 14–31.

Bovon, François. "Ces chrétiens qui rêvent. L'autorité du rêve dans les premier siècles du christianisme." In *Geschichte, Tradition, Reflexion. Festschrift für Martin Hengel*, 631–53. Edited by Hubert Cancik et al. Tübingen: Mohr/Siebeck, 1996.

———. *De Vocatione Gentium: Histoire de l'interprétation d'Act. 10, 1–11, 18 dans les six premiers siècles*. Tübingen: Mohr/Siebeck, 1967.

Boyarin, Daniel. *Dying for God: Martyrdom and the Making of Christianity and Judaism*. Stanford, Calif.: Stanford University Press, 1999.

———. "The Gospel of the Memra: Jewish Binitarianism and the Prologue to John." *HTR* 94 (2001) 243–84.

———. *A Radical Jew: Paul and the Politics of Identity*. Berkeley: University of California Press, 1994.

Bréhier, Émile. *The Hellenic Age*. Translated by Joseph Thomas. History of Philosophy. Chicago: University of Chicago Press, 1963.

———. *The Hellenistic and Roman Age*. Translated by Wade Baskin. History of Philosophy. 1931. Repr., Chicago: University of Chicago Press, 1965.

Brooten, Bernadette. *Love between Women: Early Christian Responses to Female Homoeroticism*. Chicago: University of Chicago Press, 1996.

Brown, Peter. *The Body and Society: Men, Women, and Sexual Renunciation in Early Christianity*. New York: Columbia University Press, 1988.

Buell, Denise Kimber. "Rethinking the Relevance of Race for Early Christian Self-Definition." *HTR* 94 (2001) 449–76.

Bultmann, Rudolf. *Theology of the New Testament*. 2 vols. New York: Scribner's, 1955.

Burrus, Virginia. "The Heretical Woman as Symbol in Alexander, Athanasius, Epiphanius, and Jerome." *HTR* 84 (1991) 229–48.

Bynum, Caroline Walker. *Fragmentation and Redemption: Essays on Gender and the Human Body in Medieval Religion*. New York: Zone Books, 1991.

Campenhausen, Hans von. *Ecclesiastical Authority and Spiritual Power in the Church of the First Three Centuries*. Stanford, Calif.: Stanford University Press, 1969.

———. *The Formation of the Christian Bible*. Translated by J. A. Baker. Philadelphia: Fortress, 1972.

Castelli, Elizabeth A. *Imitating Paul: A Discourse of Power*. Louisville, Ky: Westminster/John Knox, 1991.

———. "Interpretations of Power in 1 Corinthians." *Semeia* 54 (1991) 197–222.

———, and Hal Taussig, eds. "Drawing Large and Startling Figures: Reimagining Christian Origins." In *Reimagining Christian Origins: A Colloquium Honoring Burton L. Mack*, 3–20. Valley Forge, Pa.: Trinity Press International, 1996.

Cerrato, J. A., "Hippolytus' *On the Song of Songs* and the New Prophecy." *Stud. Pat.* 31 (1997) 268–73.

Chakrabarty, Dipesh. *Provincializing Europe: Postcolonial Thought and Historical Difference*. Princeton, N.J.: Princeton University Press, 2000.

Clark, Elizabeth A. "Footnotes. A More Curious History." Paper presented at the Fourteenth International Conference of Patristics, Oxford University, 18–22 August 2003.

Classen, C. Joachim. "St. Paul's Epistles and Ancient Greek and Roman Rhetoric. In *Rhetoric and the New Testament: Essays from the 1992 Heidelberg Conference*," 265–91. Edited by Stanley Porter and Thomas Olbricht. JSNTSup 90. Sheffield, England: JSOT, 1993.

Collins, R. F. "Reflections on 1 Corinthians as a Hellenistic Letter." In *The Corinthian Correspondence*, 39–61. Edited by R. Bieringer. BETL 125. Leuven: Leuven University Press, 1996.

Conzelmann, Hans. *1 Corinthians: A Commentary on the First Epistle to the Corinthians*. Hermeneia. Philadelphia: Fortress, 1975.

Crouzel, Henri. *Origen*. Translated by A. S. Worrall. San Francisco: Harper and Row, 1989. Translation of *Origène*. Paris: Lethielleux, 1985.

Daniélou, Jean. *From Glory to Glory: Texts from Gregory of Nyssa's Mystical Writings*.Translated by Herbert Musurillo. New York: Scribner, 1961.

De Boer, Martinus C. "The Composition of 1 Corinthians." *NTS* 40 (1994) 229–45.

Desjardins, Michel. *Sin in Valentinianism*. Atlanta, Ga.: Scholars Press, 1990.

Dillon, John. *The Middle Platonists 80 B.C. to A.D. 220*. Revised edition. 1977. Repr., New York: Cornell University Press, 1996.

Dodds, E. R. *The Greeks and the Irrational*. 1951. Repr., Berkeley: University of California Press, 1956.

—. *Pagan and Christian in an Age of Anxiety*. Cambridge: Cambridge University Press, 1965.

Douglas, Mary. *Natural Symbols: Explorations in Cosmology*. 1970. London: Routledge, 1996.

—. "Social Preconditions of Enthusiasm and Heterodoxy." In *Forms of Symbolic Action: Proceedings of the 1969 Annual Spring Meeting of the American Ethnological Society*, 69–80. Edited by Robert F. Spencer. Seattle, Wash.: University of Washington Press, 1969.

DuBois, Page. *Centaurs and Amazons: Women and the Pre-History of the Great Chain of Being*. Ann Arbor, Mich.: University of Michigan, 1982.

Duff, Paul Brooks. *Who Rides the Beast? Prophetic Rivalry and the Rhetoric of Crisis in the Churches of the Apocalypse*. Oxford: Oxford University Press, 2001.

Dunn, James. *Jesus and the Spirit: A Study of the Religious and Charismatic Experience of Jesus and the First Christians as Reflected in the New Testament*. 1975. Repr., Grand Rapids, Mich.: Eerdmans, 1997.

Eco, Umberto. *The Role of the Reader: Explorations in the Semiotics of Texts*. Bloomington, Ind.: Indiana University Press, 1979.

Ellis, E. Earle. *Prophecy and Hermeneutic in Early Christianity*. WUNT 18. Tübingen: Mohr, 1978.

Elm, Susanna. "Montanist Oracles." In *Searching the Scriptures: A Feminist Ecumenical Commentary and Translation*, 2:131–8. Edited by Elisabeth Schüssler Fiorenza. 2 vols. New York: Crossroad/Continuum, 1994.

Evans, R. F. "On the Problem of Church and Empire in Tertullian's *Apologeticum*." *Stud. Pat.* 14 (1976) 21–36.

Fadiman, Anne. *The Spirit Catches You and You Fall Down*. New York: Farrar, Strauss & Giroux, 1997.

Forbes, Christopher. *Prophecy and Inspired Speech In Early Christianity and its Hellenistic Environment*. Peabody, Mass.: Hendrickson, 1997.

Foucault, Michel. *Archaeology of Knowledge and the Discourse on Language*. Translated by A. M. Sheridan Smith. New York: Pantheon, 1972.

———. *The Care of the Self*. Vol. 3 of *The History of Sexuality*. Translated by Robert Hurley. New York: Vintage Books, 1988.

———. *Discipline and Punish: The Birth of the Prison*. Translated by Alan Sheridan. 2d edition. 1975. Repr., New York: Vintage Books, 1995.

———. *Madness and Civilization: A History of Insanity in the Age of Reason*. Translated by Richard Howard. 1961. Repr., New York: Vintage Books, 1988.

Frede, Dorothea. "The Philosophical Economy of Plato's Psychology: Rationality and Common Concepts in the *Timaeus*." In *Rationality in Greek Thought*, 29–58. Edited by Michael Frede and Gisela Striker. Oxford: Clarendon, 1996.

Frede, Michael. "Introduction." In *Rationality in Greek Thought*, 1–28. Edited by idem and Gisela Striker. Oxford: Clarendon, 1996.

Frend, W. H. C. "Montanism: A Movement of Prophecy and Regional Identity in the Early Church." *Bulletin John Rylands Library of Manchester* 70 (1988) 25–34.

———. "Montanism: Research and Problems." In *Archaeology and History in the Study of Early Christianity*. London: Variorum Reprints, 1988. Reprinted from *Rivista di storia e letteratura religiosa* 30 (1984) 521–37.

———. *The Rise of Christianity*. Philadelphia: Fortress, 1984.

Friedrich, G. προφήτης. *TDNT* 6 (1968) 828–61.

Gager, John G. *Kingdom and Community: The Social World of Early Christianity*. Englewood Cliffs, N.J.: Prentice-Hall, 1975.

———. *Reinventing Paul*. Oxford: Oxford University Press, 2000.

Georgi, Dieter. *The Opponents of Paul in Second Corinthians: A Study of Religious Propaganda in Late Antiquity*. 1964. Philadelphia: Fortress, 1986.

Gillespie, Thomas W. *The First Theologians: A Study in Early Christian Prophecy*. Grand Rapids, Mich.: Eerdmans, 1994.

Groh, Dennis E. "Utterance and Exegesis: Biblical Interpretation in the Montanist Movement." In *The Living Text: Essays in Honor of Ernest W. Saunders*, 73–95. Edited by idem and Robert Jewett. New York: University Press of America, 1985.

Goulder, Michael. "Σοφία in 1 Corinthians." *NTS* 37 (1991) 516–34.

Gunkel, Hermann. *The Influence of the Holy Spirit: The Popular View of the Apostolic Age and the Teaching of the Apostle Paul.* Translated by Roy A. Harrisville and Philip A. Quanbeck, II. 1888. Repr., Philadelphia: Fortress, 1979.

Hällström, Gunnar Af. *Charismatic Succession: A Study of Origen's Consept* [sic] *of Prophecy.* Helsinki: Toimittanut Anne-Marit Enroth, 1985.

Hanson, John S. "The Dream/Vision Report and Acts 10:1–11:18: A Form-Critical Study." Ph.D. diss., Harvard University, 1978.

———. "Dreams and Visions in the Graeco-Roman World and Early Christianity." *ANRW* 23.2:1395–1427.

Harnack, Adolf von. *The Mission and Expansion of Christianity.* Translated by James Moffatt. Glouchester, Mass.: Peter Smith, 1972.

Hauck, Robert J. *The More Divine Proof: Prophecy and Inspiration in Celsus and Origen.* AAR 69. Atlanta, Ga.: Scholars Press, 1989.

Heine, Ronald E. "Role of the Gospel of John in the Montanist Controversy." *Second Century* 6 (1987/88) 1–19.

Hill, David. *New Testament Prophecy.* London: Marshall, Morgan and Scott, 1979.

Hoek, Annewies van den. "The 'Catechetical' School of Early Christian Alexandria and its Philonic Heritage." *HTR* 90 (1997) 59–87.

———. "Origen and the Intellectual Heritage of Alexandria: Continuity or Disjunction?," *Origeniana Quinta: Historica, Text and Method, Biblica, Philosophica, Theologica, Origenism and Later Developments: Papers of the Fifth International Origen Congress, Boston College, 14–18 August 1989,* 40–50. Edited by Robert J. Daly. BETL 105. Leuven: Peeters, 1992.

Hunt, Allen. *The Inspired Body: Paul, the Corinthians, and Divine Inspiration.* Macon, Ga.: Mercer University Press, 1996.

Jamison, Kay R. *An Unquiet Mind.* New York: Knopf, 1995.

Jensen, Anne. *God's Self-Confident Daughters: Early Christianity and the Liberation of Women.* Translated by O. C. Dean, Jr. 1992. Repr., Louisville, Ky.: Westminster John Knox, 1996.

Jones, A. H. M. "Were Ancient Heresies National or Social Movements in Disguise?" In *Orthodoxy, Heresy and Schism in Early Christianity,* 314–32. Edited by Everett Ferguson. New York: Garland, 1993.

Keller, Mary. *The Hammer and the Flute: Women, Power, and Spirit Possession.* Baltimore, Md.: Johns Hopkins University Press, 2002.

Kennedy, George. *A New History of Classical Rhetoric*. Princeton, N.J.: Princeton University Press, 1994.

———. *A New Testament Interpretation through Rhetorical Criticism*. Chapel Hill, N.C.: University of North Carolina Press, 1984.

———. *Progymnasmata: Greek Textbooks of Prose Composition and Rhetoric*. Atlanta, Ga.: SBL, 2003.

———. *Quintilian*. New York: Twayne Publishers, Inc., 1969.

King, Karen L. "The Book of Norea, Daughter of Eve." In *Searching the Scriptures: A Feminist Ecumenical Commentary and Translation*, 2: 66–85. Edited by Elisabeth Schüssler Fiorenza. 2 vols. New York: Crossroad/Continuum, 1994.

———. "Prophetic Power and Women's Authority: The Case of the *Gospel of Mary (Magdalene)*." In *Women Preachers and Prophets through Two Millennia of Christianity)*, 21–41. Edited by Beverly Kienzle and Pamela J. Walker. Berkeley: University of California Press, 1998.

———. *What is Gnosticism?*. Cambridge: Harvard University Press, 2003.

Klawiter, Frederick C. "The Role of Martyrdom and Persecution in Developing the Priestly Authority of Women in Early Christianity: A Case Study of Montanism." *Church History* 49 (1980) 251–61.

Koester, Helmut. *Ancient Christian Gospels: Their History and Development*. Valley Forge, Pa.: Trinity Press International and London: SCM Press Ltd., 1990.

———. *Introduction to the New Testament*. 2 vols. 2d edition. New York: de Gruyter, 2000.

———. "Writings and the Spirit: Authority and Politics in Ancient Christianity." *HTR* 84 (1991) 353–72.

Kraemer, Ross Shepard. *Her Share of the Blessings: Women's Religions among Pagans, Jews, and Christians in the Greco-Roman World*. New York: Oxford University Press, 1992.

Kramer, Peter D. *Listening to Prozac*. New York: Viking, 1993.

Krawiec, Rebecca. *Shenoute and the Women of the White Monastery: Egyptian Monasticism in Late Antiquity*. Oxford: Oxford University Press, 2002.

Kümmel, Werner Georg. *Introduction to the New Testament*. Translated by A. J. Mattill, Jr. 14th revised edition. Nashville, Tenn.: Abingdon, 1966.

Labriolle, Pierre Champagne de. *La crise montaniste*. Paris: E. Leroux, 1913.

Lawlor, H. J. "The Heresy of the Phrygians." In *Orthodoxy, Heresy and Schism in Early Christianity*, 333–51. Edited by Everett Ferguson. New York: Garland, 1993.

Levison, John R. *The Spirit in First Century Judaism*. Leiden: Brill, 1997.

Lewis, Bernard. *What Went Wrong? Western Impact and Middle Eastern Response*. Oxford: Oxford University Press, 2002.

Lewis, Charlton T., and Charles Short. *A Latin Dictionary*. Oxford: Clarendon, 1975.

Lewis, I. M. *Ecstatic Religion: A Study of Shamanism and Spirit Possession*. 1971. 2d edition. London: Routledge, 1989.

Lipsius, Richard Adelbert. *Zur Quellenkritik des Epiphanios*. Vienna: Wilhelm Braumüller, 1865.

Lloyd, Genevieve. *The Man of Reason: 'Male' and 'Female' in Western Philosophy*. Minneapolis: University of Minnesota Press, 1984.

Lods, Marc. *Confesseurs et martyrs: Successeurs des prophètes dans l'Église des trois premiers siècles*. Cahiers théologiques 41. Neuchatel: Delachaux et Niestlé, 1958.

Louth, Andrew. *The Origins of the Christian Mystical Tradition from Plato to Denys*. Oxford: Clarendon, 1981.

Martin, Dale B. *The Corinthian Body*. New Haven, Conn.: Yale University Press, 1995.

Martin, Luther H. "Artemidorus: Dream Theory in Late Antiquity." *Second Century* 8 (1991) 97–108.

Matthews, Shelly. *First Converts: Rich Pagan Women and the Rhetoric of Mission in Early Judaism and Christianity*. Stanford, Calif.: Stanford University Press, 2001.

McDonald, Lee M. *The Formation of the Christian Biblical Canon*. Revised edition. Peabody, Mass.: Hendrickson, 1995.

McGinn, Sheila E. "The 'Montanist' Oracles and Prophetic Theology." *Stud. Pat.* 31 (1997) 128–35.

Meyers, Eric M. "The Crisis of the Mid-Fifth Century BCE. Second Zechariah and the 'End' of Prophecy." In *Pomegranates and Golden Bells: Studies in Biblical, Jewish, and Near Eastern Ritual, Law, and Literature in Honor of Jacob Milgrom*, 713–23. Edited by David P. Wright, David Noel Freedman, and Avi Hurvitz. Winona Lake, Ind.: Eisenbrauns, 1995.

Miller, Patricia Cox. *Dreams in Late Antiquity: Studies in the Imagination of a Culture*. Princeton, N.J.: Princeton University Press, 1994.

Mitchell, Margaret. *Paul and the Rhetoric of Reconciliation: An Exegetical Investigation of the Language and Composition of 1 Corinthians*. Tübingen: Mohr/Siebeck, 1991.

Momigliano, Arnaldo. *On Pagans, Jews, and Christians*. Middletown, Conn.: Wesleyan University Press; Scranton, Pa.: Harper & Row, 1987.

Moore-Gilbert, Bart. *Postcolonial Theory: Contexts, Practices, Politics*. London: Verso, 1997.

Nandy, Ashis. "History's Forgotten Doubles." *History and Theory* 34 (1995) 44–67.

Nasrallah, Laura. "'An Ecstasy of Folly': Rhetorical Strategies in Early Christian Debates over Prophecy." Th.D. diss., Harvard Divinity School, 2002.

———. "'Now I Know in Part': Historiography and Epistemology in Early Christian Debates about Prophecy." In *Walk in the Ways of Wisdom: Essays in Honor of Elisabeth Schüssler Fiorenza*, 244–65. Edited by Melanie Johnson-DeBaufre, Cynthia Kittredge, and Shelly Matthews. Valley Forge, Pa.: Trinity Press International, 2003.

Neusner, Jacob. "In the View of Rabbinic Judaism, What, Exactly, Ended with Prophecy?" In *Mediators of the Divine: Horizons of Prophecy, Divination, Dreams and Theurgy in Mediterranean Antiquity*, 45–60. Edited by Robert M. Berchman. Atlanta, Ga.: Scholars Press, 1998.

Neyrey, Jerome. *Paul, In Other Words: A Cultural Reading of His Letters*. Louisville, Ky.: Westminster/John Knox, 1990.

Nussbaum, Martha C. *The Fragility of Goodness: Luck and Ethics in Greek Tragedy and Philosophy*. New York: Cambridge University Press, 1986.

———. *The Therapy of Desire: Theory and Practice in Hellenistic Ethics*. Princeton, N.J.: Princeton University Press, 1994.

Oepke, Albrecht. ἔκστασις. *TDNT* 2 (1964) 449–58.

Osborn, E. "Was Tertullian a Philosopher?" *Stud. Pat.* 31 (1997) 322–34.

Overholt, Thomas W. "The End of Prophecy: No Players Without a Program." *JSOT* 42 (1988) 103–15.

Padel, Ruth. *In and Out of the Mind: Greek Images of the Tragic Self*. Princeton, N.J.: Princeton University Press, 1992.

———. "Women: Model for Possession by Greek Daemons." In *Images of Women in Antiquity*, 3–19. Edited by Averil Cameron and Amelie Kuhrt. Detroit, Mich.: Wayne State University Press, 1993.

Pagels, Elaine. "Visions, Appearances, and Apostolic Authority: Gnostic and Orthodox Traditions." In *Gnosis: Festschrift für Hans Jonas*, 415–30. Edited by Barbara Aland. Göttingen: Vandenhoeck & Ruprecht, 1978.

Perkins, Judith. *The Suffering Self: Pain and Narrative Representation in the Early Christian Era*. New York: Routledge, 1995.

Plank, Karl. *Paul and the Irony of Affliction*. Atlanta, Ga.: Scholars Press, 1987.

Pogoloff, Stephen. *Logos and Sophia: The Rhetorical Situation of 1 Corinthians*. SBLDS 134. Atlanta, Ga.: Scholars Press, 1992.

Poirier, John C. "Montanist Pepuza-Jerusalem and the Dwelling Place of Wisdom." *JECS* 7 (1999) 491–507.

Porter, Stanley and Thomas Olbricht, eds. *Rhetoric and the New Testamaent: Essays from the 1992 Heidelburg Conference*, 265–91. JSNTSup 90. Sheffield, England: JSOT, 1993.

Pourkier, Aline. *L'hérésiologie chez Épiphane de Salamine*. Paris: Beauchesne, 1992.

Price, Simon. "The Future of Dreams: From Freud to Artemidorus." *Past and Present* 113 (1986) 3–37.

———. "Latin Christian Apologetics: Minucius Felix, Tertullian, and Cyprian." In *Apologetics in the Roman Empire: Pagans, Jews, and Christians*, 105–29. Edited by Mark Edwards et al. Oxford: Oxford University Press, 1999.

Purcell, Rosamond Wolff, and Stephen Jay Gould. *Illuminations: A Bestiary*. New York: Norton, 1986.

Quasten, Johannes. *Patrology*. 4 vols. Westminster, Md.: Newman, 1964.

Rankin, D. I. "Was Tertullian a Jurist?" *Stud. Pat.* 31 (1997) 335–42.

Reid, Stephen. "The End of Prophecy in the Light of Contemporary Social Theory: A Draft." In *SBL 1985 Seminar Papers*, 515–23. Edited by Kent Harold Richards. Atlanta, Ga.: Scholars Press, 1985.

Robeck, Cecil M., Jr. *Prophecy in Carthage: Perpetua, Tertullian, and Cyprian*. Cleveland, Ohio: Pilgrim, 1992.

Rossing, Barbara. *The Choice Between Two Cities: Whore, Bride, and Empire in the Apocalypse*. HTS 48. Harrisburg, Pa.: Trinity Press International, 1999.

Runia, David. "Philo and Origen: A Preliminary Survey." In *Origeniana Quinta: Historica, Text and Method, Biblica, Philosophica, Theologica, Origenism and Later Developments: Papers of the Fifth International Origen Congress, Boston College, 14–18 August 1989*, 333–38. Edited by Robert J. Daly. BETL 105. Leuven: Peeters, 1992.

———. *Philo of Alexandria and the* Timaeus *of Plato*. Leiden: Brill, 1986.

Sanders, Todd K. "A New Approach to 1 Corinthians 13.1." *NTS* 36 (1990) 614–18.

Schmithals, Walter. *Gnosticism in Corinth: An Investigation of the Letters to the Corinthians*. Translated by John E. Steely. Nashville, Tenn.: Abingdon, 1971.

Schneemelcher, William. "General Introduction." In *Gospels and Related Writings*. Vol. 1 of *New Testament Apocrypha*. Edited by Edgar Hennecke, William Schneemelcher, and R. McL. Wilson. Westminster: John Knox, 1991.

Schottroff, Luise. "Animae naturaliter salvandae: Zum Problem der himmlischen Herkunft des Gnostikers." In *Christentum und Gnōsis*, 65–97. Edited by Walther Eltester. Berlin: Alfred Töpelmann, 1969.

———. "A Feminist Hermeneutic of 1 Corinthians." In *Escaping Eden: New Feminist Perspectives on the Bible*, 208–15. Edited by Harold C. Washington et al. New York: New York University Press, 1999.

Schüssler Fiorenza, Elisabeth. *The Book of Revelation: Justice and Judgment*. Philadelphia: Fortress, 1985.

———. *But She Said: Feminist Practices of Biblical Interpretation*. Boston: Beacon Press, 1992.

———. *In Memory of Her: A Feminist Theological Reconstruction of Christian Origins*. New York: Crossroad, 1983.

———. *Jesus and the Politics of Interpretation*. New York: Continuum, 2000.

———. *Jesus: Miriam's Child, Sophia's Prophet: Critical Issues in Feminist Christology*. New York: Continuum, 1994.

———. "Re-Visioning Christian Origins: In Memory of Her Revisited." In *Christian Origins: Worship, Belief, and Society*, 225–50. Edited by Kiernan J. O. Mahoney. JSNTSup 241. New York: Sheffield Academic Press, 2003.

———. "Rhetorical Situation and Historical Reconstruction in 1 Corinthians." *NTS* 33 (1987) 386–403.

———. *Rhetoric and Ethic: The Politics of Biblical Studies*. Minneapolis: Fortress, 1999.

———. "The Rhetoricity of Knowledge: Pauline Discourse and its Contextualizations." In *Religious Propaganda and Missionary Compe-tition in the New Testament World*, 443–69. Edited by Lukas Bormann and Kelly Del Tredici. Leiden: Brill, 1994.

Schweitzer, Albert. *The Quest of the Historical Jesus*. Translated by W. Montgomery. 3d edition. 1906. Repr., London: Adam and Charles Black, 1956.

Sider, Robert Dick. *Ancient Rhetoric and the Art of Tertullian*. Oxford: Oxford University Press, 1971.

Sigountos, James G. "The Genre of 1 Corinthians 13." *NTS* 40 (1994) 246–60.

Smit, Joop. "Argument and Genre of 1 Corinthians 12–14." In *Rhetoric and the New Testament: Essays from the 1992 Heidelberg Conference*, 211–30. Edited by Stanley Porter and Thomas Olbricht. JSNTSup 90. Sheffield, England: JSOT, 1993.

———. "Two Puzzles: 1 Corinthians 12.31 and 13.3: A Rhetorical Solution." *NTS* 39 (1993) 246–64.

Smith, Jonathan Z. *Drudgery Divine: On the Comparison of Early Christianities and the Religions of Late Antiquity*. Chicago, Ill.: University of Chicago Press, 1990.

Stendahl, Krister. "Glossolalia: The New Testament Evidence." In *Paul among Jews and Gentiles and Other Essays*, 109–24. Philadelphia: Fortress, 1976.

Stewart-Sykes, Alistair. "Papyrus Oxyrhynchus 5: A Prophetic Protest from Second Century Rome." *Stud. Pat.* 31 (1997) 196–205.

Stowers, Stanley K. "Paul on the Use and Abuse of Reason." In *Greeks, Romans, and Christians: Essays in Honor of Abraham J. Malherbe*, 253–86. Edited by David Balch et al. Minneapolis: Fortress, 1990.

Tabbernee, William. *Montanist Inscriptions and Testimonia: Epigraphic Sources Illustrating the History of Montanism*. NAPS Monograph Series 16. Macon, Ga.: Mercer University Press, 1997.

———. "'Our Trophies are Better than your Trophies': The Appeal to Tombs and Reliquaries in Montanist-Orthodox Relations." *Stud. Pat.* 31 (1997) 206–17.

Taves, Ann. *Fits, Trances and Visions: Experiences Religion and Explaining Experience from Wesley to James*. Princeton, N.J.: Princeton University Press, 1999.

———. "Knowing through the Body: Dissociative Religious Experience in the African- and British- American Methodist Traditions." *Journal of Religion* 73 (1993) 200–22.

Theissen, Gerd. *The Social Setting of Pauline Christianity*. Edited and translated by John H. Schütz. Edinburgh: T&T Clark, 1982.

Thomassen, Einar. *Le Traite tripartite (NH I, 5)*. Bibliothèque Copte de Nag Hammadi Section "Textes" 19. Quebec: Presses de l'Université Laval, 1989.

Trevett, Christine. "Eschatological Timetabling and the Montanist Prophet Maximilla." *Stud. Pat.* 31 (1997) 218–24.

———. *Montanism: Gender, Authority and the New Prophecy*. Cambridge: Cambridge University Press, 1996.

Tuckett, Christopher. "Jewish Christian Wisdom in 1 Corinthians?" In *Cross-ing the Boundaries: Essays in Biblical Interpretation in Honour of Michael D. Goulder*, 201–19. Edited by Stanley Porter. Leiden: Brill, 1994.

Turner, Victor. *The Ritual Process: Structure and Anti-Structure*. 1969. New York: Aldine de Gruyter, 1995.

Tylor, Edward B. "Animism." In *Reader in Comparative Religion: An Anthropological Approach*, 13–23. Edited by William A. Lessa and Evon Z. Vogt. Evanston, Ill.: Row, Peterson and Company, 1958.

———. *Primitive Culture*. 7th edition. 2 vols. in 1. 1871. Repr., New York: Brentano's, 1924.

Voigt, Heinrich Gisbert. *Eine Verschollene Urkunde des Antimontanistischen Kampfes*. Leipzig: Fr. Richter, 1891.

Watson, Duane F. "Paul's Rhetorical Strategy in 1 Corinthians 15." In *Rhetoric and the New Testament: Essays from the 1992 Heidelberg Conference*, 231–49. Edited by Stanley Porter and Thomas Olbricht. JSNTSup 90. Sheffield, England: JSOT, 1993.

Weber, Max. *On Charisma and Institution Building: Selected Papers*. Edited by S. N. Eisenstadt. Chicago, Ill.: University of Chicago Press, 1968.

Weiss, Johannes. *A History of the Period A.D. 30–150*. Vol. 1 of *Earliest Christianity*. Translated by Frederick C. Grant. New York: Harper and Brothers, 1959.

Williams, Michael. *Rethinking "Gnosticism": An Argument for Dismantling a Dubious Category*. Princeton, N.J.: Princeton University Press, 1996.

Wilson, Robert. *Prophecy and Society in Ancient Israel*. Philadelphia: Fortress, 1980.

Winston, David. *Philo of Alexandria:* The Contemplative Life, The Giants and Selections. Classics of Western Spirituality. New York: Paulist Press, 1981.

Wire, Antoinette Clark. *The Corinthian Women Prophets: A Reconstruction through Paul's Rhetoric*. Minneapolis: Fortress, 1990.

Young, Robert. *Colonial Desire: Hybridity in Theory, Culture, and Race*. London: Routledge, 1995.

# Index

Abram, 37–38, 40–41

Adam. *See* Anti-Phrygian source; ecstasy

*afflatus*, 122, 131–32, 153

*amentia*. *See* madness

*anima, De,* 111–26; genre and rhetorical form of, 111–13; sister's vision of the soul in, 147–48; and unified soul, 117–19, 135–36, 153. *See also* Tertullian

Anti-Phrygian source, 155–96; catalog of prophets in, 179, 187–91; and contempt for "ecstasy of folly," 3, 49, 178, 194, 197–98; dating and extent of, 167–70; and God's *philanthropia*, 48, 181, 185, 195; interpretation of Adam's ecstasy in, 47–51; prophetic gifts in, 11, 172–74; reason and mental instability in, 178–87; and Tertullian, 44–45, 155, 168–69; understanding of history in, 51, 173–76, 187–93, 195. *See also* ecstasy; Epiphanius

Artemidorus, 9+n21, 29+nn2–3, 30+n4, 31+n6, 136

Aune, David, 18+n50, 22n59, 161+n17

authority, 198–201; changing claims and view of, 12–13; charismatic type of, 13–14; and Paul, 61–62, 69, 76; and Tertullian, 96, 145. *See also* model of charismatic origins and decline

barbarian, topos of Greek and, 46–47, 103–6, 177–78

Campenhausen, Hans von, 10n27, 18–19, 160+nn13–14

Chakrabarty, Dipesh, 24, 202. *See also* postcolonial criticism

charisma. *See* model of charismatic origins and decline; Douglas, Mary

Cicero, Marcus Tullius, 1+nn2–3, 2, 9+n20, 111

compulsion. *See* prophets

1 Corinthians, and the discourse of folly, 62, 69, 70–76, 89, 93–94; and the discourse of periodization of history, 11, 27, 70, 72–74, 88–90, 93–94,

130; epistemic boundaries in, 61, 64, 71, 77, 88–90, 95; issue of opponents of, 64–65+n7, 71n27; Paul as father/founder of the community in, 69, 75–76; ranking of spiritual gifts in, 58, 78, 81, 83–87, 198–99; rhetoric of "one body" in, 69, 77–84, 86; rhetorical form of, 63–64, 72n32, 76n41. *See also* Paul; periodization of history

2 Corinthians, fool's speech in, 87, 186+n74; issue of opponents in, 65

Delphic oracle, 9, 34

*Didache*, 2+n4, 66

Dionysius, 35, 177

discourse. *See* Foucault, Michel; periodization of history; rationality

divination, 1, 9

Dodds, E. R., 160+n14, 161+n16

Douglas, Mary, 15–16+nn44–45, 66n15, 202

dreams, importance in antiquity of, 1–4, 6–7+n15; importance in Bible of, 9+nn24–25; taxonomy of, 53–56; Tertullian's understanding of, 52–58, 136–40, 148, 152–53; theories of, 1–2. *See also* Artemidorus; ecstasy; Tertullian

ecstasy, Adam's, 45–51, 53–58, 120, 132–34, 154, 168, 191; Anti-Phrygian understanding of, 7, 50; as intoxication or madness, 41–44, 50, 129–53; as possible communication from divine,

12, 31. *See also* Anti-Phrygian source; Tertullian

Epiphanius, 2n5, 168n33, 169n38, 170n40, 175n53; Anti-Phrygian source of, 4, 27–28, 140, 149, 152n58, 153–56, 162–71, 173n48, 184; feminization of heresy by, 164–65+n25

epistemology, 44, 62–64, 95–96, 103, 108–9, 110, 119–20, 127, 129–30, 140

Eusebius, 50n46, 98n4, 156–57, 164n25, 171, 173n48, 175n54, 179, 187n77

Foucault, Michel, construction of history by, 23; "discourse" in writings of, 5+nn12–13, 6; and dreams in, 7n15; discussion of madness by, 7n17, 8n18, 23n66

Frend, W. H. C., 157–58+n5

glossolalia, 11n30, 68–69, 73, 80, 84n70, 85–87, 91–93, 199

Gnosticism, and 1 Corinthians, 65, 71, 73n34; and "Montanism," 157n4; and Tertullian, 109

Gunkel, Hermann, 10+n26, 22n59

Harnack, Adolf von, 18+n50, 19n53, 157n4, 159+n12

Hermogenes. *See under* Tertullian

historiography. *See* model of charismatic origins and decline; model of struggle; periodization of history

kyriarchy, 30+n5. *See also* Schüssler Fiorenza, Elizabeth

kyriarchy, 30+n5. *See also* Schüssler Fiorenza, Elizabeth

Lewis, I. M., 17+n47, 202
*logos*, and ancient philosophy, 5–6, 108; Philo's use of, 198; as sympathetic mediator between God and human, 44

madness, Anti-Phrygian's rhetoric of, 49–50, 156, 171, 175–76, 178–93, 196, 198, 201; discourse of rationality and, 5+n12, 6, 12–13, 15, 73, 91–93, 156, 194, 204; as discussed in Paul's writings, 130; and Platonism, 32–36; in Tertullian, the relation between prophecy and, 134; Tertullian's use of the term *amentia*, 120, 134–40, 141–43, 153; understanding by Plato of, 32–36. *See also* rationality; Tertullian
Marcion. *See under* Tertullian
*Martyrdom of Perpetua and Felicitas*, 175–76
Maximilla, 51, 159+n9, 164n25, 166, 170–75, 176–81, 193n93, 200; oracles of, 16, 149, 156, 172–75, 179, 182–87, 191, 194–95
medicine, in antiquity, 8, 9n21, 77, 107, 116n63; and modern treatment of prophetic experiences, 7–8. *See also* Soranus
model of charismatic origins and decline, and classification of "primitive" peoples, 15; and devolution into institutions, 15; and early Christian historiography, 12, 18–19, 154, 161, 203; and origins as pure, 13; and Turner's tripartite schema of institution and spirit, 1; and Tylor's theory of evolution in religion, 14. *See also* Turner, Victor; Tylor, Edward; Weber, Max
model of struggle, 20–25, 62, 198, 203; and moments of rupture and negotiation, 202; and postcolonial critics, 23–25, 202; and rhetorical-critical method, 20–22
"Montanism," in early Christian historiography, 3–4+n11, 10, 155–62, 166–67; Tertullian and, 12, 99–101. *See also* Anti-Phrygian source
Montanus, 16, 47, 51, 158–60, 164n25, 170, 172, 176, 193n93; oracles of, 16, 156, 170–71, 179, 180–83+n67, 191–95

Nandy, Ashis, 24, 202. *See also* postcolonial criticism
"New Prophecy." *See* "Montanism"

"one body," 77–83. *See also under* 1 Corinthians
oracles, 145–46. *See also* Delphic oracle; Maximilla; Montanus
Origen, 2n8, 10n27, 11n29, 36n15, 37n17, 46n36, 80n57, 152n58, 179n59

Paraclete, 28, 100, 126, 130, 146–47, 149–54, 162n19, 175, 178n58, 183nn67–68

Paul, the Anti-Phrygian's and Tertullian's use of, 4, 67–69, 133 +n8, 144, 178, 185–86+n73, 187n76, 188; and Judaism, 12, 62+n1, 67+n17; knowledge of divine in future as understood by, 198; modern scholarship on rationality and, 7, 67–68, 86n73, 91–93. *See also* 1 Corinthians; 2 Corinthians

periodization of history, discourse of, 3–5, 11–19, 30, 51, 70, 90, 130, 148–52, 174–76, 187–93, 195, 197–98; new perspectives on historiography and, 20–21, 23–24

Philo, ecstasy and intoxication in, 38, 40–45, 59, 198; and Middle Platonism, 36–37; taxonomy of ecstasy in, 36–44; theory of the *logos* in, 44; use of Dionysian language in, 38, 42–43

Phrygians, 46–47, 158, 165–66, 176–78, 191. *See also* "Montanism"; Anti-Phrygian source

Plato, ecstasy in *Phaedrus* of, 32–36; theory of the soul of, 109, 116–19, 136; *Timaeus* of, 119. *See also under* Tertullian

Plutarch, 9, 180n61

*pneumatika,* 77, 83–87

*pneumatikoi,* 69-76. *See also* "spiritual people"

postcolonial criticism, 13n33, 24–25, 104n24, 202–3

Priscilla. *See* Maximilla

prophecy. *See* ecstasy; madness; Paul; Philo; prophets

prophetic experiences, 2

prophets, and compulsion, 87n76, 180, 184–87, 192–93; described as divine instrument, 86n74, 181, 193

rationality, discourse of madness and, 5–11, 12–13, 15, 73, 91–93, 156, 171, 179–80, 194, 201–2, 204; and Enlightenment theory of progress, 18, 202; modern constructions of, 7–8, 10, 26, 202; and prophecy, 5–11

reason. *See logos*

Revelation, Book of, and early Christian prophecy, 67–69; Tertullian's use of, 116, 126

rhetorical criticism, 21–22

Schüssler Fiorenza, Elisabeth, and 1 Corinthians, 63n3, 67, 68n20, 71n31, 72n32, 76n41, 77n46, 79n53, 82nn64–65, 83n68, 92n91; kyriarchy in, 30+n5; and model of struggle, 21–23

sense perception, treatment by Anti-Phrygian of, 49, 190; treatment by Philo of, 40, 198; treatment by Tertullian of, 52–53, 119–20

*somnia. See* dreams

Soranus, 95, 99n11, 105, 107n33, 114n58

soul. *See anima, De*; Anti-Phrygian source; Plato; Tertullian

"spiritual people," in 1 Corinthians, 66, 69, 70–76, 80, 91, 94, 199; in Tertullian's thought, 57–58, 120–22, 129–30, 142–48, 152, 154, 199

Stoicism, and dreams, 1–2; and Paul, 78n51, 81, 93; and Tertullian, 98, 101–3, 105–6, 107–9, 110, 113, 117, 119, 126, 136

Tertullian, antiphilosophical stance in, 101–11, 200; argument with Hermogenes, 106, 111–14; argument with Marcion, 103–4, 106, 129, 141–45, 148, 152–54, 177; characterization of Valentinians in, 109, 119–21, 122, 133; and classical rhetoric, 97–99, 110n42, 112; critique of Plato by, 99, 101–3, 105–9, 117, 122–23, 126; distinction between soul and spirit in writings of, 130–32; dreams and sleep in, 51–52, 54–58, 59, 136, 198; equivalency of *ecstasis* and *amentia* in, 55, 137–40; epistemic value of dreams in, 52–53, 138–40; and "Montanism," 97, 100–1+n18, 153, 155, 162; and the soul's corporeality, 53, 115–16, 147–48; and the soul's unity, 117–18, 120–22, 125, 127, 130–35, 139, 199; understanding of history of, 11–12, 149–52; and value of sense perception, 52, 119–20, 127, 135, 140. *See also anima, De*

Turner, Victor, 17+n49, 202

Tylor, Edward, 14–15+nn38–40, 24–25

Valentinians. *See under* Tertullian

visions. *See* dreams; ecstasy; prophecy; prophetic experiences

Weber, Max, 13–14, 17, 154

# Harvard Theological Studies

52. Nasrallah, Laura Salah. *"An Ecstasy of Folly": Prophecy and Authority in Early Christianity*, 2003.

51. Brock, Ann Graham. *Mary Magdalene, The First Apostle: The Struggle for Authority*, 2003.

50. Trost, Theodore Louis. *Douglas Horton and the Ecumenical Impulse in American Religion*, 2002.

49. Huang, Yong. *Religious Goodness and Political Rightness: Beyond the Liberal-Communitarian Debate*, 2001.

48. Rossing, Barbara R. *The Choice between Two Cities: Whore, Bride, and Empire in the Apocalypse*, 1999.

47. Skedros, James Constantine. *Saint Demetrios of Thessaloniki: Civic Patron and Divine Protector, 4th–7th Centuries C.E.*, 1999.

46. Koester, Helmut, ed. *Pergamon, Citadel of the Gods: Archaeological Record, Literary Description, and Religious Development*, 1998.

45. Kittredge, Cynthia Briggs. *Community and Authority: The Rhetoric of Obedience in the Pauline Tradition*, 1998.

44. Lesses, Rebecca Macy. *Ritual Practices to Gain Power: Angels, Incantations, and Revelation in Early Jewish Mysticism*, 1998.

43. Guenther-Gleason, Patricia E. *On Schleiermacher and Gender Politics*, 1997.

42. White, L. Michael. *The Social Origins of Christian Architecture*. Vol. I and II, 1997.

41. Koester, Helmut, ed. *Ephesos, Metropolis of Asia: An Interdisciplinary Approach to its Archaeology, Religion, and Culture*, 1995.

40. Guider, Margaret Eletta. *Daughters of Rahab: Prostitution and the Church of Liberation in Brazil*, 1995.

39. Schenkel, Albert F. *The Rich Man and the Kingdom: John D. Rockefeller, Jr., and the Protestant Establishment*, 1995.

38. Hutchison, William R. and Hartmut Lehmann, eds. *Many Are Chosen: Divine Election and Western Nationalism*, 1994.

37. Lubieniecki, Stanislas. *History of the Polish Reformation and Nine Related Documents*. Translated and interpreted by George Huntston Williams, 1995.

–   Davidovich, Adina. *Religion as a Province of Meaning: The Kantian Foundations of Modern Theology*, 1993.

36. Thiemann, Ronald F., ed. *The Legacy of H. Richard Niebuhr*, 1991.

35. Hobbs, Edward C., ed. *Bultmann, Retrospect, and Prospect: The Centenary Symposium at Wellesley*, 1985.

34. Cameron, Ron. *Sayings Traditions in the Apocryphon of James*, 1984.

33. Blackwell, Albert L. *Schleiermacher's Early Philosophy of Life: Determinism, Freedom, and Phantasy*, 1982.

32. Gibson, Elsa. *The "Christians for Christians" Inscriptions of Phrygia: Greek Texts, Translation and Commentary*, 1978.

31. Bynum, Caroline Walker. Docere Verbo et Exemplo: *An Aspect of Twelfth-Century Spirituality*, 1979.

30. Williams, George Huntston, ed. *The Polish Brethren: Documentation of the History and Thought of Unitarianism in the Polish-Lithuanian Commonwealth and in the Diaspora 1601–1685*, 1980.

29. Attridge, Harold W. *First-Century Cynicism in the Epistles of Heraclitus*, 1976.

28. Williams, George Huntston, Norman Pettit, Winfried Herget, and Sargent Bush, Jr., eds. *Thomas Hooker: Writings in England and Holland, 1626–1633*, 1975.

27. Preus, James Samuel. *Carlstadt's Ordinaciones and Luther's Liberty: A Study of the Wittenberg Movement, 1521–22*, 1974.

26. Nickelsburg, George W. E. *Resurrection, Immortality, and Eternal Life in Intertestamental Judaism*, 1972.

25. Worthley, Harold Field. *An Inventory of the Records of the Particular (Congregational) Churches of Massachusetts Gathered 1620–1805*, 1970.

24. Yamauchi, Edwin M. *Gnostic Ethics and Mandaean Origins*, 1970.

23. Yizhar, Michael. *Bibliography of Hebrew Publications on the Dead Sea Scrolls 1948–1964*, 1967.

22. Albright, William Foxwell. *The Proto-Sinaitic Inscriptions and Their Decipherment*, 1966.

21. Dow, Sterling, and Robert F. Healey. *A Sacred Calendar of Eleusis*, 1965.

20. Sundberg, Jr., Albert C. *The Old Testament of the Early Church*, 1964.

19. Cranz, Ferdinand Edward. *An Essay on the Development of Luther's Thought on Justice, Law, and Society*, 1959.

18. Williams, George Huntston, ed. *The Norman Anonymous of 1100 A.D.: Towards the Identification and Evaluation of the So-Called Anonymous of York*, 1951.

17. Lake, Kirsopp, and Silva New, eds. *Six Collations of New Testament Manuscripts*, 1932.

16. Servetus, Michael. *The Two Treatises of Servetus on the Trinity: On the Errors of the Trinity, 7 Books, A.D. 1531. Dialogues on the Trinity, 2 Books. On the Righteousness of Christ's Kingdom, 4 Chapters, A.D. 1532*. Translated by Earl Morse Wilbur, 1932.

15. Casey, Robert Pierce, ed. Serapion of Thmuis's *Against the Manichees*, 1931.

14. Ropes, James Hardy. *The Singular Problem of the Epistles to the Galatians*, 1929.

13. Smith, Preserved. *A Key to the Colloquies of Erasmus*, 1927.

12. Spyridon of the Laura and Sophronios Eustratiades. *Catalogue of the Greek Manuscripts in the Library of the Laura on Mount Athos,* 1925.

11. Sophronios Eustratiades and Arcadios of Vatspedi. *Catalogue of the Greek Manuscripts in the Library of the Monastery of Vatopedi on Mt. Athos,* 1924.

10. Conybeare, Frederick C. *Russian Dissenters,* 1921.

9. Burrage, Champlin, ed. *An Answer to John Robinson of Leyden by a Puritan Friend: Now First Published from a Manuscript of A.D. 1609,* 1920.

8. Emerton, Ephraim. *The* Defensor pacis *of Marsiglio of Padua: A Critical Study,* 1920,

7. Bacon, Benjamin W. *Is Mark a Roman Gospel?* 1919.

6. Cadbury, Henry Joel. 2 vols. *The Style and Literary Method of Luke,* 1920.

5. Marriott, G. L., ed. Macarii Anecdota*: Seven Unpublished Homilies of Macarius,* 1918.

4. Edmunds, Charles Carroll and William Henry Paine Hatch. *The Gospel Manuscripts of the General Theological Seminary,* 1918.

3. Arnold, William Rosenzweig. *Ephod and Ark: A Study in the Records and Religion of the Ancient Hebrews,* 1917.

2. Hatch, William Henry Paine. *The Pauline Idea of Faith in its Relation to Jewish and Hellenistic Religion,* 1917.

1. Torrey, Charles Cutler. *The Composition and Date of Acts,* 1916.

## Harvard Dissertations in Religion

In 1993, Harvard Theological Studies absorbed
the Harvard Dissertations in Religion series.

31. Baker-Fletcher, Garth. *Somebodyness: Martin Luther King, Jr. and the Theory of Dignity,* 1993.

30. Soneson, Jerome Paul. *Pragmatism and Pluralism: John Dewey's Significance for Theology,* 1993.

29. Crabtree, Harriet. *The Christian Life: The Traditional Metaphors and Contemporary Theologies,* 1991.

28. Schowalter, Daniel N. *The Emperor and the Gods: Images from the Time of Trajan,* 1993.

27. Valantasis, Richard. *Spiritual Guides of the Third Century: A Semiotic Study of the Guide-Disciple Relationship in Christianity, Neoplatonism, Hermetism, and Gnosticism,* 1991.

26. Wills, Lawrence Mitchell. *The Jews in the Court of the Foreign King: Ancient Jewish Court Legends,* 1990.

25. Massa, Mark Stephen. *Charles Augustus Briggs and the Crisis of Historical Criticism*, 1990.

24. Hills, Julian Victor. *Tradition and Composition in the* Epistula apostolorum, 1990.

23. Bowe, Barbara Ellen. *A Church in Crisis: Ecclesiology and Paraenesis in Clement of Rome*, 1988.

22. Bisbee, Gary A. *Pre-Decian Acts of Martyrs and* Commentarii, 1988.

21. Ray, Stephen Alan. *The Modern Soul: Michel Foucault and the Theological Discourse of Gordon Kaufman and David Tracy*, 1987.

20. MacDonald, Dennis Ronald. *There Is No Male and Female: The Fate of a Dominical Saying in Paul and Gnosticism*, 1987.

19. Davaney, Sheila Greeve. *Divine Power: A Study of Karl Barth and Charles Hartshorne*, 1986.

18. LaFargue, J. Michael. *Language and Gnosis: The Opening Scenes of the Acts of Thomas*, 1985.

12. Layton, Bentley, ed. *The Gnostic Treatise on Resurrection from Nag Hammadi*, 1979.

11. Ryan, Patrick J. *Imale: Yoruba Participation in the Muslim Tradition: A Study of Clerical Piety*, 1977.

10. Neevel, Jr., Walter G. *Yamuna's* Vedanta *and* Pancaratra*: Integrating the Classical and the Popular*, 1977.

9. Yarbro Collins, Adela. *The Combat Myth in the Book of Revelation*, 1976.

8. Veatch, Robert M. *Value-Freedom in Science and Technology: A Study of the Importance of the Religious, Ethical, and Other Socio-Cultural Factors in Selected Medical Decisions Regarding Birth Control*, 1976.

7. Attridge, Harold W. *The Interpretation of Biblical History in the* Antiquitates judaicae *of Flavius Josephus*, 1976.

6. Trakatellis, Demetrios C. *The Pre-Existence of Christ in the Writings of Justin Martyr*, 1976.

5. Green, Ronald Michael. *Population Growth and Justice: An Examination of Moral Issues Raised by Rapid Population Growth*, 1975.

4. Schrader, Robert W. *The Nature of Theological Argument: A Study of Paul Tillich*, 1976.

3. Christensen, Duane L. *Transformations of the War Oracle in Old Testament Prophecy: Studies in the Oracles Against the Nations*, 1975.

2. Williams, Sam K. *Jesus' Death as Saving Event: The Background and Origin of a Concept*, 1972.

1. Smith, Jane I. *An Historical and Semantic Study of the Term "Islam" as Seen in*

This book was produced at the offices of Harvard Theological Studies, located at the Harvard Divinity School, Cambridge, Massachusetts.

Managing Editor:       Margaret Studier

Copy Editor:          Gene McGarry

Typesetters:          Paul D. Jones
                      Rachel Haut-Castañeda Billings
                      Mindy Newman

The index was prepared by Laura S. Nasrallah.

The Greek font (SymbolGreekII) used to print this work is available from Linguist's Software, Inc. PO Box 580, Edmonds, WA 98020-0580 USA tel (425) 775-1130 www.linguistsoftware.com.